An Introduction to LATIN AMERICAN POLITICS

—— *The Structure of Conflict* ——

SECOND EDITION

MARTIN C. NEEDLER

University of New Mexico

PRENTICE-HALL, INC., Englewood Cliffs, New Jersey 07632

Library of Congress Cataloging in Publication Data

Needler, Martin C.
   An introduction to Latin American politics.

   Bibliography: p.
   Includes index.
1. Latin America—Politics and government—
1948-   . 2. Latin America—Politics and
government—1830–1948. 3. Latin America—
Foreign relations. I. Title.
F1414.N39 1983   980′.03   82-9820
ISBN 0-13-486035-7   AACR2

to
JAN

© 1983, 1977 by Prentice-Hall, Inc.
Englewood Cliffs, New Jersey 07632

Printed in the United States of America

10 9 8 7 6 5 4 3 2 1

Editorial/production supervision and interior design by Paul Spencer
Cover design by Ray Lundgren
Manufacturing buyer: Ron Chapman

ISBN 0-13-486035-7

Prentice-Hall International, Inc., *London*
Prentice-Hall of Australia Pty. Limited, *Sydney*
Prentice-Hall Canada Inc., *Toronto*
Prentice-Hall of India Private Limited, *New Delhi*
Prentice-Hall of Japan, Inc., *Tokyo*
Prentice-Hall of Southeast Asia Pte. Ltd., *Singapore*
Whitehall Books Limited, *Wellington, New Zealand*

Contents

Preface
to the
Second Edition

It is gratifying that readership has been such as to call for a second edition of this book. It has been revised in the light of readers' comments to make it a more usable introduction to the complexities of Latin American politics.

In the five years that have elapsed between the publication of the first and second editions, the principal trends have been: amelioration of the harshness of the dictatorial regimes in southern South America; rapid though mixed economic growth, with some political liberalization, in Brazil and Mexico; heightened mobilization of marginal Indians and mestizos in northern South America and Central America. This last trend has strengthened democratic tendencies in Peru and Ecuador, but in Central America it has led to intermittent civil war.

The role of the United States government in these events has not been insignificant; for that reason, it behooves U.S. citizens of goodwill to become familiar with the countries with which we share a hemisphere, so as to form an active and concerned public. This book is intended as a contribution to that end.

MARTIN C. NEEDLER

Preface
to the
First Edition

The study of politics is in essence the study of conflict. The important questions are, then: How do societies divide into groups among which conflict is waged? What are the techniques by which conflict is engaged in? How, if at all, is conflict managed or resolved? These are the questions, as applied to Latin America, that we will be examining in this book.

It was perhaps Marx rather than anyone else who taught us to view politics as conflict, and there is no doubt that, for the most part, we are still living on the stock of ideas bequeathed to us by Marx. And it still makes sense to begin the search for the bases of social cleavage with an examination of class structure, although one then must take into account the existence of bases of important cleavage and conflict other than class. As it happens, in Latin America today the situation with respect to class is particularly complex, in that a variety of different economic systems coexist, each of which generates its own characteristic set of social classes and sub-classes.

The basic facts of geography, demography, economics, and culture provide a variety of alternative bases of cleavage, out of which alternative definitions of the conflict situation can be formed. Thus, for example, the set of political parties found in one country may have no exact counterpart elsewhere because of the different definitions of the conflict situation that have become accepted in different countries. One of the critical functions of political leadership, seen in this light, is to offer new conceptions of the central political issues, which can redefine group allegiances so as to create new political majorities.

The richness of Latin American societies in alternative bases of social cleavage has made it possible to interpret those societies in radically different ways, so that a variety of schools of interpretation exist that have few points of contact with each other. At the same time, this situation is a producer of political instability, since the character of the predominant coalition of political forces can change frequently, each coalition breaking up as the critical issues are redefined. Because of the irreducible variety of social groups formed by these multiple cleavages, it makes sense to examine Latin American countries one by one, since different cleavages are the important ones in different countries, and even similar groups may play different roles in the differing political systems of individual countries. In this book, therefore, we will examine the specific structure of conflict in individual countries and groups of countries, after an initial examination of the bases of political cleavage and the modes of conflict and conflict management prevalent in the area as a whole.

Traditionally, domestic politics is treated separately from international relations. However, for the Latin American countries, whose economies are integrated into the world market, which are faced by the hegemony in the hemisphere of a single dominant power, the United States, this approach is unrealistic. The character of its external relations, especially in their effect on its economy, is a critical factor in understanding the political dynamics of a Latin American country. Accordingly, in this book "international relations" factors are integrated into the discussion of domestic politics, and countries are grouped along lines determined not only by geography but also by the realities of international politics and economics.

1

Introduction

TRADITIONAL LATIN AMERICA

Although Latin America is a region undergoing rapid change, the weight of the past remains heavy. Before we can understand the region as it is today, we must examine the demographic, economic, and social patterns inherited from previous eras. These, in turn, have their origins in the fundamental geographic realities of the area.

Geographic Divisions

Latin American societies can be divided roughly into those of the highlands, the plains, and the lowlands. Before the Europeans arrived, indigenous societies and economies varied among these three types of regions. Generally speaking, in the highlands stable societies based on the planting of food staples, such as corn, beans, and potatoes, were created, large populations developed, and complex civilizations arose. In the plains areas, a nomadic form of life developed based primarily on hunting. In the hot lowlands, economic activity consisted of informal agriculture and fishing, and society and civilization remained simple.

After the European conquest of the area, the distinctions among these types of regions were maintained. In the mineral-rich highlands, mining activities developed, and the Spanish conquerors established themselves as feudal overlords of the masses of Indian agriculturalists. In the sparsely populated plains areas, the nomadic Indians were driven off or killed, the areas were repopulated by European immigrants, and the raising of cattle, horses, and sheep was established. In the hot lowlands, tropical crops, such as sugarcane, tobacco, and, later, cotton and bananas, were grown for European markets. However, the lowland Indians refused to adapt to a plantation regime of forced labor and rapidly died out through overwork and disease, were killed in the repression of uprisings, and even committed suicide. To replace them, black slaves were imported from Africa.

Nineteenth-Century Social and
Economic Structures

Thus geographic, economic, and historical circumstances combined to give rise to the typical socioeconomic structures that characterized the classic Latin American societies of the nineteenth century. In the sierra, or highland areas, of Mexico, Guatemala, Ecuador, Peru, and Bolivia, an indigenous version of late medieval feudalism existed complete with lords of the manor and Indian serfs, together with extensive mining. In highly stratified societies, a tiny upper class commanded great resources while the masses remained impoverished and miserable.

In the temperate plains areas of southern South America, in Argentina, Uruguay, and the extreme south of Brazil, small numbers of European immigrants enjoyed comfortable living standards based on the high returns of an animal-raising economy. Social conditions were more equal, and literacy became general.

In the islands of the Caribbean and the surrounding coastal lowlands, and in northeast Brazil, plantation economies continued to produce for Western European and North American markets. The end of slavery brought increased possibilities for social mobility, but social class continued to be correlated with race. Paradoxically, however, the social distance between white and black or brown in the tropics was generally less than in the Indian countries, where the classes were also separated by the gulfs of language and culture.

A fourth type of society developed in some intermediate areas where the quality of the land did not make it worthwhile either to bring in African slaves or to drive out the Indians and replace them with European settlers; here the concentrations of Indians had been too low to permit the development of large cities or to withstand the ravages of imported diseases to which the Indians had no immunity. The few Europeans who came to these areas mingled with the few Indians who remained, producing societies that were racially mestizo. Without gold, slaves, or vast quantities of rich land, these mestizo societies became poor backwaters; their populations lived at essentially the subsistence level during their early years as colonies. Only subsequently, when the mining of products other than gold and silver became profitable, or when, in the nineteenth century, the introduction of coffee culture suddenly brought value to hilly land previously regarded as worthless, did the mestizo areas begin to enjoy any substantial income.

Economic Systems

The economies of the Latin American countries have traditionally been divided into two sectors: one that produced primarily for local consumption, and another that grew crops or extracted minerals for export. The export sector typically operated as an enclave; it used foreign capital, managers, and technicians and exploited local resources but transferred the products abroad, with a negligible impact on the development of the local economy.

Excessive dependence on Western European and North American markets produced a state of economic colonialism in which the foreign headquarters of large agricultural or mining companies controlled Latin American economies through their production and marketing decisions. Such companies exerted undue political influence in their countries of operation either directly or through pressure on their home governments to intervene. Governments in Western Europe and North America were usually receptive to the pleas of companies to defend their interests when the need arose. However, ideological, strategic, and political motivations sometimes counterbalanced purely economic motives in determining the policies of such governments; they did defend corporate interests, but that was not the only thing that moved them to act.

Apart from the lack of autonomy inherent in external dependence, dependence on external markets had further disadvantageous effects. Exports principally consisted of only one or two items, the prices of which fluctuated as supply and demand conditions in the world market changed, thus contributing to considerable economic, and therefore political, instability.[1] It is true that countries concentrate on production of a single item that they are well equipped to produce, because, in general, it pays better. The revolutionary government of Cuba became aware of this truth after attempting a radical diversification of the economy away from sugar, only to discover that Cuba could earn more by growing and selling sugar than by doing anything else.[2] Nevertheless, it is clear that diversification is desirable in order to stabilize the economy by rendering it less dependent on price fluctuations. New items need to be produced in addition to the traditional product rather than instead of it.

Political Life

Traditionally, political life was the province of a small minority of the population, usually those with better education, more wealth, and more European ancestry. These traditional ruling groups, or "oligar-

---

[1]It is by now a truism that political instability follows economic fluctuations. The evidence on this point is detailed in Martin C. Needler, "The Latin American Military Coup: Some Numbers, Some Speculations," paper presented at the American Political Science Association meeting in Washington, D.C., September 1972, reprinted in Steffen Schmidt and Gerald Dorfman, eds., *Soldiers in Politics,* Los Altos, Calif.: Geron-X, 1974.

[2]Ernesto Guevara, "The Cuban Economy," *International Affairs,* vol. 40, no. 4, October 1964.

chies," were never completely exclusive. A poor boy of humble rural antecedents might work his way up through the army to a position of wealth and influence; however, these changes in status were rare, and the masses as a whole remained excluded from power.

The "oligarchy" was cosmopolitan in outlook. Many members of the oligarchy had been educated abroad and were more interested in the culture of France, Spain, or England than in what was going on among the Indians or the poor in the hinterlands of their own country.

Where upper class economic interests were tied into the export sector, England, France, and the United States were the external points of reference. For the more isolated rural upper class, whose economic position was based on landholding and the production of crops for local, and even domestic, consumption, more traditional and more religious, Spain remained the overseas model.

The major axis of overt political competition during the nineteenth century therefore was that between the Liberals, oriented to France and England, sometimes with export interests but, in any case, more urban and engaged typically in business and the professions, and the Conservatives, whose principal economic base was large landholding and who remained devoutly religious and Hispanophile. Formal constitutional arrangements might be based on democratic institutions and phraseology copied from Western Europe and North America; however, the entrenched system of minority rule and a rigid class structure made genuine democracy quite unfeasible, and actual politics was based on the rivalries of oligarchic families and military cliques, with revolts and coups d'état as likely to produce changes in government as were elections.

Although there were occasional dissenting priests, the hierarchy of the Catholic church constituted a support of the system. The elements of religious doctrine that justified the status quo as a manifestation of God's will, counseled obedience, and stressed the virtues of humility and patience were stressed. There were also close social and family connections between the upper ranks of the church hierarchy and the conservative economic elite.

Individual military officers were frequently of nonelite social origins, and their interests were not always identical with those of the upper classes. More often than not, however, the armed forces as an institution played a role supportive of the existing system in maintaining the existing distribution of property and repressing dissent.

Participation in political life was, of course, drastically limited. Although only a limited range of interests was represented by those who participated, politics were, nevertheless, unstable. The rivalries of aristocratic cliques, the incursions of crude military leaders, and occasional outbreaks of fighting led to a high degree of political instability punctuated by interludes of stability under dictatorship.

CHANGE IN THE
TRADITIONAL ORDER

The changes that have taken place in this traditional order spring from various roots and may occur in different sequences from one country to another, but, for our present purposes, they can be regarded as different aspects of a single process of change.

Rapid Population Growth

The first aspect of this process of change is rapid population growth (Table 1). Latin America, like other developing areas, finds itself in the stage of what has been called "the demographic transition." Traditional societies with low living standards typically have high birth rates, but they also have high death rates, so that the population remains roughly constant or grows or decreases only slightly. A sophisticated and high-income society, on the other hand, typically has low death rates because of improved standards of health and nutrition; however, it also has low birth rates because of widespread knowledge of birth control techniques and because having fewer children appears to be more rational to parents who live in a city under crowded conditions where growing children cannot help effectively in the family's everyday economic activities.

In a transitional society, however, health and nutritional standards improve rapidly, so that death rates drop long before the attitudes and behaviors spread that lead to a reduction in the birth rate. Accordingly, a period ensues in which high birth rates and low death rates mean very rapid population growth. Most of the Latin American countries are today in this phase of demographic transition. The exceptions are Haiti, which still remains in the phase of high birth rates and high death rates, on the one hand, and, on the other, Argentina and Uruguay, which have passed to the phase of low birth rates and low death rates. Some of the highest population growth rates in the world today are found among Latin American countries.

In the rural areas, the increase in population means increased pressure on the available land and either demands for change or the actual beginning of change in land ownership.

TABLE 1 Latin American Social and Economic Data, 1975–80

	POPULATION (MILLIONS)	RATE OF POPULATION GROWTH (%)	DENSITY PER MILE²	URBAN (%)	GNP PER CAPITA US $. MARKET PRICES	LITERACY (%)	LIFE EXPECTANCY (YEARS AT BIRTH)
Argentina	26.7	1.3	24	80	2,280	93	68
Bolivia	5.4	2.7	14	37	550	40	47
Brazil	122.9	2.9	34	59	1,690	67	61
Chile	10.9	1.7	37	83	1,690	88	63
Colombia	26.1	2.3	56	62	1,010	78	61
Costa Rica	2.2	2.5	110	40	1,810	89	69
Cuba	9.8	1.6	180	53	1,410	96	72
Dominican Republic	5.3	3.0	260	44	990	68	58
Ecuador	8.0	3.3	63	42	1,050	75	60
El Salvador	4.4	2.9	510	40	670	57	58
Guatemala	6.8	2.9	150	35	1,020	46	52
Haiti	5.0	1.7	480	21	260	10	45
Honduras	3.6	3.4	77	28	530	51	53
Mexico	67.6	3.3	82	63	1,590	74	61
Nicaragua	2.6	3.3	45	48	660	57	50
Panama	1.9	2.7	59	51	1,350	78	66
Paraguay	2.9	2.9	17	37	1,060	74	61
Peru	17.3	2.8	32	57	730	61	58
Uruguay	2.9	0.2	39	81	2,090	90	68
Venezuela	14.4	3.4	37	82	3,130	77	66

Sources: *Selected Economic Data for the Less Developed Countries*, RC-W-136, Agency for International Development, May 1977, and *1980 World Bank Atlas*. Population and GNP figures are for 1979, the others are from various years. Figures for Cuban life expectancy and urbanization, however, are from the *Statistical Abstract for Latin America, 1978*; for Cuban population density from the *Area Handbook for Cuba, 1977*; for Cuban literacy, from the *National Basic Intelligence Factbook, 1975*.

Urbanization

Population growth also means very substantial migration to the cities, or urbanization. The region's population is steadily becoming more urban, although the patterns of rural-urban migration are rather different in different countries. Chile, for example, is witnessing the classic pattern of "step" migration, in which rural people tend not to move directly into the big cities but, rather, first go to the smaller towns. Residents of small towns drift toward the provincial capitals, and it is from the provincial capitals that most of the migrants to the national capital come. The pattern in Mexico is rather different, with substantial movement directly from villages to Mexico City, perhaps because Mexico City is located in the heavily populated center of the country and is quite accessible from areas of dense rural population. In addition to this movement, by whatever route, to the large cities, migration also occurs to new boom areas, such as those where tourism is developing or where oil has been found.

Political awareness and participation. Urbanization provides the matrix for a whole set of associated changes in the social and political fabric of developing countries. Along with urbanization comes a great expansion in literacy and exposure to national communications networks: newspapers, radio, television, and word-of-mouth information. The increasing sophistication that results from these changes implies growing realism and rationality; at least in the second generation of urban residents, though usually not in the first (the aspirations of the migrants themselves are frequently fully satisfied by the move to the city), it also means a rise in the level of aspirations and a desire for greater social mobility.

The urbanization and communications revolutions also bring about a rise in political participation.

Public services. Urbanization means a very heavy increase in the demand for the provision of public services, especially housing, but also water, electricity, and sewage disposal. It may well be cheaper to provide such services to urban dwellers than to the corresponding number of rural dwellers; it is easier and less expensive to string the wires that will provide electricity to 10,000 people in an urban district than to provide electricity to the same number of people scattered in three or four villages around the countryside. If they had remained in the countryside, however, it might not have occurred to them to want the services; they might not have been able to organize effectively to demand them; and the government could more easily have ignored such demands if it wished to do so.

Housing. The need for housing has become especially great. Many lower-class urban dwellers, after an initial period of living with relatives or sharing rooms in old downtown slum areas, occupy open land in various parts of the city, usually without legal title, and construct improvised housing of their own. Some governments still try to bulldoze such shantytowns, arguing that the squatters have no legal title to the land and that the shantytowns are an eyesore. However, most students of the question now agree that the more rational solution is to realize that neither government nor private business can provide adequate housing for lower-class urban residents at prices that they can afford; it is therefore more reasonable to make arrangements for transfer of title to the land to the squatters, to provide public utilities services to the new shantytowns, and to make available building materials and technical assistance, so that the shantytowns can be rebuilt, by the labor of their occupants, into lower-class communities that meet acceptable housing standards.[3]

Employment. The massive urbanization movement has overstrained not only the supply of decent housing but also the supply of jobs, and many lower-class residents of the city are occupied with tasks that not only pay low wages but that also make no productive contribution to the economy, such as street vending, theft, and "guarding" parked cars. In other words, movement to the cities has not occurred in response to the demand for workers in cities and, in a sense, not even in response to poverty in the rural areas. There appears to be a preference for living in urban areas because of the amenities of urban life quite apart from the economic facts of income and employment. For this reason, although they may reduce its magnitude, it is probably not possible for governments to bring an end to the movement to the cities by manipulating economic incentives and disincentives.

At the same time, this preference for urban life may strike at any rational basis for the national economy from the viewpoint of its comparative advantage in the international division of labor. Thus, for example, Argentina has hundreds of square miles of some of the richest agricultural land in the world, but it is not being used for growing crops; if it is used at all, it is only for grazing animals. At the same time, the country is very highly urbanized, with one third of the whole national population living in greater Buenos Aires. It would do no good to tell a *porteño* (as the inhabitants of the capital are called) that instead of eking out a straitened existence as a clerk in an office he could make more money as a farmer; he would simply not be interested.

[3]William Mangin, "Latin American Squatter Settlements: A Problem and a Solution," *Latin American Research Review,* vol. 2, no. 3, Summer 1967.

ECONOMIC DEVELOPMENT

Regional differences become particularly marked in the process of economic development. Some areas may be consciously designated "poles of development" by governments that act to focus modern economic activity in these areas in the hope that such concentrations will pass the "critical mass," become self-sustaining, and give a dynamic impetus to the development of the surrounding area.

Even where there is no conscious attempt to create poles of development, it is clear that the development process does not begin uniformly across the whole country but is initiated in certain specific areas. These areas are typically the capital city, and perhaps other very large cities; the ports, or points that are centers for border trade; and areas where geographic circumstances have provided a specific product, such as oil, other minerals, or tourism, for which market conditions are favorable.

Because of this uneven distribution of the development process in its early stages, there will inevitably be grounds for criticism of the process, because, despite the gains made in some areas, other areas remain backward. In many cases, conditions will become worse for sectors of society that do not participate in the benefits of economic growth. For example, the expansion of the money supply that accompanies growth may result in higher prices, which means a drop in the standard of living for those whose incomes have remained constant. This is especially the problem where growth is based on some economic activity that produces a great amount of new wealth but that requires a very small labor force, such as oil. First in Venezuela, then in Ecuador, oil in this way made the country rich but further impoverished the masses. In fact, the experience of countries now considered to be developed suggests that the benefits of growth eventually begin to spread throughout the society.[4] However, government must be alert to facilitate this process and even in developed countries there are typically regions in which backwardness and low standards of living persist.

Thus economic development is marked by fits and starts, by sudden setbacks, by obstacles and bottlenecks. Nevertheless, it would be a mistake to regard such negative phenomena as the only features of the economic scene in Latin America and to lose sight of the fact that development is, indeed, occurring. One needs to take account of both the problems and the progress, the steps forward and the steps backward, the bottlenecks and the breakthroughs. The forward movement of

[4]Jeffrey G. Williamson, "Regional Inequality and the Process of National Development: A Description of the Patterns," *Economic Development and Cultural Change,* vol. 13, no. 4, Part II, July 1965.

development is most apparent in the countries with large internal markets for manufactured products, namely Brazil, Colombia, and Mexico, but is also visible in Venezuela and Ecuador, where petroleum has provided a new resource base, and in Cuba and Peru, where profound political changes, although accompanied by social and political dislocation, have made possible the elimination of some obstacles to growth.

ARENAS OF CONFLICT

Political conflict takes place in different arenas, social battlegrounds that differ from each other in accessibility to the different combatants, in weapons used, and in visibility to the public. One of these arenas is the constitutional one, where conflict takes place between executive and legislature, where elections are held, and where judges decide cases at law. In this arena, where weapons are votes and legal decisions, presidents can be removed by impeachment or electoral defeat. But two other arenas of conflict exist that are equally important, one less public than the constitutional arena, the other more public. One of these arenas is the private one, the world of personal contacts and influence, of family pressures, bribery, blackmail, and graft. This is a world where the weapons are not votes and legal decisions but rather money, threats, and promises. The third arena of conflict is the streets, where conflict takes the form of demonstrations, strikes, and riots, and the weapons used are violence and the threat of violence. If a president leaves office after defeat in the private arena or in the streets, it is not by impeachment but by revolt, forced resignation, or perhaps assassination.

These three arenas overlap and interpenetrate, and the same struggle may shift from one arena to another. Thus action in the streets may be a prelude to private negotiations or can set the mood for an election or a congressional debate. Use of the different arenas of conflict varies between different countries, with a larger proportion of conflict occurring in the constitutional arena in politically more developed countries such as Chile or Costa Rica. In the politically least developed countries, such as Haiti and Paraguay, most politics tends to be private politics, almost court intrigue, with very occasional resort to the streets at times of crisis. The streets are most used in countries of an intermediate stage of development.

Political development in this sense refers to the amount of freedom tolerated in political activity, the respect for political rights shown by governments, the absence of fraud or coercion in elections, and, in general, the fidelity of government authorities to the letter and spirit of the constitution. The countries more developed in a social and economic sense, those with high indicators of literacy, health, and income, are usually, although not always, the more developed politically.[5]

ECONOMIC POLICY ISSUES

In the struggle for power in Latin America, the central issue in political debate has increasingly become the issue between economic nationalists and economic internationalists or liberals, that is, the question of to what extent national economies should remain integrated into the world capitalist system: Should free movement of goods and capital exist? Or should restrictions be imposed in the interest of developing home industry, limiting the impact of market fluctuations, and especially limiting the power over the economy held by foreign interests?

[5]Political development is used here in the same sense as in the author's *Political Development in Latin America: Instability, Violence, and Evolutionary Change,* New York: Random House, 1968; or in Samuel E. Finer's *The Man on Horseback,* 2nd ed., New York: Praeger, 1974. The concept is used in somewhat different though comparable senses by the various authors who have written in this field. Other leading books on the topic are Samuel P. Huntington, *Political Order in Changing Societies,* New Haven: Yale University Press, 1970; Lucian Pye, *Aspects of Political Development,* Boston: Little, Brown, 1966; Cyril E. Black, *The Dynamics of Modernization: A Study in Comparative History,* New York: Harper and Row, 1966. Also see Fred W. Riggs, "The Theory of Political Development," in James C. Charlesworth, ed., *Contemporary Political Analysis,* New York: The Free Press, 1967.

2

Mexico

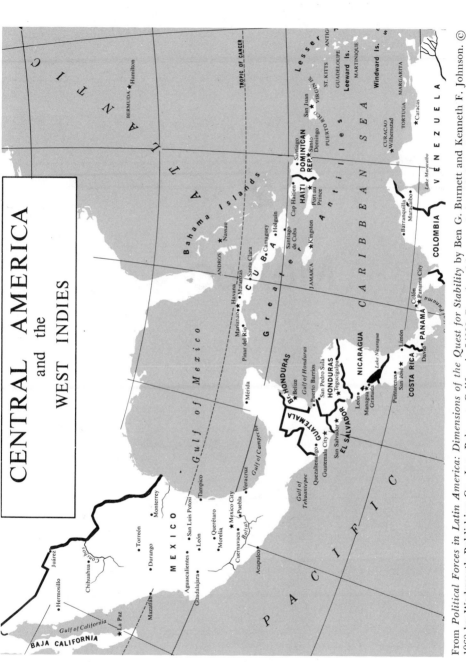

CENTRAL AMERICA
and the
WEST INDIES

From *Political Forces in Latin America: Dimensions of the Quest for Stability* by Ben G. Burnett and Kenneth F. Johnson. © 1968 by Wadsworth Publishing Co., Inc., Belmont, California 94002. Reprinted by permission of the publisher, Duxbury Press.

MEXICAN HISTORY SINCE
THE REVOLUTION

Modern Mexican history begins with the Revolution of 1910. This was one of the great revolutions: like the French Revolution or the Russian Revolution, it involved extensive fighting and, indeed, extended civil war and led not only to a change in government but also to a complete transformation of society.

Major Cleavages in Mexico
Since 1910

Apart from the clash of personal ambitions that characterizes politics everywhere, the major cleavages in Mexico since the Revolution have been, in succession: the conflict between Revolutionaries and counterrevolutionaries; the struggle among Revolutionary factions for

PRESIDENTS OF MEXICO, 1917–1982

1917–20	Venustiano Carranza
1920	Adolfo de la Huerta
1920–24	Alvaro Obregón
1924–28	Plutarco Elías Calles
1928–30	Emilio Portes Gil
1930–32	Pascual Ortiz Rubio
1932–34	Abelardo Rodríguez
1934–40	Lázaro Cárdenas
1940–46	Manuel Avila Camacho
1946–52	Miguel Alemán
1952–58	Adolfo Ruiz Cortines
1958–64	Adolfo López Mateos
1964–70	Gustavo Díaz Ordaz
1970–76	Luís Echeverría
1976–82	José López Portillo
1982–	Miguel de la Madríd Hurtado

control of the government; conflict over the role of the church; after the Revolution was consolidated and the mechanisms for the orderly transfer of power established, conflict over social and economic policy; and, finally, in the current phase, conflict over the democratization of the regime. Although these were the dominant conflicts during each of the successive phases of the formation of modern Mexico, some were not completely resolved and persisted into succeeding phases; in addition, in each phase, the major conflicts were supplemented by secondary lines of cleavage over separate issues and by personal conflicts between rival leaders.

Armed Struggle, 1910–1917

In 1910, Francisco Madero began a revolution against the government of the long-time dictator Porfirio Díaz. Although the revolution finally succeeded, Madero was president for only fifteen months before being overthrown and killed during a counterrevolution led by Victoriano Huerta. The Revolutionaries resumed fighting, and the Huerta presidency lasted only slightly longer than that of Madero; however, armies that represented different Revolutionary tendencies, based on distinct regions of the country and headed by rival leaders, most importantly Francisco Villa, Emiliano Zapata, and Venustiano Carranza, fought among themselves until Carranza established himself, first as provisional president, and in 1917 as elected constitutional president. Thus the phase of conflict between Revolutionary and counterrevolutionary was succeeded by a struggle among various Revolutionary tendencies and leaders that was not finally brought to an end until Alvaro Obregón, the general who commanded Carranza's forces during the fighting, overthrew Carranza in 1920. The Revolution of 1920 was the last successful revolt in Mexican history. Several other revolts, begun around each election time over the question of who would succeed to the presidency, occurred during the 1920s, but essentially the regime of the Revolution was consolidated and stabilized during Obregón's term of office.

Alvaro Obregón

It was the government of Obregón (1920–24) that gave concrete form to Revolutionary aspirations for social justice. One contribution of Obregón was the establishment of a political stability which, although it meant a continuation of the Mexican tradition that the candidate of the incumbent regime always wins the presidential elections, effectively barred a president from succeeding himself and thus allowed for continuous change in the occupancy of political positions. Obregón also began two lines of Revolutionary policy that have remained fundamental for Mexican government to this day: the distribution of land to landless peasants and the protection of workers through the encouragement of labor organizations and the establishment of various social security programs.

Plutarco Elías Calles and Lázaro Cárdenas

Obregón's policies in these three respects—political stability without *continuismo,* the continuation of the incumbent president in office; land reform; and the encouragement of labor organization, together with the granting of extensive social benefits—were reaffirmed and amplified by the first president to serve a six-year term, Lázaro Cárdenas (1934–40). In the ten years that had elapsed between Obregón's presidency and that of Cárdenas, these objectives had become blurred, or were pursued half-heartedly, or in a distorted fashion. The president who succeeded Obregón, Plutarco Elías Calles, became skeptical about the economic effects of land reform; protection of the rights of labor degenerated into acquiescence in racketeering by union leaders; and the principle of no reelection, while maintained in form, was weakened as Calles became the strong man who dominated the governments of his successors. During this period, also, two further issues became of major political importance: the rights of foreign investors and the relation between church and state. As Calles became more conservative on the agrarian question, he also became more favorably disposed to foreign, that is, United States, investment. However, he retained his intense dislike of the Catholic church and enforced the anticlerical provisions of the 1917 Constitution and subsequent anticlerical laws to the extent that devout Catholics rose in revolt in the Cristero Rebellion (1927) and a terrible civil war was fought, with frightful atrocities on both sides. The presidents who succeeded Calles—Ortiz Rubio, Portes Gil, and Rodríguez[1]—softened the hostility between church and state, and the

[1]Obregón was reelected for the first six-year term under a constitutional amendment that permitted a president to return to office after skipping a term. However, he was assassinated before taking office, and Congress elected a provisional president, Emilio Portes Gil, until new elections could be held. Pascual Ortiz Rubio won the elections and was to have served out the four years and ten months that remained of Obregón's term, but he resigned after two and one-half years and ten months that remained of Obregón's term, but he resigned after two and one-half years in office, and Congress elected Abelardo Rodriguez to complete the term. A good detailed history of Mexico in the 1920s and 1930s is J. W. F. Dulles, *Yesterday in Mexico,* Austin: University of Texas Press, 1964.

dispute was finally laid to rest during the term of Cárdenas and his successor, Manuel Avila Camacho. Cárdenas also had reservations about the policy of unlimited freedom for foreign capital and, provoked by the contempt shown by foreign oil companies for Mexican laws, expropriated and nationalized the companies' properties. Despite strong pressure to do so, President Roosevelt refrained from intervening on behalf of the companies. Cárdenas also nationalized the railroads and greatly amplified the scope of the land reform program, setting up some of the plantations expropriated as collective farms. For the most part, land distributed under the program had been farmed by individual peasants, although the land is not held by individuals but by a land-holding community, usually a village but sometimes only part of it, or parts of several villages, called the *ejido*.

Cárdenas was also responsible for the present organization of the ruling party into three sectors: agrarian, labor, and "popular," which represented, respectively, peasants, workers, and the Revolutionary middle class. There was briefly also a military sector of the party, which was abolished by President Avila Camacho.

Presidents After Cárdenas

The terms of office of the presidents who followed Cárdenas were less exciting and marked by less innovation. The government was immune now from counterrevolution or military revolts by disgruntled Revolutionary heroes, and the religious question, while not finally settled, was permanently held in abeyance; thus the major question of public policy became that of economic growth and social change. Miguel Alemán (1946–52), who succeeded Avila Camacho, followed a policy of stepped-up growth that required freedom for foreign investors, strong support for Mexican businessmen, and correspondingly less attention to the needs of workers and peasants. A modified version of this policy was also followed by Adolfo Ruiz Cortines (1952–58) and Gustavo Díaz Ordaz (1964–70). Adolfo López Mateos (1958–64) and Luís Echeverría (1970–76) instead followed more left-wing policies that placed restrictions on foreign investments, paid more attention to the needs of poorer sectors of society, and, in general, were concerned not only with how fast total production grew but also with how the income from such growth was distributed among the different classes of the population. José López Portillo (1976–82) attempted a balanced policy midway between these two alternatives, and it appeared likely that Miguel de la Madrid Hurtado (1982–) would follow in López Portillo's footsteps in this respect.

NEW DIRECTIONS FOR
POLICY

Since 1976, petroleum production in Mexico has increased rapidly, and the country has become the world's fourth leading exporter. The wealth brought by oil exports, has, however, been a mixed blessing. While alleviating balance of payments problems, it has encouraged imports and discouraged the production of goods within the country. Borrowing abroad has become easier, and Mexico's foreign debts have grown. Easier money has contributed to greater corruption, always a major problem in Mexico, and to inflation.

Intimidated by the prospect that Mexico might become another Venezuela, importing everything but oil and unable to provide jobs, López Portillo undertook an expensive but successful attempt to stimulate agricultural production. Serious problems of inflation, unemployment, and maldistribution of income remained for his successor, however.

Her role as major oil exporter enabled Mexico to speak with a louder voice in international politics. Always treading a narrow path between asserting independence of the United States and remaining on good terms with her major trading partner, Mexico's Revolutionary heritage has always made her sympathetic with popular insurgent movements that some United States governments have treated only as disguised advanced parties for Soviet imperialism. In the early 1980's that made for divergences between United States and Mexican policies, although the Mexicans tried to play a moderating and mediating role with respect to the revolutionary movements in Central America, rather than one frankly antagonistic to the United States.

POLITICAL PARTIES

The political structure created by Obregón was given institutional form by Calles as a political party. Baptized by Calles the Partido Nacional Revolucionario, or PNR, it was renamed by Cárdenas the Partido de la Revolución Mexicana and has been called since 1946 the Partido Revolucionario Institutional, or PRI. Conceived of by Calles as the party of all Revolutionaries, excluding only those who did not accept the Mexican Revolution, it was thus based on the lines of cleavage of the first phase of postrevolutionary political conflict. Except to some degree for the conflict over the role of the church, therefore, the line of division between the ruling party and other political parties has not corresponded to the lines of cleavage over subsequent conflicts, which have cut across party identification, dividing the ruling party into factions and involving people outside of the ruling party.

This effect has been especially notable in the struggle over government social and economic policy. In the 1920s, conflict took place between peasants and unionized workers over where the emphasis of government social policy should lie, but since the 1940s workers and peasants have generally found themselves on the same side of economic issues, opposed to investors and employers of labor in both agriculture and industry. The lines of economic conflict in Mexico today thus resemble those in the industrialized countries of Western Europe in being primarily between poor and well-to-do, between capital and labor.

In the industrial sector, this struggle does not occur within the ruling party as such; the party statutes are explicit in excluding from membership in the PRI those who employ more than six people. Business interests participate in the political struggle, however, through direct pressure on the president and other officials, either in personal contacts or through the actions of the powerful trade associations, which also attempt to influence public opinion by means of campaigns in the press. In the agricultural sector, the struggle does go on to some extent within the PRI, however. The *ejidatarios* (members of the *ejidos)*, who have received land under the government land reform program, together with the professional society of agronomists, constitute the agrarian sector of the PRI; in the "popular" sector of the party, however, is an organization called the National Confederation of Small Property Owners, which, although it ostensibly enlists only small private farmers, actually serves as a mouthpiece for large commercial farmers too.

The role of the National Confederation of Small Property Owners indicates the versatility of the popular sector of the party. In principle, it was designed as a means by which progressive members of the bourgeoisie could affiliate with the party, but Cárdenas placed the federation of government employees in the popular sector, since the labor sector of the party would be all powerful if it included the bureaucrats' union. In recent years, the popular sector has, in fact, become the dominant sector within the PRI, far out-distancing the other sectors in such ways as the number of seats in the chamber of deputies won by its members. The greatest addition to popular sector strength has been through the Federation of Proletarian Districts, an organization that enrolls in the party the dwellers in the shantytowns and slum districts that have mushroomed in the country's major cities. The popular sector today thus represents a curious alliance between the best educated and the best situated members of the middle class and the poorest of dwellers in the city.

THE LOCUS OF POLITICAL POWER

As the Mexican political system has evolved, power has shifted within the regime. In the early postrevolutionary period, the government was dominated by the military heroes of the Revolution. In a period in which fighting still occasionally occurred and always threatened, military leadership was natural, but the Revolution was gradually civilianized. As the effects of Obregón's policies became felt, the government won the support of the masses, and military revolts came increasingly to be seen as a losing proposition. Revolutionary generals died off, retired, or were sent into exile as a result of unsuccessful revolts. Obregón began the professionalization of the private armies that had fought in the Revolution, requiring officers to attend courses of military training if they wanted to retain their commissions.

Army officers continued to play key roles in party and government affairs but on a decreasing scale, and civilians have occupied the presidency continuously since 1946. The practice of having military officers as presidents of the PRI died out in the 1960s. Governorships and cabinet positions gradually became the preserve of civilians, so that today the only career military officers in the cabinet are the two men who serve as Secretary of Defense and Secretary of the Navy.

Under Cárdenas, labor leaders played a major role in politics; under Alemán, the balance was redressed, and businessmen became a political force. Since 1952, however, the dominant factor in Mexican politics has been the career bureaucrats, who have come to occupy all of the top government positions. Through the popular sector of the PRI, bureaucrats have also come to wield major power within the party, but the party itself is today not important as a policy-making body, serving instead primarily as a mechanism for rallying support to the government, by running election campaigns, offering careers to the ambitious, organizing public demonstrations in support of the government's policies, and serving as a two-way communications network that both provides information from local areas and insures that the president's control is effective throughout the republic.

MINOR POLITICAL PARTIES

Partido de Acción Nacional

Although the political system is dominated by the PRI, the minor parties also have their role to play. The largest of the minor parties is the Partido de Acción Nacional, or PAN. Founded in 1939, it originally accepted the role written into the Revolutionary drama by Calles for it as the party of the counterrevolution and stressed the rights of private property and the rights of the church, which had been abrogated by Revolutionary legislation. The PAN's image of itself, and its policy line, has fluctuated over the years. Sometimes it took the posture of an elite group of Catholic intellectuals criticizing the course the Revolution was taking without ever contemplating that it might itself gain power. At other times, it came under the influence of extreme right-wing activists, such as those in the Sinarquista movement, who believed in violent direct action and were influenced by European fascism. Finally, under more moderate leadership in the 1960s, the PAN assumed the role of loyal opposition, competing in elections and accepting its minority status. In this role, the PAN "accepts" the Revolution and its policy outcomes, arguing only for a shift or emphasis in policy. In church-state relations, the PAN wants recognition in law of the modus vivendi that has been reached in practice, which consists essentially in leaving the anticlerical legislation of the early days of the Revolution undisturbed on the statute books and in the constitution but not enforcing it. In economic affairs, the PAN urges greater consideration for small business and the conversion of ejido plots into outright private ownership. The party also takes a "good government" line, criticizing bribery of public officials, fraud in elections, and interference by central government authorities with the autonomy of the states and municipalities. The PAN is welcomed by the PRI as a loyal opposition that gives substance to the PRI's electoral rhetoric that the government party is still needed to defend the Revolution against its enemies.

As Mexican society has developed and the middle class has grown, the PAN has slowly but steadily increased its voting strength. In presidential elections, the party took 7.82 percent of the vote in 1952, 9.42 percent in 1958, 10.98 percent in 1964, and 13.83 percent in 1970. (Due to internal dissension, it did not nominate a presidential candidate in 1976.) As the leading opposition party to the PRI, the PAN from time to time picks up support from dissident elements in the ruling party, disappointed over the choice of PRI candidates or over some local scandal or act of repression. Thus local-level surges in support for the PAN occur from time to time, providing it with majorities in municipal elections. It is the only party other than the PRI that wins some congressional district seats—four out of three hundred in 1979. In addition, it receives the largest number of seats from the one hundred reserved for minority parties by the 1979 reform legislation, which gave it an additional thirty-nine seats in the 1979–82 legislature.

The Partido Democrático Mexicano lies further to the right than the PAN and, ironically, espouses a pro-clerical and anti-democratic ideology. It received ten Chamber seats in the 1979 election.

Other Minor Political Parties

The other minor political parties lie ideologically to the left of the PRI. They thus constitute part of the "Revolutionary family," unlike the PAN and the PDM, and therefore are not wholly distinct from the all-embracing government party. These minor parties sometimes oppose the PRI, sometimes ally with it; they are influenced by the PRI, and two of them, the PPS and the PARM, may be subsidized by it. There is an ideological overlap between these parties and the left wing of the PRI, so for individuals the question of which party to join may be as much one of tactics, family traditions, and personal career prospects as it is of fundamental ideological commitment. The most significant of the minor parties of the left used to be the Popular Socialist Party or PPS, which manages to capture two or three percent of the national vote. Although the Popular Socialists are today essentially a satellite of the PRI, the PPS is a pro-Soviet Marxist party with Stalinist tendencies. Collaborating with the PRI, on the premise that the socialist revolution cannot come about until Mexican capitalism has reached its maximum development, the PPS is now close in ideology and tactical line to the labor sector of the PRI.

Mexican Communist party. Interestingly enough, the Mexican Communist party, the PCM, is less loyal to Moscow and has taken a more flexible line, especially in international affairs, than the PPS. Thus the PPS endorsed the Soviet invasions of Czechoslovakia in 1968 and Afghanistan in 1979; the PCM opposed them. The Popular Socialists support the Soviet Union in its dispute with China, while the PCM takes a more open attitude, trying to maintain good relations with all foreign Communist parties, including those of the Soviet Union, China, Yugoslavia, and Romania.

Democratization of the System

With its election of eighteen deputies in 1979, the PCM became the leading left-wing opposition party. It has taken its responsibilities very seriously, showing itself well-prepared in debate and making clear that it considers itself a democratic party whose role is to educate voters and participate in the electoral process; it does not wish to be considered a Leninist revolutionary sect. Its general orientation is close to that of the Communist Party of Spain, and it might be called "Eurocommunist."

For the 1982 elections the PCM joined with some smaller left-wing groups to form the PSUM, the Unified Mexican Socialist Party.

The Trotskyite Socialist Workers Party, Partido Socialista de los Trabajadores, or PST, is also represented in the Chamber of Deputies. A variety of minuscule leftist groupings are affiliated with the PST or the PCM for electoral purposes.

The Mexican Workers' Party, the Partido Mexicano de los Trabajadores, or PMT, led by Heberto Castillo, may become a force (relatively speaking) in the future, but it did not contest legislative elections in 1979.

Representation of the minor parties in the Chamber of Deputies was made possible by the political reform legislation passed under López Portillo in 1979, which made it easier for parties to register legally and increased the number of seats which minority parties could win on a proportional representation basis to one hundred.

MEXICO: A HYBRID REGIME TYPE

The complexities of the Mexican system require that it be considered a hybrid regime type, with residual revolutionary elements and careful democratic reformist strategies constituting aspects of the system that moderate its basic authoritarian features. Moreover, the balance among these different tendencies shifts from one presidential term to another. Under Echeverría, a sincere attempt was made to identify Mexico internationally with the countries of the Third World, and the United States was clearly unhappy with positions taken by Mexico at the United Nations, such as its denunciations of United States dominance in the hemisphere and of its efforts to undermine the Allende government in Chile. The government's economic policies control and guide the role of foreign investment in the economy, and though the foreign companies can live with these restraints, they would clearly prefer it if they were not there. The distribution of income from Mexico's growing and vital economy is highly unequal among classes and regions of the republic, but progressive presidents make efforts to reduce that inequality, as did Echeverría and his successor, José López Portillo.

Dominance of the President

Echeverría's choice of López Portillo as his successor demonstrated clearly the dominance of the president in the political system, since any method of choosing the regime's candidate other than absolute presidential discretion would surely have resulted in a different choice.[2] In view of the dominant role of the president in the system, some observers have regarded it as one of personal dictatorship, the only constraint being that the dictator has to be changed every six years. In a more sophisticated interpretation, the regime is an authoritarian system, in the terms outlined in the writings of Juan Linz. In view of the substantial role of United States business interests in the economy, some observers view the authoritarian character of the system as working on behalf of the forces of international capitalism. This is not an unreasonable position to take; it can be coupled with evidences of dependency and "internal colonialism," in the manner of the classic analysis of Pablo González Casanova,[3] to present Mexico in the stereotyped guise of an economic colony of the United States ruled on behalf of international capitalism by a corrupt local oligarchy. But while this may be part of the picture, to consider it as the whole picture ignores the genuine nationalism and leftist orientation of many members of the political leadership.

MEXICO AS A DEVELOPING COUNTRY

The concept of development is much favored today to explain what is happening in the poorer countries of the world. For many of those countries, reality can be made to fit the model of "development" only by stretching and straining it almost to the breaking point. For Mexico, on the other hand, the concept of development fits perfectly; in fact, it is impossible to understand Mexican reality outside a developmental perspective.

The key to the political crisis through which Mexico is passing is that Mexico has a political system adapted to bringing about development in a backward, predominantly peasant, society that has recently emerged from civil war and wants social peace above all. It is a system designed to blur differences, to disguise clashes of interest, and to preserve outward calm, at the same time that the economy grows, that population becomes more urbanized and sophisticated, and that society becomes more differentiated. It is a governmental system suited to the tasks of "guided democracy," which plays a strong leadership role vis-à-vis a backward, ignorant, and apathetic population.

[2]This has confirmed the correctness of the position taken by Daniel Cosío Villegas in his book *La sucesión presidencial en México,* Mexico, D.F.: Ediciones Joaquin Mortiz, 1975.

[3]*La democracia en México,* Mexico, D.F.: Ediciones Era, 1964.

Here, however, the central paradox of Mexican politics emerges. If such a government begins to succeed in its tasks, if the population does indeed become more sophisticated, if a middle class grows, if the number of university students expands, then that type of more modern, sophisticated society requires a different type of government, one that is responsive to demands for wider participation, that is open to a critical opposition, and that accepts conflict as legitimate. Much as a good doctor tries to treat a patient so that his own services will no longer be necessary, so a strong developmental regime must strive to make itself obsolete. The change in the base, one might say, must be reflected by a change in the superstructure.

In that superstructure, however, in that governmental apparatus, are very real people who do not like to contemplate the loss of power, prestige, and wealth that the possibility of opening up the regime to broader participation, of allowing effective criticism, implies. As a result, measures that appear to signify a greater degree of openness and political participation are introduced but with the hope that they will mollify and coopt the critics of the regime without changing its basic character. So far, that strategy has been successful.

SUMMARY

The significant cleavages in Mexican politics since the Revolution of 1910 have been, in turn, the conflict between Revolutionaries and counterrevolutionaries; the struggle among Revolutionary factions for control of the government; conflict over the role of the Church; conflict over social and economic policy; and conflict over the democratization of the regime. After the conclusion of the civil war, the government of Alvaro Obregón (1920–24) stabilized Mexican politics and began the fundamental policies of land reform and the promotion of labor organization. After setbacks in these policies, they were pushed further by Lazaro Cárdenas (1934–40), who nationalized the railroads and the foreign oil companies, stepped up land reform, and reorganized the ruling party, now the PRI, into separate sectors for workers, peasants, and the middle class. Subsequent presidents have oscillated between left- and right-wing emphases. The country now has a mixed economy and a long-dominant political party currently trying to maintain firm control of the country while responding to the demands of the expanding middle class and student populations for greater openness and participation and trying to find solutions to complex and difficult economic problems. The regime is of a partially authoritarian type, its authoritarianism modified in a democratic direction by mass mobilization in the party's constituent organizations, the emphasis on economic and social development, and the rule of no presidential reelection.

3

Central America

GENERAL DESCRIPTION

The five countries of Central America—reading from northwest to southeast, Guatemala, El Salvador, Honduras, Nicaragua, and Costa Rica—are among the smallest, both in population and in area, in Latin America. Yet it is surprising how the microcosm of Central America contains a wide variety of geographic zones, of demographic structures, and of political systems. One can learn a lot from comparing and contrasting the Central American countries as they are arrayed along some key social and political dimensions.

Demographic Structures

One such dimension is the demographic. As one moves south and east away from the pre-Hispanic population centers in Guatemala, the size of the national populations diminishes. For political purposes, it is more significant that as one moves southeast populations become less Indian. About half of the population of Guatemala itself is Indian, in the cultural sense of speaking primarily Indian languages and exhibiting non-modern traits in dress, food, and attitudes. In El Salvador, the proportion of the population that is Indian is probably no more than ten percent, with the rest mestizo. Honduras and Nicaragua are overwhelmingly mestizo, while in Costa Rica, the southernmost state, the purely European element is the strongest of any of the five countries. In both Nicaragua and Costa Rica, there are small black and mulatto populations in some coastal areas.

Economic Distinctions

Exports. Coffee is the dominant crop throughout the area; it is the leading export of Guatemala, El Salvador, and Costa Rica. However, Guatemala has begun to export petroleum, which should become a more significant economic factor in the years ahead. The principal exports of Honduras and Nicaragua are bananas and cotton, respectively. Sugar and rice cultivation and cattle raising are subsidiary activities that produce export revenues, with corn and beans raised for domestic consumption.

Economic and social indicators. In indicators of economic and social well-being, such as literary, life expectancy, and gross national product per capita, Costa Rica leads the states in the area, while Honduras is the least developed in these respects. Except for Honduras, the area experienced high rates of economic growth during the 1960s, especially under the stimulus of the Central American Common Market, an arrangement under which each state of the area favored imports from the others over imports from outside Central America, and there was agreement not to compete in certain new industries. However, the Common Market all but collapsed in the early 1970s. Honduras withdrew, correctly arguing that it bore a heavy share of the costs of the arrangement while receiving few benefits from it. Costa Rica partially withdrew from participation because its higher labor costs meant that it could not compete effectively with the lower wage rates of the other countries, and because of this factor and an overvalued currency unit it had therefore built up balance of payment deficits with the other countries of the isthmus. Trade between El Salvador and Honduras was broken off in the aftermath of the 1969 "soccer war" between the two countries; the economy of Nicaragua was severely damaged as a result of the earthquake that devastated Managua during the "Black Christmas" of 1972; and Guatemala was even more severely affected by the earthquake it experienced in early 1976. Nevertheless, under the stimulus of the common market arrangement, an impetus was given to the industrialization of the area, especially in Guatemala and El Salvador. These countries were the ones that already had something of an economic base facilitating industrialization, partly because their domestic populations were large enough to make possible a certain amount of industry catering to the home market and, in the case of El Salvador, because population density made it impossible for the labor force to be completely absorbed into agriculture.

Political Crises

In the late 1970s, the region was shaken by extreme political crises. The venality and brutality of Anastasio Somoza Debayle, the ruler of Nicaragua, provoked the formation of a broad multiclass coalition against him which supported the Sandinista Liberation Army in its final victorious struggle to overthrow the dictator. The example of victorious revolution in Nicaragua stimulated the efforts of revolutionaries in El Salvador, on the one hand, and, on the other, provoked the United States and some junior Salvadorean officers into abandoning the country's dictator in an attempt, which seemed unlikely to succeed, to forestall revolution through rather tentative and ambiguous reforms.

Urge to Unity

The Central American Common Market is only the most recent expression of the urge to unity that has always existed in the Central American isthmus. The five countries were united politically in the early days of independence, and attempts at unification by force of arms continued during the nineteenth century. At present, the movement to unity remains no more than an aspiration embodied in constitutional provisions, in the identical colors of the national flags, and in the pious sentiments of the national anthems. A common political organization for the five states, ODECA, does exist but is of no practical effect. The desire for unity is continuously in conflict with the fear of the four smaller states that Guatemala, the largest state of the isthmus, would dominate any federation, with the rivalries and hostilities between El Salvador and Honduras, with the boundary disputes between Honduras and Nicaragua, and with the political animosities existing between authoritarian and democratic regimes.[1]

To understand the dynamics of their political situations and social structures, it is necessary to examine each country in turn.

GUATEMALA

Its Indian Character

Guatemala is more than half Indian in population, heir to the flourishing and highly developed Maya civilization. The Indian population is primarily distributed in independent villages and as workers on large estates in the central portion of the country. Many Indians also travel as seasonal farm workers to the cotton and sugar plantations in the coastal lowlands, concentrated on the Pacific side of the country that is the home of its export agriculture. (Like all Central American countries, except El Salvador, Guatemala has both Atlantic and Pacific coasts.)

---

[1] On the question of Central American unity, see Joseph S. Nye, Jr., "Central American Regional Integration," *International Conciliation*, no. 562, March 1967.

The People and Their Political Tendencies

While the rural landowner interest remains of first importance, Guatemala is no longer merely a traditional underdeveloped country. In the cities, and especially in Guatemala City itself, there is a substantial middle class of quite recent origin, primarily in government employment and the professions but also increasingly in industry. The organized working class is small as yet, and in politics it has generally been content to follow the lead of progressive elements of the middle class. For most of the country's recent history the political struggle thus has taken place essentially between traditional conservative landholding elements and the mildly progressive sectors of the urban middle class backed by the small urban working class; it has centered on modest reform measures and issues of civil liberties, constitutional government, and military intervention in politics. As in other similar cases, if it appeared that a genuine threat to law and order and the rights of property existed, a substantial portion of the middle class went over to the conservative side. Under the influence of the civil wars taking place in Nicaragua and El Salvador in the late 1970s and early 1980s conflict heightened and became more vicious.

The Arbenz Government

The specific political tendencies in combat have developed out of the violent history of the last forty years in Guatemalan politics, which began with the election as president of Juan José Arévalo in 1944. The moderate center-left government of Arévalo prepared the way for the election in 1950 of Jacobo Arbenz Guzmán, a former colonel who attempted to move the country much further left in an authentically revolutionary direction. Expressing sympathy with the international policies of the Soviet Union, Arbenz was given active support by the Partido Guatemalteco de Trabajo, the Guatemalan Communist Party, which took an active role in Arbenz's government, especially in its land reform program. This program entailed the expropriation with only nominal compensation of large estates, including the extensive properties owned by the North American United Fruit Company. Conscious of the danger that his program would be resisted by conservative interests that would attempt to use the army against him, President Arbenz organized a militia force, which the Guatemalan army refused to arm and train. He thereupon arranged for the shipment of arms for his militia from suppliers in Eastern Europe. It is not clear whether, in the mind of John Foster Dulles, then the United States Secretary of State, President Arbenz's crimes consisted more in getting arms from Eastern

Europe, in expropriating the United Fruit Company, or in taking a pro-Soviet line internationally; in all probability, such distinctions were not made, and it was simply felt that "communism," however demonstrated, was intolerable in Central America. In 1954, the United States Central Intelligence Agency (CIA) organized, trained, and armed an invasion force that operated from Honduran territory, led by a former colonel in the Guatemalan army, Carlos Castillo Armas. The Guatemalan army, itself hostile to Arbenz, refused to fight against the invasion force, and, in an agreement negotiated by a representative of the United States, Castillo Armas became president while Arbenz went into exile.[2] Its spurious "success" in overthrowing a leftist president through an exile invasion helped mislead the CIA into thinking that the Bay of Pigs invasion would overthrow Fidel Castro, seven years later.

PRESIDENTS OF GUATEMALA, 1944-82

1944–50	Juan José Arévalo
1950–54	Jacobo Arbenz Guzmán
1954–58	Carlos Castillo Armas
1958–64	Miguel Ydígoras Fuentes
1964–66	Enrique Peralta Azurdia
1966–70	Julio César Méndez Montenegro
1970–74	Carlos Arana Osorio
1974–78	Eugenio Kjell Laugerud García
1978–82	Romeo Lucas García
1982–	Efraín Ríos Montt

Castillo Armas and Counterrevolution

As president, Castillo Armas led a stringent counterrevolution. Land that had been expropriated and distributed to Indian peasants was restored to its former owners. If the Indians would not go peacefully, they were shot. This experience was traumatic for the Indian population, which had started to participate in politics but which subsequently relapsed into defensive aloofness. An election was held to ratify Castillo Armas as legal president of Guatemala, a plebiscite without opposition candidates in which each voter had to tell the electoral officials orally how he wanted to vote. It was hardly surprising that the vote for Castillo Armas was all but unanimous. However, Castillo Armas was assassinated in 1958 by a member of his own guard, in an incident whose

[2]United States sources for these events are generally biased against Arbenz. See Ronald Schneider, *Communism in Guatemala, 1944–1954,* New York: Praeger, 1959, for a detailed account. A pro-Arbenz perspective is given in Guillermo Toriello Garrido, *La batalla de Guatemala,* México, D.F.: Ediciones Cuadernos Americanos, 1955.

antecedents remain obscure, although a committee of the Guatemalan congress ultimately reported that it believed the Dominican dictator, Rafael Trujillo, was responsible for the act.

Guatemalan Politics Since 1958

In 1958, a well-meaning but not very able conservative former soldier and government official, Miguel Ydígoras Fuentes, was elected president after his partisans had threatened revolt unless the results of a previous election they alleged to have been fraudulent were annulled. Although uninspired, the government of Ydígoras did try to keep within the norms of constitutional government. In fact, Ydígoras was overthrown toward the end of his term when the army commander, Colonel Enrique Peralta Azurdia, believed that he might hold a fair election that could be won by ex-president Arévalo, feared now by the army commanders as the man whose government had prepared the way for that of Arbenz.

Peralta himself headed a provisional regime from 1964 to 1966, during which time a new constitution was adopted that reduced the president's term to four years and made the franchise universal. Previously, illiterate women had not been allowed to vote.

In another unsatisfactorily explained incident, the leading candidate in the 1966 elections, the leader of the moderate center-left Partido Revolucionario, Mario Méndez Montenegro, was found shot in what was officially called a suicide. Mario's brother, Julio César Méndez Montenegro, thereupon became the party's candidate and was elected. Before the military allowed him to take office, however, he had to agree to a series of limitations on his power as president, including giving a free hand to the army to wage war against the leftist guerrillas active in the country. During his four years as president, in fact, Méndez was able to be little more than a figurehead for the military, whose counter-guerrilla campaign, while successful, was waged by means of ferocious tactics that included the massacre of innocent villagers. The far left thereupon turned to urban terrorism, kidnapping, and assassination, which were, in turn, answered by a right-wing counterterrorist campaign, which resulted in a total breakdown of personal security in the country. Right-wing terror activities, spearheaded by the fearsome Mano Blanca organization, soon dwarfed the efforts of the left and extended to the assassination, often after torture, not only of leftist activists but also of leading political figures of the center-left and center and of friends and members of the families of those suspected of leftist sympathies, including innocent peasants and students. The terror continued, with government connivance, after the commander of the military antiguerrilla campaign, Colonel Carlos Arana Osorio, was elected president for the 1970–74 term with the support of a timid and frightened middle class, eager for "law and order."

The main two conservative political parties, the Partido Institucional Democrático, or PID, founded by Colonel Peralta, and the Movimiento de Liberación Nacional, or MLN, an extremely reactionary group founded by Castillo Armas, some of whose leaders are implicated in right-wing terrorism, supported the dominant Arana regime, which represented military and landowner interests especially. The Partido Revolucionario (PR) of Méndez Montenegro, supported by elements of the urban middle class and now occupying a center position in the political spectrum, included both elements willing to cooperate with the right-wing parties and those remaining with the party's traditional center-left orientation. Some of the more leftist elements in the PR, such as the mayor of Guatemala City during the Arana Osorio regime, Manuel Colom Argüeta, left the PR and organized their own party, the FURD, close in political orientation to the Christian Democrats (Partido Social Cristiano Guatemalteco), and presented a common candidate with the Christian Democrats in the 1974 presidential elections. Further to the left is the illegal Partido Guatemalteco de Trabajo, the Guatemalan Communist Party, which was dealt a heavy blow when the entire leadership of the party was killed in 1973, apparently on orders of the Arana administration. Finally, a fraudulent election gave the presidency in 1974 to another general, Eugenio Kjell Laugerud García.

Laugerud seemed to appreciate the gravity of the political situation in the country and attempted to move toward the center, forming a congressional alliance with the Partido Revolucionario. There appeared some hope for a moderate and reformist solution to the country's problems in an alliance between the PR and Laugerud's PID, leaving isolated to the right the MLN and the Central Auténtico Nacionalista formed by Colonel Arana. For the term beginning in 1978, this centrist-moderate alliance elected General Romeo Lucas García for President, and, for Vice-President, Francisco Villagrán Kramer of the PR, a progressive specialist in international law. Nevertheless, the right wing, panicked by the Sandinista victory in Nicaragua and the growing civil war in El Salvador, stepped up its campaign of terror. Assassinations increased, extending not only to left-wingers but also to progressive and centrist leaders, including Colom Argüeta, and indeed to any officials of the university student association and professors of note, especially in the social sciences. Finally, in 1980, Villagrán Kramer himself resigned the vice-presidency and went into exile to avoid assassination. In 1981, Amnesty International published a report making clear that the right-wing terror campaign was covertly directed by Lucas García himself.

The elections of March 1982 resulted, predictably, in a victory for the government candidate, General Aníbal Guevara. Younger officers, sympathetic with MLN and Christian Democratic complaints of fraud but probably more concerned over promotions and the senior officers' monopoly of corruption, organized a coup and installed as president retired General Efraín Ríos Montt, who had been the Christian Democrats' presidential candidate in 1974. Since become a Protestant evangelist of somewhat erratic behavior, Ríos Montt seemed unlikely, even if he could stay in power, to be able to heal the open wounds of Guatemalan society.

An Overview

The Guatemalan political system thus reflects the agony of a society undergoing acute crisis. Convinced that a nation dominated by great concentrations of wealth and marked by the colossal gulf between Indian and non-Indian segments of society can only change as a result of a thoroughgoing revolution, and having before their eyes the example of how a progressive regime was overthrown by violence directed from outside the country, the far left puts its hopes in violent revolution. Conservative landed interests and military officers, presented with this possibility, fight back ruthlessly. Elements of the middle class become frightened and accept the "law and order at any price" position of the right, which justifies terror and violence. More progressive members of the middle class, together with the limited segments of the lower classes who are politically active, attempt to promote mild social change through constitutional and democratic means, knowing that fair elections would give them a majority of the vote. But democratic procedures threaten the landowners' wealth and the generals' power, and right-wing terrorism is directed against the center even more than against the left.

EL SALVADOR

General Description

El Salvador resembles Guatemala in some social and economic features, but in other respects its characteristics are quite distinctive. Fundamentally El Salvador is a mestizo rather than an Indian society; the proportion of Indians, by linguistic and cultural definition, has been steadily dropping and now stands at fewer than ten percent of the total population. Economic power, based primarily on landownership, but increasingly based on urban real estate, banking, and manufacturing, has long been concentrated in the hands of a few leading families, proverbially in El Salvador *los catorce* or "the fourteen" families, though the number today is actually considerably higher than the proverbial figure. Despite the growth of industry, coffee remains the leading export.

Demographic Characteristics

The most distinctive feature of Salvadorean society is its extreme population density. By 1980 the country's population, increasing at three and one-half percent per year, had passed four million. With a land area of about 8260 square miles, this figure gives El Salvador a population density of well over four hundred people per square mile, which is clearly excessive in a country where sixty percent of the work force is engaged in agriculture. While Salvadorean society thus faces substantial economic problems, its rate of growth in gross national product had traditionally been high, and the country seemed to be gradually pulling ahead of its Central American neighbors, except for Costa Rica, in social indicators like literacy and life expectancy.

The secret of El Salvador's encouraging economic performance, despite the formidable obstacles, seemed to lie in the distinctive character of its population, a character whose origins were not wholly clear, though it had doubtless been influenced heavily by the fact of population density. Although the epithet applied to Salvadoreans by some of their neighbors, "the Japanese of Central America," was hardly justified, it seemed clear that, perhaps because of the intense competition made necessary by population pressure, Salvadoreans tended to be more dynamic, fast-moving, and energetic than their Central American neighbors. The Salvadoreans had been in the forefront of promoting Central American unification and had been very active in the Central American Common Market, which allowed the incipient industry of the country to develop further. Perhaps also related to the pressure of population has been the generally high level of violence in interpersonal relations in El Salvador, which, like Mexico, was always one of the world's leaders in statistics of homicides per capita. Culturally, El Salvador resembles Mexico in other ways, and, indeed, the Indian population of the country, through partly Mayan as in Guatemala, also contains Nahuatl speakers related to the population of central Mexico.

The 1969 war with Honduras (see the later section) put an end to optimistic prognoses for the Salvadorean economy. Not only did it deal an all-but-fatal setback to the process of Central American economic integration from which Salvadorean industry had benefited, but it also meant the repatriation to overcrowded, underemployed El Salvador of hundreds of thousands of Salvadoreans who had been living in Honduras. These events were the catalyst for the political turmoil that followed.

The Salvadorean Political System

The political system of El Salvador is, at the time of writing, in a state of flux. From the repression of the 1934 uprising until 1979, the system was one in which the principal actors were the military and the coffee aristocracy. A certain influence was acquired by the developing middle class and the urban working class, but military officers retained control of the system throughout. There was divergence within the military, with some officers being unconditional servants of the oligarchy, and others, albeit a smaller number, sympathizing with the aspirations of the urban middle and working classes and even of agricultural workers, but the bulk of the officer class put first their own interests and the interests of the military institution. These institutional interests, however, were normally consonant with the interests of the oligarchy in the maintenance of law and order, good relations with the United States, and business as usual. When, in 1972 and 1977, elections were held in which the majority vote went to candidates of the rising urban elements, led by the Christian Democrats, the military went along with electoral fraud and the imposition of the more conservative military candidates. This made it clear that the system would not be allowed to evolve peacefully in a progressive and democratic direction, and that the only hope for fundamental change and the end of the stranglehold of the oligarchy on the country had to be by revolutionary means.

Political activism extended to the countryside. The progressive currents in the Catholic Church whose modern-day acceleration had begun with the collaboration of Christian and Socialist elements in the Western European resistance to Hitler and had given rise to the modern Christian Democratic parties, had received new impetus from the papacy of John XXIII. "Liberation theology" and the "consciousness-raising" educational programs of Catholics in the Brazilian Northeast had spread the view among clergy and committed laity that people's material circumstances had to be improved before they could devote themselves to spiritual concerns, that they were truly saved only if they understood their situation and made their religious commitments knowingly, and that their spiritual nature was better fulfilled if their full humanity was recognized, that is, if they were treated not as beasts of burden but as beings with rights.

This doctrine helped to contribute to the beginnings of economic and political organization in the countryside as farm workers began to believe that their misery and grinding poverty were not divinely ordained. After the overthrow of the Somoza dictatorship in Nicaragua in 1979, some progressive younger officers, with United States encouragement, became afraid that the heavy repression that President

Humberto Romero had believed necessary to maintain him in office would be counterproductive and would lead to the radicalization of the entire country, as had occurred in Nicaragua. They hoped instead that a certain amount of reform and a moderate line of policy might take the steam out of the opposition to the regime.

Romero was overthrown in October 1979 by some younger officers led by Colonels Jaime Abdul Gutiérrez and Adolfo Majano. Progressive civilians were invited to collaborate in the resulting junta and cabinet. Nevertheless, the younger officers, although they purged military ranks to some extent, shrank from eliminating the dominant position of the army in the country's life and maintained the existing chain of command. What this meant was that the army and the other "security forces"[3] continued to run the country, and to run it in accordance with the interests of the landowners, no matter what members of the junta and the cabinet decided. This situation became intolerable for the progressive members of the junta and cabinet, who resigned on January 1, 1980, after failing to effect any change in the situation. The Christian Democrats, whose leaders had remained aloof from the first junta, then entered a new junta which was eventually presided over by José Napoleón Duarte, the unsuccessful presidential candidate of 1972. The Christian Democrats, and the United States government, which became more heavily involved as their sponsor and principal support, believed it would be possible to create a third force between the left-wing insurgents, now organized as a guerrilla army, and the right-wing oligarchs and die-hard military authoritarians.

In pursuit of that objective, and under heavy United States pressure, the junta decreed a hasty land reform, together with the nationalization of the banks and the export of commodities. In fact, however, the junta remained dependent on the military, which continued to be the effective power in the country and whose anti-guerrilla campaign became a terrorist policy of assassinations and massacres of revolutionaries and bystanders alike. Extravagant aid afforded limitless opportunities for military corruption. Many military officers, after initially resenting the land reform forced on them by the United States, saw the opportunity of transferring land titles to their own names after the land had been expropriated from the original landowners. Where it did not go to military officers, much of the expropriated land went to members of an organization known as ORDEN, which had consisted of a network of informers and police agents in the countryside. At the time of

---

[3]The responsibility for internal policing, especially dealing with "agitators" who make trouble for landowners, has been in the hands of the National Guard and the Treasury Police, which are commanded by army officers but are regarded as less competent, more corrupt, and more brutal than the army itself.

writing the outcome of the slow-motion civil war in El Salvador was not clear. In deciding that its own interests were threatened and interposing itself forcibly into the situation, it appeared that the United States had thrust aside the old landowning oligarchy, at least temporarily, and broken the dependence of the military on the oligarchy, and had itself become the army's sponsor. That is, El Salvador had left the traditional South American pattern of rule by the military in the interests of the landowning class and had instead entered the Caribbean pattern exemplified by pre-revolutionary Cuba or Nicaragua, or the Dominican Republic, in which the army or national guard ruled, not in the interest of the local landowning class, but in its own interest, the personal interest of its commander, and the interest of the United States. The military had changed constituencies.

By the end of 1981 the guerrilla forces, the "Farabundo Martí Liberation Front," had made clear that they could not be defeated by the Salvadorean military, though they had not yet proved able to conquer power themselves. Under these circumstances, several foreign governments urged negotiations between the government and the rebels, represented by the Revolutionary Democratic Front, or FDR, for a cease-fire, a compromise government, fair elections, and a genuine reform policy. Instead, the U.S. government backed elections, boycotted by the left, which resulted in a Constituent Assembly in which the Christian Democrats, favored by the U.S., were outvoted by two right-wing parties representing the traditional landowners, PCN and ARENA. Pressure from the U.S. prevented the election as provisional president of Major Roberto d'Aubuisson, leader of ARENA, former intelligence officer, and reputed organizer of death squads, who became president of the assembly. The provisional presidency went to a politically ambiguous banker, Alvaro Magaña, as the military and landowners felt they now had a green light to abort the land reform and prosecute a civil war they thought they could win if only they were ruthless enough with possible rebel sympathizers.

PRESIDENTS OF EL SALVADOR, 1948–82

1948–50	Provisional military junta
1950–56	Oscar Osorio
1956–60	José María Lemus
1960–62	Provisional military junta
1962–67	Julio A. Rivera
1967–72	Fidel Sánchez Hernández
1972–77	Arturo A. Molina
1977–79	Humberto Romero
1979–82	Civil-military juntas
1982–	Alvaro Magaña

THE 1969 HONDURAS-EL
SALVADOR WAR

The 1969 "Soccer War" between El Salvador and Honduras escalated out of the mistreatment of Hondurans playing in an international soccer game between the countries in San Salvador, but its causes were, of course, more deep-lying. As has been stressed, a fundamental problem in El Salvador is demographic pressure, with the land available being inadequate for the farming population. At the same time, El Salvador's neighbor Honduras has a smaller total population, about two and one-half million in 1969, spread out over a land area about six times larger than that of El Salvador, which, in 1969, gave El Salvador a population density perhaps eight times that of its neighbor. Inevitably, Salvadoreans drifted into Honduras, legally or illegally, to find unoccupied land. This practice was resented by the Hondurans all the more since the Salvadoreans were typically more dynamic and hard-working than the Hondurans and soon came to take leading positions in the localities where they had settled. This situation led on occasion to mistreatment of the Salvadorean settlers by their Honduran neighbors, sometimes by "vigilante" actions that gave both sides cause for complaint: the Salvadoreans because of the discrimination against them, the Hondurans because they felt the Salvadoreans had no business being there in the first place. This bad feeling was augmented by the course taken by the Central American Common Market, which was of substantial benefit to the Salvadoreans, but proved disadvantageous to Honduras. In addition, the boundary line between the two countries was inadequately demarcated, and Hondurans feared a tendency by the Salvadoreans to annex Honduran territory. "The boundary stones walk at night," the Hondurans complained.

In 1969, the Salvadoreans opened hostilities and rapidly drove into Honduras, but their advance became stalled because of several factors. Condemnation from the Organization of American States (OAS) was made more effective because the OAS members placed sanctions on the supply of fuel to El Salvador and the Salvadorean armored vehicles ran out of gasoline. Although initial Honduran resistance on the ground was not effective, the Honduran air force established superiority in the air. A cease-fire was established without a fundamental settlement of the underlying causes that led to the fighting. However, each of the parties felt it had won a victory, the Salvadoreans because they had occupied Honduran territory and vindicated the right of Salvadorean nationals, the Hondurans because, although caught by surprise, they had stopped the Salvadorean advance and had established air superiority.

In 1981 a territorial settlement was speedily agreed to which eliminated the "no man's land" which had been used as a base by Salvadorean guerrillas. Thereafter the two armies shared in anti-guerrilla operations which made life miserable for the desperate peasant families of the area.

HONDURAS

General Description

Honduras is sometimes called "the Cinderella of Central American," and it is true that, by social and economic indicators, the country is the least developed in what is, after all, an underdeveloped region. "The country of the 70's" it was once called by President Ramón Villeda Morales, not because it was up-to-date, but because its population was seventy percent rural, seventy percent illiterate, and seventy percent born illegitimate. The capital city, Tegucigalpa, located in the mountainous central portion of the country, has fewer than 150,000 inhabitants and is hardly more than a small town. The growth in gross national product per capita barely keeps up with the rate of growth in population, which is high. The second city, San Pedro Sula, in the center of the banana-growing region on the Pacific north coast, is somewhat more dynamic; however, banana cultivation is itself subject to recurrent disasters in the form of hurricanes and plant diseases.

The United Fruit Company

It is true that the United Fruit Company, the major fruit grower, no longer controls governments the way it used to. After being forced to do so by legislation, the banana company today makes much of its role of good citizen, providing housing, health care, and schools for its employees and their families. Nevertheless, any Honduran government treads with great care where the interests of United Fruit are concerned, and a land reform law proposed under the Villeda Morales administration (1957–63) was amended to ineffectualness after the fruit company and other landowners objected to it. Forcible confrontation has given way to more subtle techniques, however, and President López Arellano was removed in 1975 after it was charged that he had accepted a million-dollar bribe not to impose higher taxes on the company, in a bizarre series of developments that included the suicide, in New York, of the president of United Brands, the fruit company's parent organization.

The Military and Politics

The efforts of Honduran governments are, however, generally feeble and ineffective in any case. The armed forces are virtually immune from control by the President; the military enjoy a specially protected constitutional status under which assignments and promotions are decided within the military, and the armed forces even present their own budget to Congress without its being subject to presidential review. Moreover, the armed forces commander-in-chief is elected for a fixed term by Congress, not appointed by the President. Politically, the armed forces have usually been identified with one of the two traditional parties, the Nationalists. Villeda Morales was overthrown before the end of his term at the end of 1963, because the Liberal candidate to succeed him, Modesto Rodas Alvarado, who appeared likely to be the winner in the scheduled election, talked about subjecting the military to civilian control.

Oswaldo López Arellano, the Air Force general who led the coup against Villeda and dominated Honduran politics for some time thereafter, served first as provisional president and then was elected to a six-year term (1965–71) by a constituent assembly chosen with heavy government intervention. The general incompetence of the government caused enough disaffection that López could not get the support necessary to extend his term of office, and elections were held in 1971, the first popular elections for president that Honduras had seen in twenty years. (Villeda had been elected by a Constituent Assembly.)

PPRESIDENTS OF HONDURAS, 1957–82

1957–63	Ramón Villeda Morales
1963–71	Oswaldo López Arellano
1971–72	Ramón E. Cruz
1972–75	Oswaldo López Arellano
1975–78	Arturo Melgar Castro
1978–82	Policarpo Paz García
1982–	Roberto Suazo Córdova

The Pacto Nacional

In an attempt to reduce interparty conflict and begin a new era in the country's politics, representatives of the parties signed a pact, the *Pacto Nacional*, to share power equally in the cabinet and the supreme court, with the party winning the presidency to have the tie-breaking vote in the congress and the losing party a one-man majority on the

45

court.[4] The fact that the Liberals were more identified with the unpopular Central American Common Market helped the Nationalist candidate, Ramón Ernesto Cruz, to win the 1971 elections, but disaffection set in with Cruz's refusal to abide by some of the provisions of the two-party pact, and López Arellano, who had stepped down from the presidency to the position of commander of the armed forces, used this disaffection as a base to stage a coup in December 1972 that returned him to the presidency.

Beginnings of Social Change

Conscious of the lack of enthusiam that had prevented him from getting enough support in his effort to succeed himself the previous year, López Arellano attempted to broaden the base of his support by taking a more nationalist and developmentalist line and appealing to the labor union and peasant organizations that are a recent development in Honduran politics. Emboldened by evidences of presidential support, peasant organizations began to agitate for land reform. This volatile situation was inherited by the weak and internally divided military government, under the leadership of Colonel Arturo Melgar Castro, that took over from López Arellano in 1975 when it was charged that he had accepted bribes from the United Fruit Company not to go along with the efforts of Panama and other Central American countries to raise taxes on banana exports. While some elements in the government encouraged peasant militance, others joined with the private armies of aroused landowners in crushing peasant demonstrations and land occupations with bloodshed.

Yet peasant organizations continued to grow and more progressive parties, such as PINU, the Partido de Innovación y Unidad, began to make their appearance outside the traditional Nationalist-Liberal framework. There were visible signs of economic growth as Honduras became a beneficiary of the decisions of the World Bank and USAID to concentrate development assistance on the poorest countries, and as foreign investors were impressed by the relative peacefulness and moderation on Honduran politics, which contrasted so strongly with the violence of its Central American neighbors.

Colonel Melgar's attempts to construct a personal power base contributed to his removal and replacement by Colonel Policarpo Paz García in 1978. Paz García presided over elections to a constituent assembly in 1980; the strong pro-democratic stand of the Carter Ad-

---

[4]James A. Morris, *The Honduran Plan Político de Unidad Nacional 1971–1972: Its Origins and Demise,* El Paso, Texas: University of Texas at El Paso Center for Inter-American Studies, 1975.

ministration in the United States was an important factor in ensuring that those elections were fair, despite all expectations, and the Liberals won a slight majority. Nevertheless, they imprudently permitted Paz to remain as president pending the organization of presidential elections.

Although at first Honduras seemed immune from the terrorism and civil war that ravaged its neighbors, El Salvador and Nicaragua, it was bound to be affected sooner or later. Ex-Somocista National Guardsmen from Nicaragua formed right-wing bands that pillaged the countryside and terrorized peasants. Salvadorean rebels used the no man's land of territory left undemarcated by the settlement of the 1969 soccer war as a sanctuary area; late in 1980 El Salvador agreed to a hasty demarcation favorable to Honduras in order to eliminate the problem, after which the Honduras army collaborated with the Salvadorean in anti-insurgent activity at the border. Refugees from the Salvadorean fighting nevertheless took asylum in Honduras. A small insurrectionary movement, comparable to those in El Salvador and Nicaragua, was organized. Some Americans and Guatemalans tried to interest the Hondurans in contingency plans for concerted action against the Sandinista government in Nicaragua. The President elected in late 1981 and inaugurated in January 1982, Roberto Suazo Córdova, although a Liberal, seemed ready to cooperate in the right-wing adventures being proposed. It appeared that for better or worse, the beginnings of economic development, political modernization, and ideological warfare had finally arrived in the Cinderella of Central America.

NICARAGUA

General Character

In some respects, Nicaragua resembles the countries of the Caribbean, such as Cuba or the Dominican Republic, more than it does its Central American neighbors. Partly, this is because the climate of the central portion of the country surrounding the capital, Managua, is more tropical than that of the highland capitals of Guatemala City or Tegucigalpa, or even San José de Costa Rica, on its inland plateau to the south. But, politically and economically, the major role played in Nicaragua by the United States resembles the heavy involvement of the Caribbean, rather than the limited interest and intermittent intervention of the Central American pattern.

United States interest in the country.   Historically, United States interest in Nicaragua derived from the fact that the isthmus contains a canal route alternative to that of Panama, a route that would connect the Pacific and Atlantic Oceans with the major lake, Lake Nicaragua, in the central part of the country. Accordingly, the United States became concerned to have friendly governments in power and was early drawn into involvement in Nicaraguan politics, intervening to forestall civil wars growing out of contested elections between Liberals and Conservatives, elite political parties based on the rivalry between the towns of León and Córdoba. Like other such parties, the Conservatives tended to be somewhat more pro-clerical and landowner-oriented than the Liberals. Finally, the United States Marines were sent in as a permanent occupation force that remained in the country more or less continuously from 1912 to 1933. As in the comparable cases of Haiti and the Dominican Republic, United States governments of the early twentieth century naively conceived of the problem of the maintenance of peace and constitutional procedures as the simple mechanical task of enforcing law and order; therefore, the preparation made for Nicaraguan autonomy, as the Marines made ready to withdraw, was the training of a constabulary force that would, in theory, be nonpolitical and nonpartisan and would assure public order and make constitutional government possible.

The attempt by the United States to implant and maintain constitutional governments was not a consistent concern of United States administrations but rather was a special project of the erstwhile political scientist Woodrow Wilson. For most United States governments, it was enough that the governments of the region were friendly to United States interests. As President Franklin D. Roosevelt was reported to have said of Anastasio Somoza, "He may be an s.o.b., but he's our s.o.b." What happened in Nicaragua, as in Santo Domingo, was that soon after the United States withdrawal, the commander of the constabulary force—in Nicaragua the Liberal party politician and commander of the National Guard by virtue of his cabinet post as Minister of War, Anastasio Somoza García—himself assumed power, ruling the country, though not always as president, for twenty years (1937–56), and founding a dynasty.

The Somoza Dynasty

The regime established by Anastasio Somoza was in the classic authoritarian pattern. The dominant institution, the Somoza family, was connected by alliances and marriages with other leading families, and maintained its hegemony despite changes in individual presidents. Other institutions of the regime that persisted in their own right but were tied into the system of Somocista hegemony were the military force, the National Guard, of which first Anastasio Somoza Sr., and then Anastasio Somoza Jr., were commanders; the Liberal party, also controlled by the family; and the landowning, entrepreneurial, and financial elite, likewise dominated by Somoza economic interests. The United States was identified in a variety of ways with the Somozas, and after the assassination attempt on Anastasio Somoza Sr., he was flown to a United States hospital in the Canal Zone, where an unsuccessful attempt was made to save his life. This close relationship continued under Anastasio Jr., who attended West Point.

On his assassination in 1956, Somoza García was succeeded by the next in line of constitutional succession, the president of the Senate, his oldest son Luis Somoza Debayle, who served first as provisional president and then was elected in his own right for a term that ended in 1963. Luis attempted the partial, or at least the cosmetic, de-Somozaization of the system, presiding over the drafting of a new constitution, promulgated in 1962, under which a president served for five years and then was forbidden either to succeed himself or to be succeeded by any close relative.

Luis Somoza was succeeded by a political associate of the family, René Schick Gutiérrez, who died in office and was succeeded by Lorenzo Guerrero. But Luis Somoza also died during this period, so that when his younger brother, Anastasio Jr., was elected to the presidency in 1957, there was nothing except the need for another constitutional revision to prevent "Tachito," as he was called, who resembled his strong-willed father "Tacho" rather than his more moderate older brother, from following in the father's footsteps and perpetuating himself in power indefinitely. During his presidency, Tachito retained the command of the National Guard he had held since his father's death, and although he stepped down from the presidency in 1972 at the end of his term, to be succeeded by a makeshift "triumvirate" that wielded executive power while a constituent assembly rewrote the constitution to make it possible for Tachito to resume the presidency, he remained throughout the effective ruler of the country.

PRESIDENTS OF NICARAGUA, 1956–81

1956–63	Luis Somoza Debayle
1963–66	René Schick Gutiérrez
1966–67	Lorenzo Guerrero Gutiérrez
1967–72	Anastasio Somoza Debayle
1972–74	Triumvirate
1974–79	Anastasio Somoza Debayle
1979–	Revolutionary junta

Under the Somoza dynasty, the Somozas controlled not only the country's politics but also its economy. The family's interests reached everywhere in the economy, to the extent that it was sometimes impossible to distinguish between the interests of the family and those of the Nicaraguan state. The Somozas owned the Nicaraguan airline and shipping line, together with over half of the country's agricultural land, and a lot of the best real estate in Managua. Nevertheless, all that was not enough for Somoza Debayle, and his greed led to his downfall.

In 1972, just before Christmas, an earthquake struck Managua, leading to colossal death tolls and destruction of most of the city. Countries all over the world sent relief supplies for the stricken, homeless, and starving population. To the horror and disgust of the Nicaraguan people and foreign observers, these supplies were blatantly stolen by the National Guard, who diverted them to their own use or resold them on the black market. Despite his millions, Somoza himself profiteered from the disaster. In spite of studies that showed the area to be unsafe from future earthquakes, he decreed that the city be rebuilt on land he personally owned.

In retrospect, it is clear that the aftermath of the "Black Christmas" marked the beginning of the end for the Somoza dynasty. Previously, other economic interests besides those of the Somozas survived in the country's agriculture—cotton, cattle, coffee, and sugar were principal crops—and in its small-scale consumer good industries. While most government loans and subsidies went to the Somoza family and their relatives and collaborators, some economic activity was left over for other entrepreneurs. After the earthquake, however, Somoza's greed seemed to know no bounds. He may have been egged on by his son and heir, Anastasio Somoza Portocarrero, now returned from military academy in the United States and given a National Guard commission, who appears to have been an even more unpleasant character than his father. The increasing rapacity of the Somozas and the National Guard that served them steadily alienated virtually the entire population not tied in directly with the regime, including the non-Somoza economic elite.

As the repression grew worse, opposition to the regime escalated. A minor insurgent movement, named after the Nicaraguan patriot Augusto Cesar Sandino, began to gain adherents like a snowball. Sandino had led the resistance to the occupation of Nicaragua by the United States Marines between 1919 and 1933. The Marines' counter-insurgency campaign, which resembled in its unpleasantness and ineffectualness similiar United States campaigns from the Philippines to Vietnam, never succeeded in putting down Sandino, who lived to be betrayed and assassinated by Anastasio Somoza García. As the Sandinista movement picked up strength, staging daring coups such as the seizure of the National Palace and the holding of the legislators hostage, repression escalated, forcing many young men to join the rebels since they were likely to be shot for rebel sympathies in any case.

Matters came to a head in January 1979, with the assassination of Joaquín Chamorro, the editor of the leading opposition paper, *La Prensa*. Chamorro came from an old and distinguished Conservative family, whose opposition to the Somozas was based in the first instance on the fact that they were Liberals. Previously, the Somozas had tolerated some Conservative opposition for public relations purposes. So long as it was ineffectual, it made the regime plausibly democratic and helped rally behind them the majority of the population, which was Liberal. Finally, however, *La Prensa* touched a nerve with a campaign revealing Somoza's involvement in a blood plasma export company. It seemed that Somoza had robbed the Nicaraguan people till they had nothing left but their blood, and now wanted that too. The dictator's son, Somoza Portocarrero, organized the assassination, which was the last straw in alienating elite elements from the dynasty. The Sandinistas went from strength to strength, and the frantic genocidal tactics of the National Guard simply guaranteed that whatever population survived would hate the Somozas undyingly. The United States staged a last-minute attempt to achieve a non-Somoza, non-Sandinista solution, but such a solution no longer had any Nicaraguan constituency, and Somoza fled, taking with him a good part of the national treasury.

The Sandinistas inherited a country devastated by civil war, which had never really recovered from the earthquake of 1972.

There had originally been three different tendencies in the Sandinista movement, but they had differed primarily in their strategies for seizing power. With the impending collapse of the Somoza regime, these differences had become no longer relevant and the three tendencies were unified in the overthrow of the regime and the establishment of the revolutionary government that succeeded it. Nevertheless, at some future time divergences of opinion based on the original groupings within the movement may perhaps reemerge, especially as there were differences in social class origin among the followers of the different tendencies within the movement.

The Sandinistas are, of course, revolutionary socialists, but, the expropriation of the vast properties of the Somoza family kept the new revolutionary government busy enough trying to keep the properties still functioning and producing without contemplating the wholesale expropriation of the rest of the economy. At the same time, it was felt that such expropriations would be a breach of faith with the business and farming interests that had joined with the Sandinistas in the final push to overthrow Somoza. Nevertheless, differences of approach were bound to emerge between the young revolutionary socialists who had fought in the hills and the older members of the private sector who collaborated with them in the first government of the revolution. These differences focused on economic policy and on the country's future political organization, especially the holding of elections and whether the Sandinistas would remain as the single dominant party or whether there would be a plural system of competing parties. Although the Sandinistas had the monopoly of armed force (the National Guard was disbanded) as well as a majority in the political organs that were established, they appreciated the need to be moderate and pragmatic in their policies. The United States remained a major factor in their calculations, and there were clearly limits to how much socialism and authoritarianism the United States would tolerate before using its economic might to crush the Sandinista government. Accordingly, the government took a moderate line. For example, it agreed to assume the debts contracted abroad by the Somoza government, even though much of the money borrowed had gone to buy arms that were used against the Sandinistas or into the Somozas' foreign bank accounts; in preference to having the loans repudiated, banks accepted a consolidation and refinancing of the debts on easy terms.

The principal organs of power in the new government were, of course, the Sandinista army; the directorate of the FSLN (Frente Sandinista de Liberación Nacional), the Sandinista movement; a governing junta; the cabinet; and a consultative Council of State. The original junta consisted of five members: Humberto Ortega Saavedra, at age 32 a senior Sandinista commander; Moïses Hassan Morales, a Sandinista physicist; Sergio Ramírez, a writer and intellectual of Sandinista sympathies, though not a combatant; Violeta Barrios de Chamorro, the widow of the slain editor; and Alfonso Robelo Callejas, an industrialist and political leader of the private sector. Within a year of the assumption of power of July 1979, Violeta Barrios had resigned, giving grounds of health, and Alfonso Robelo had resigned because elections were not being scheduled. Robelo continued to be active in politics at the head of his own Movimiento Democrático Nacional, or MDN. Sra. Chamorro has gone to live abroad, but the Chamorro family continues to dominate newspaper publishing in the new Nicaragua. Joaquín Chamorro Barrios, her son, is publisher of *La Prensa,* which takes a critical attitude to the government. His brother edits *Barricada,* the Sandinista paper; and his uncle Xavier, who left *La Prensa,* taking most of its staff with him, because of its critical attitude to the government, publishes a more pro-government newspaper, *El Nuevo Diario.* Straining to make clear that government policies were still moderate, pragmatic, and acceptable to the United States, two other non-Sandinistas had been appointed to the junta to replace Robelo and Violeta Barrios; however the junta was finally cut in 1981 to three members, but the balance was still maintained: Ortega, Ramírez, and, representing the private sector, Rafael Córdova Rivas.

The junta's role is symbolic rather than effective. Power resides much more in the directorate of the FSLN and in the armed forces' leadership. Humberto Ortega, the chairman of the junta, is one of the key figures on the Sandinista directorate; his brother Daniel is Commander-in-Chief of the Sandinista Army, which makes a potent combination. The other key figure is Tomás Borge, the Minister of Interior, and one of the most popular Sandinista leaders. Borge, now over fifty years old, the senior figure among the Sandinistas, is well regarded for his moral character and impassioned oratory. The other most popular leader was Edén Pastora, a dashing younger figure, who acquired celebrity as the commander of the raid that seized the legislative palace. However, in 1981 Pastora resigned his cabinet post and went off, à la Che Guevara, to fight as a guerrilla in an unidentified (presumably Central American) country. The following year he surfaced in Costa Rica to announce he was disillusioned over the failure to hold elections and would lead his own opposition movement from exile.

Clearly, the road ahead for Nicaragua's revolutionary government was an extremely difficult one, and not only because of the sheer magnitude of the problems of restoring a shattered economy, trying to feed the hungry, shelter the dispossessed, and instruct the illiterate. Ex-National Guardsmen, based across the border in Honduras, conducted sabotage raids. The private sector was restive and non-Sandinista politicians exigent. The United States under President Reagan was unsympathetic. And the conflagration engulfing El Salvador might at any moment spread throughout Central America.

Footnote: Somoza Debayle took refuge in safely dictatorial Paraguay, the only country that would have him. During 1980 he was assassinated in a rocket attack on his automobile in an incident that has never been fully clarified. While it would be logical to suspect Sandinista agents, the ease with which he was killed and with which the assassins made their getaway in tightly policed Paraguay lent substance to rumors that his amorous escapades had offended powerful figures in the Paraguayan regime.

COSTA RICA

General Character

Costa Rica is distinctive not only in Central America but in Latin America generally, and to understand Costa Rica it is necessary to come to grips with the causes of this distinctiveness. Unlike their neighbors in the isthmus, the Costa Ricans have a deep-rooted constitutional government in which political violence is almost unknown, elections are free, power passes peacefully from one party to another, there is no military intervention in politics—indeed, there is no army as such—and public life is informed with a spirit of democracy and equality. Middle-class attitudes are dominant, and extremes of poverty and wealth are not glaring or acute. Population is concentrated in the central portion of the country, in the Meseta Central, where the climate is mild and agreeable, rather than on the coasts.

Geographic and Demographic Factors

What is the secret of the success this fortunate land has made of its national existence? As in any historical problem, causal relations are complex and arise out of the interaction of several causal factors. The land that today is Costa Rica held a very small Indian population before the arrival of the Spaniards and lacked the quantities of precious metals that attracted settlers elsewhere. As a result, the country was settled only by an unusual group of migrants to the new world, not those who came to secure instant riches through luck or the work of others, but those who had a vocation and a desire to farm their own land but had no property in Spain. These were principally younger sons, excluded from inheritance by the custom of entail, who came from the areas of northern Spain where family farming was traditional, especially in Catalonia and the Basque country. Because of a variety of reasons of history and climate, these areas had preserved the tradition of the family farm, rather than the latifundio and ranching types of land exploitation that had developed elsewhere in the peninsula. This combination of geographic and demographic factors produced in Costa Rica a society of small and medium farmers, a sort of egalitarian yeomanry such as Thomas Jefferson had dreamed of.[5] Some latifundia were established, but, although they cover a great deal of territory, they form a minor note in Costa Rican society, where most of those in agriculture are either working on their own farms or else are hired hands on a family farm in the neighborhood. Just as there is no class of large landowners, there is no great mass of landless peasants, renters, or sharecroppers working on haciendas, such as is commonly found in other Latin American countries, although there were signs of the beginnings of such a class at the end of the 1960s, as the unoccupied land available for settlement on the Meseta finally was exhausted.

[5]The most comprehensive statements of the case are to be found in James L. Busey, *Notes on Costa Rican Democracy,* Boulder: University of Colorado Press, 1962, and Carlos José Gutiérrez, "Libertad y derecho político," *Revista de Ciencias Jurídicas,* no. 1, May 1963.

PRESIDENTS OF COSTA RICA, 1950–82

1950–54	Otilio Ulate Blanco
1954–58	José Figueres Ferrer
1958–62	Mario Echandi Jiménez
1962–66	Francisco Orlich Bolmarich
1966–70	José Joaquín Trejos Fernández
1970–74	José Figueres Ferrer
1974–78	Daniel Oduber Quirós
1978–82	Rodrigo Carazo Odio
1982–	Luis Alberto Monge

While an urbanization movement has set in in Costa Rica, as it has elsewhere in the world (helping to bring down the birth rate that had until recently been one of the world's highest), the spirit of Costa Rican society is still that of a rural property-holding democracy, bourgeois but egalitarian, and urban life in Costa Rica lacks the activity and excitement that city life implies elsewhere.

Political Life Since 1948

Political life in Costa Rica is not invariably peaceful, however. A revolt did take place in 1948, against the attempt of the incumbent government to rig the elections, and the present political system dates from changes introduced by the provisional civilian junta that held office from 1948 to 1950 under the leader of that successful revolt, José Figueres Ferrer. Figueres's popular movement was transformed into the Party of National Liberation, Partido de Liberación Nacional (PLN), which remains the country's leading party and which has twice since 1950 carried Figueres to the presidency.[6] The other Costa Rican parties, more conservative than the slightly left-of-center PLN, and appealing on the whole to the more well-to-do, realized that they would have to unite to have any chance of electing presidential candidates, and they generally contest elections under the coalition banner of Unificación Nacional. At least in the years when Figueres himself is not running, the two rival camps of Liberación Nacional and Unificación Nacional are fairly evenly balanced, with the result that for twenty years, between 1954 and 1974, the presidency alternated every four years between the two, making Costa Rica a model of the peaceful transition of power, until the PLN won the presidency against a divided opposition in 1974, for its second consecutive victory. The PLN and Figueres also took

[6]At the time, an ex-president could be reelected after skipping two terms. Now, no reelection at all is allowed.

a leading role with respect to similar parties of the "democratic left" elsewhere in Latin America. In fact, a school to train younger leaders of social democratic parties has functioned fairly continuously in Costa Rica.

Figueres's image, and that of his party, deteriorated, however, because of his increasingly erratic pronouncements and behavior, and especially because of his entanglement with the fugitive United States financier Robert Vesco, who was for several years given asylum in Costa Rica. Vesco's money helped to start a process of the corruption of the PLN, whose reputation for financial rectitude had been badly battered by the end of Daniel Oduber's presidential term in 1978.

The anti-PLN forces elected Rodrigo Carazo president in 1978, but the PLN staged a comeback in 1982. Carazo had proved unable to improve economic performance, which deteriorated further as immigration by Salvadoreans and others from Central America's battlegrounds led to growing unemployment. Suspicion of financial irregularities attached to members of the Carazo family and administration, while some conservatives opposed the wholehearted support Carazo had given to the anti-Somoza Sandinista insurrection in Nicaragua, although the Sandinista cause was favored by Costa Ricans generally.

However, Costa Ricans feared that if the fighting in El Salvador were to spread beyond that country's borders, conservative forces in Guatemala and Honduras might attempt to overthrow the Sandinista government in general warfare that could involve Costa Rica. Some voices were even heard in favor of the creation of a Costa Rican army, a course of action also favored by conservative elements in the United States government. It seemed likely, however, that Costa Ricans were too conscious of the advantages of their peaceful ways of doing things to abandon them lightly.

On the economic front, per capita growth has usually been quite steady, and Costa Rica has gradually moved ahead in income levels relative to other Latin American countries. For some time, it has enjoyed the highest per capita income in Central America. Difficulties have set in in recent years, however. The price of the country's major export, coffee, has fluctuated, and in 1970 Irazú, the volcano that overlooks the Meseta Central, erupted, causing a setback to the country's agriculture; however, the downpour of volcanic ash enriched the soil and helped to increase coffee yields in subsequent years.

A severe drought in 1973 affected not only agriculture but also the supply of hydroelectric power for the country's industry. That industry had grown in response to the stimulation of the Central American Common Market and constitutes an appreciable factor in the national economy, although it is principally limited to the production of articles of prime necessity, that is, food, clothing, and building materials. Costa

Rica has, however, been in a difficult position with respect to the other countries of the Central American Common Market. It has enjoyed a higher standard of living, thus making its labor and social welfare costs higher, so that goods produced elsewhere in Central America are often cheaper than those made in Costa Rica. As a result, the country found itself buying more than it was selling. Given the government's reluctance to devalue the colón, a balance of payments deficit developed that forced a modification of the Common Market rules, under which Costa Rica imposed some barriers to imports from the other Common Market countries. Devaluation only came after the economy had been further weakened by speculation and high levels of foreign debt.

In the overall picture, however, such temporary economic difficulties have so far been dwarfed by the political and social strengths, especially the absence of the class polarization created by the existence of classes of large landowners and landless peasants, that make Costa Rica a pleasant and fortunate society among the Latin American nations and an exception to the patterns that apply generally in the region.

SUMMARY

The five small countries of Central America present a microcosm of the geographic, demographic, and political variations met with in Latin America. The size of the national populations, like the proportions of Indians in those populations, drops as one moves from northwest to southwest through the Central American isthmus, from Guatemala to El Salvador, Honduras, Nicaragua, and Costa Rica. National populations are concentrated on the Pacific side of the isthmus, except in Honduras, which has no Pacific coast. The countries of the region have formed a Common Market, which has contributed to some economic improvement, especially in Guatemala and El Salvador, but has faced a variety of problems, some growing out of the extreme backwardness of Honduras or the high level of wages in Costa Rica.

Guatemala

In Guatemala, the rural population is composed principally of Indians working on large estates in the highlands, on their own traditional property holdings, or as seasonal workers on lowland plantations. The conservative landowning interest is opposed by growing urban middle and working classes that support the Christian Democrats and other center and center-left parties. The traditional sectors of society retain control by force and fraud, relying on the army but also on terrorism and assassination campaigns against the left. The extreme left engages in similar campaigns and in guerrilla warfare.

El Salvador

The general social and political structure of El Salvador resembles that of Guatemala in the sense that large landowners (whose workers are culturally mestizo rather than Indian) are pitted against a growing urban middle-class and working sector, in a struggle which has become a virtual civil war, although growing United States involvement may mean that the United States government replaces the landowners as the real constituency of the military, as was the case in pre-revolutionary Nicaragua. The very high density of population has resulted in a bustling competitive society and also in the occupation by Salvadoreans of land across the frontier in Honduras, which had led to friction and, on occasion, the outbreak of fighting between the two countries.

Honduras

Honduras is the "Cinderella of Central America." Lacking a Pacific coast, export agriculture—that is, banana production—is concentrated on the Atlantic coast, where it is subject to the ravages of hurricanes. The soil is of poor quality, and Honduras has the lowest living standard in the region, with pervasive malnutrition leading to debility and even mental retardation. The traditional Nationalist and Liberal parties compete for power, which is often preempted by the military, whose governments are no more effectual than those of civilians. Some forces for change are, however, becoming evident with the growth of a small working class and an urban middle-class sector, and with some mobilization of campesinos demanding land.

Nicaragua

Nicaragua is more fortunate geographically then Honduras, although it is subject to destructive earthquakes. Agriculture is diversified, with cotton the leading export. A revolutionary government is attempting to rebuild the earthquake- and war-torn economy along egalitarian and partially socialist lines despite harrassment from exiles and hostile foreigners.

Costa Rica

Although Costa Rica is becoming more urban, it is still basically a society of hard-working small farmers of European stock. Living standards are high, although the country faces various economic problems, and political life has for some time seen the peaceful alternation in power of moderate center-left and center-right parties.

4

The Caribbean

INTRODUCTION

The Caribbean is the region of Latin America that has traditionally been most subject to United States influence. It is not Latin America as a whole, but Central America and the Caribbean, that is the "back yard" of the United States; it is to this area that Marines have been sent; it is political developments in this area that cause the most concern to the United States government and the American public; it is really the Caribbean, and not the Western Hemisphere as a whole, to which the Monroe Doctrine applies.[1] In this chapter, we will deal with the Latin Caribbean, that is, the republics of Haiti, the Dominican Republic, and Cuba, leaving out of consideration Puerto Rico, which has a special political relationship with the United States that falls short of independence, and the smaller island countries of the Caribbean, some independent, some still dependencies of Britain and other European powers. In this group of Caribbean countries, we shall also consider Panama, which lies on the mainland as a land bridge between Central America and South America and does not clearly belong to one or the other. The distinctive economic, social, and political characteristics of Panama place it more logically in the same category as the Caribbean countries.

Although politically independent, these four countries are heavily dependent economically, and their political autonomy is, in fact, severely limited. Except for Haiti, their political independence has lasted for a far shorter period than that of the other countries of Latin America. Cuba secured independence in 1902, after being a Spanish colony throughout the nineteenth century and coming briefly under United States control after the Spanish-American War. Panama gained independence from Colombia, of which it had been a province, only in 1903, with United States intervention a determining factor. Santo Domingo

---

[1]Dexter Perkins, *A History of the Monroe Doctrine,* revised edition, Boston: Little, Brown, 1955.

became independent early but lost its independence to Spain and to the Haitians for several periods during the nineteenth century. Moreover, each of these countries has, at least partially, been militarily occupied by the United States during the twentieth century.

Apart from these political and military interventions, the countries of the region show a high degree of economic dependence. The island countries were developed precisely because their climate made it possible to grow tropical products that Europe could not provide for herself, and they have remained throughout their history dedicated almost exclusively to the provision of such products, importing all of the manufactured goods they need, heavily dependent on fluctuations in world market prices, and at the mercy of economic decisions taken in board rooms in New York or Western Europe.

PANAMA

General Description

Panama is a difficult country to categorize. Geographically, it belongs neither in Central nor in South America. Racially, it is both mestizo and mulatto, with small European and Indian populations. It combines high scores on economic and social indicators (seventy-five percent are literate and the gross national product is more than $1000 per capita) with high levels of unemployment and underemployment, political instability, and violence. The themes of political oratory have long been radical, and yet there is a wealthy and well-entrenched elite. Nationalist sentiment is very strong, but foreign interests are extremely powerful.

The Panama Canal

The dominant fact about Panama, and the key to explaining many of these paradoxes, is the Panama Canal. The canal was built by the United States, was until very recently owned and operated by the United States, and is ostensibly defended by United States troops. A strip of land ten miles wide on either side of the canal, known as the Canal Zone, was from 1901 to 1979 administered by the United States under a treaty signed at the time of Panama's independence. That independence was secured from Colombia with United States warships preventing the landing of Colombian troops to put down the rebels, after the Colombian Congress had refused to approve the terms of a treaty with the United States under which the canal was to be built. In the three-quarters of a century that followed, the Panamanians became dissatisfied with the terms of that treaty, which they agreed to under circumstances that allowed them little choice.

The central position of the canal helps to account for some of the anomalies, inconsistencies, and paradoxes in the country's political and social situation. As in other countries with a high income-producing externally oriented sector unintegrated with the national economy, a strong government sector, financed by revenue from the canal, is able to provide a level of services in advance of the rest of the country's economy. Thus, for example, classes of high school graduates are produced for whom no jobs are available. High school students, in fact, form the spearhead of radical politics in Panama, playing a role filled by university students elsewhere in Latin America.[2]

Although the existence of the Canal has created social imbalances, in a sense it also helped to maintain social peace. Until the mutation in the political system that occurred in 1968 with the assumption of power by a "progressive" military regime, at least, Panama had been ruled by fluctuating cliques of members of the country's wealthy elite. At first sight, it seems implausible that such a situation could still exist in a literate and socially mobilized society where the masses were aware of politics, newspapers were published freely, and elections were held. However, elite dominance could continue because popular resentment could always be directed away from the oligarchy toward the United States, whose role was so visible and whose position was so vulnerable and, in the Canal Zone, so accessible. The United States and the Canal Zone thus served as a social lightning rod for the Panamanian oligarchy. During election campaigns, political assassinations occurred, and riots and demonstrations took place, but the rioters always ended up by marching on the Canal Zone and not by storming the presidential palace.

PRESIDENTS OF PANAMA, 1952–82

1952–55	José Antonio Remón
1955	José R. Guizado
1955–56	Ricardo M. Arias Espinosa
1956–60	Ernesto de la Guardia
1960–64	Roberto F. Chiari
1964–68	Marco A. Robles
1968	Arnulfo Arias
1968–69	Military junta, various presidents
1969–79	Demetrio Lakas
	(chief of government: Omar Torrijos)
1979–	Arístides Royo

[2]Daniel Goldrich, *Sons of the Establishment: Elite Youth in Panama and Costa Rica,* Chicago: Rand McNally, 1966.

Panamanian Politics in the
1960s

In 1960–68, two elected presidents served out their terms, espousing a mild reformism of the Alliance for Progress variety that was in keeping with the spirit of the times. After a turbulent election in 1968, however, the popular caudillo, former president Arnulfo Arias, returned to power. Having been removed from office during a previous term, and having been frustrated by the National Guard in an attempt to have the incumbent president impeached, Arias began at once to eliminate potential opposition in the Guard, not only retiring the incumbent commander but also violating previous practice by passing over his second in command in choosing his replacement. Regarding this as political interference in internal military matters, the Guard removed Arias from office after he had served only eleven days, in a coup led by the officer fourth in the chain of command, Omar Torrijos. Torrijos soon established himself as a military strongman in the classic Latin American tradition, building an unassailable position by returning to the country and reestablishing his authority through sheer force of character when an attempt was made to remove him as commander of the Guard during a visit he made to Mexico.

Omar Torrijos and the "Panamanian Revolution." Showing himself equally skillful at building popular support, keeping on good terms with foreign companies, and maneuvering within the military, Torrijos took a policy line that was nationalist and progressive at the same time as it was pro-business and mildly dictatorial. In the tradition of his oligarchic predecessors, Torrijos maintained a nationalist image by a strong position of confrontation with the United States over the canal, and he expelled the Peace Corps. An agrarian reform provided for expropriation of large estates, along with credit to small farmers and irrigation works. Some initiatives were taken in health and education, and union membership in some fields was made compulsory. Torrijos spoke of the "Panamanian revolution" and earned praise from Fidel Castro. Yet, at the same time, Panama became an international banking center. Funds were attracted by interest rates slightly higher than those that prevailed in Europe and by provisions for numbered accounts and secrecy, on the Swiss model, and a business boom resulted. Politically, Torrijos avoided a whole series of problems by not himself taking the presidency, which was occupied by an old friend of his, Demetrio Lakas, instead exercising effective power as commander of the National Guard and "chief of government."

The National Guard itself is relatively small by Latin American standards; its personnel number about six thousand. Initially, political parties were dissolved, and there were some political prisoners and occasional intervention in the press, but the dictatorship remained relatively mild.

In 1979, in the major achievement of the Torrijos government, which was also one of the principal achievements of the Carter administration, a new treaty governing the Panama Canal was concluded and approved by a bare two-thirds of the United States Senate and a bare two-thirds of the Panamanian electorate in a referendum. The provisions of the treaty represented the maximum common denominator of the positions of the two sides. Neither was satisfied with its terms, but neither was completely dissatisfied with them. Under provisions of the treaty, the Canal Zone was abolished and its territory reintegrated into the national territory of Panama. However, the United States retained its military bases, though their number was reduced. The canal would revert to Panama in twenty years, that is, by 1999. Meanwhile it would be administered by an authority on whose governing board the United States had a majority of one. The chief administrator would be an American for the first ten years, a Panamanian for the second decade. A vastly increased share of canal revenues would go to Panama. Panama undertook not to allow construction of another canal without the approval of the United States.

A second, sea-level, canal is in fact a possibility. The present canal, which raises and lowers ships by a system of locks, is subject to silting and is not large enough to take the supertankers that carry most of the world's oil. And despite the increase in fees under the new management, there are lines of ships waiting to transit the locks. However, the problem may instead be solved by a trans-isthmian oil pipeline, and by alternative techniques.

Although Panama exports bananas, shrimp, palm oil, sugar, and coffee, and although half of the national work force is in agriculture, income from the canal in various forms constitutes the country's principal "export." This includes not only income from fees paid by ships transiting the canal, but also wages of the Panamanians who work on it, and money from purchases made by passengers in those ships and from oil refined in the republic and sold to the ships using the canal.

Following the conclusion of the canal treaty, Torrijos appeared to regard his principal political task as accomplished and withdrew from his position as chief of government. Torrijos's candidate for president, Arístides Royo, was chosen by a popular assembly elected without partisan candidates and under Torrijos's influence. And a new party, the Democratic Revolutionary Party, Partido Revolucionario Democrático or PRD, was formed to represent the views of Torrijos's national revolution, with technical assistance from the Mexican PRI and the PRD of the Dominican Republic. It was thus to be a party of the center-left.

Speculation about the genuineness of Torrijos's withdrawal from politics was cut short by the general's death in an airplane crash at the end of July 1981. While the shape of Panamanian political life to come remained unclear, most people assumed that the commanders of the National Guard would play the leading role.

HAITI

General Description

Although Haiti occupies the western portion of the island of Hispaniola, which it shares with the Dominican Republic, in many ways the country is dissociated from the rest of Latin America. Differing in language, culture, and traditions from other countries of the area, Haiti has many elements in common with the French-speaking states of West Africa. At the same time, Haiti retains cultural ties with France, the former colonial power, and its external economic relations are dominated by the United States. The concept "Latin America" is at its most attenuated when it includes Haiti.

Population.   Haiti was the second country in the hemisphere after United States, and the first Latin American country, to become independent; it had been a plantation economy owned by the French and worked by black slaves. In addition to French officials, white planters, and black slaves, the society contained two other classes, the poor whites and the mulatto *affranchis,* or freedmen. The latter class had originated usually as the offspring of white planters and slave women. Often acknowledged by their fathers and sometimes sent to France for their education, the free mulattoes surpassed the poor whites in cultural attainments and wealth and complicated a social situation in which color would otherwise have correlated with status. They were thus placed in an anomalous situation and were subjected to prejudices and legal disabilities inconsistent with their educational and economic attainments.

Independence from France;
Division of Classes

In this situation, the French Revolution aroused mutually contradictory hopes and aspirations among mulattoes, poor whites, and slaves in Haiti. As the social classes petitioned and allied themselves with the different factions that came to power in the mother country, other European powers became involved in the wars of the Revolutionary and Napoleonic period. Turbulence and fighting, both internecine and international, broke out on the island. Warfare, temporary alliances, treachery, and massacres characterized the political life on the island as successive French governments shifted policies. The French succeeded temporarily in reestablishing control, only to lose it through incompetence and miscalculation. The final outcome was not only independence for Haiti from France but also freedom for the slaves under the leadership, until his betrayal by Napoleon, of the masterful strategist and statesman Toussaint L'Ouverture, a black ex-slave. The whites fled the island or were massacred, and the class division became what it has remained to this day, a cleavage between black masses and educated mulatto elite. The masses are on the whole rural and illiterate; they speak Créole, a sort of elaborated pidgin whose vocabulary is principally French in origin but whose grammar and syntax are drastically different from French. Their effective religion is Vodun, a religion of animal sacrifice and spirit possession based on West African cults. The elite also speaks Créole but uses French for formal and public communication. The elite is observantly Catholic, or occasionally agnostic, on the French pattern. Its members are predominantly professionals, though many also own land or engage in business activities.

Unlike the traditional pattern in the Spanish-speaking countries, however, the masses are not peons, share-croppers, or renters on land owned by the upper classes. The war for independence, which was also a slave insurrection, was at the same time a movement for agrarian reform, and today most of those who work the land own their own tiny plots.[3] Hilly and eroded, the crumpled landscape of Haiti is crowded by a population packed more densely than any in the hemisphere, except that of El Salvador. The peasants scratch out a living at what can hardly even be called a subsistence level, supplementing a starchy diet with tropical fruit, while chicken and goats, the poor man's cattle, scratch around the rocks looking for nourishment.

Members of the elite, themselves economically insecure, have traditionally been dependent on government employment and favors, with politics an aspect of the economic struggle. The picture has improved somewhat since 1972, as the government has moved eagerly into development activities with the funding and under the tutelage of international agencies. Tourism has experienced some small growth,

[3] Almost seventy percent of agricultural units are below two hectares in size. Gérard Brisson, "Les rélations agraires dans l'Haiti contemporain," cited in Gérard Pierre-Charles, *Haiti: Radiografía de una dictadura,* Mexico, D.F.: Editorial Nuestro Tiempo, 1969, pp. 132–133. There are, however, also large plantations, typically owned by North Americans, that produce sugar cane, sisal, and fruit; although most of the population in agriculture works on its own tiny plots, in fact two-thirds of the land is held in units larger than ten hectares.

and there has been encouraging development of light assembly industry in clothing, sporting equipment, and electronic components, which has been able to take advantage of inexpensive but readily trainable Haitian labor. At the same time, some attempt is being made to increase the very low yields obtained from the coffee bushes that provide the peasants' chief cash crop and the country's major export.

Political History

During the nineteenth century, the political history of the country was a bizarre record of anarchy, dictatorship, monarchies, and empires, punctuated by civil wars and wars against the neighboring Dominican Republic. The United States intervened in 1915, with a customs receivership growing out of foreign debt claims becoming transformed into a full-fledged occupation of the country by the Marines. While the Marines made their mark in public works, roads, and schools, they also left a legacy of bloody repression and deliberate racism. The Marines departed in 1934, leaving the country politically in the hands of the mulatto elite that had beeen favored during the occupation and militarily under a national guard (since renamed "army"), which was small (about 5000 men), well disciplined, and, like the constabulary forces created by the occupations in Nicaragua and the Dominican Republic, ostensibly nonpartisan and nonpolitical. Thereafter, power was shared in a sort of unstable fluctuating system by members of the mulatto elite and the army commanders, who were often black. Uprisings and military interventions occurred typically around elections, when incumbent presidents attempted to extend their mandates. However, there was a certain amount of very limited economic and social development, especially under the administration of Dumarsais Estimé (1946–50), and a gradual growth, through the workings of the educational system in the capital, of a small black middle class opposed to the monopoly of the best positions by mulattoes.

PRESIDENTS OF HAITI, 1930–82

1930–41	Sténio Vincent
1941–46	Elie Lescot
1946	Military junta
1946–50	Dumarsais Estimé
1950	Military junta
1950–56	Paul Magloire
1956–57	Six successive provisional governments
1957–71	François Duvalier
1971–	Jean-Claude Duvalier

The presidential election of 1957.   The range of interest groups, classes, and sectors relevant to politics was displayed in the course of the jockeying for the 1957 presidential elections. There were four principal candidates. Louis Déjoie, a wealthy businessman, had the support of business and also some mass following. Clément Jumelle attracted mildly progressive intellectuals and professionals, most of whom were mulatto. Daniel Fignolé appealed to the masses in Port-au-Prince. The winner was, of course, François Duvalier, by dint of astute preelection maneuvering and army support as much as by his popular support in the countryside, where he had worked as a physician in public health programs. He was also popular with the rural masses because he had a tolerant or sympathetic attitude to Vodun. His ethnological writings had accepted African survivals and popular practices as part of the national tradition, instead of despising them or being ashamed of them, which was the typical elite attitude. He was also acceptable to the United States, since he had collaborated with United States government agencies in public health work and had attended the University of Michigan School of Public Health, though doubtless Jumelle and Déjoie would have been equally acceptable. Duvalier had the decisive support of the military, who probably believed that the quiet-spoken aging physician would be the easiest to control as president.

The Duvalier era.   Once in power, Duvalier did redeem, at least in a symbolic way, his commitment to the blacks; in fact, mulattoes were discriminated against. A striking statue of the "unknown runaway slave" was erected in a square in front of the presidential palace; the use of Créole was permitted in debates of the national congress; the national colors, originally the red, white, and blue of the French tricolor with the white eliminated, were changed by Duvalier to red and black. Concrete achievements, as distinct from merely symbolic ones, were sparse, however. A dam was built, and a new town, Duvalierville, was constructed; very soon, however, the Duvalier regime was dominated by what the president called "security problems." Repression became brutal dictatorship. Opponents went into exile to escape assassination, imprisonment, and torture. The impromptu armies of gangsters that defended the regime were kept happy by being allowed to graft and extort money. The economy deteriorated.

Declaring himself reelected before the end of his first term because the legend "François Duvalier, President" had appeared at the head of the ballot for Congressional candidates, Duvalier subsequently had the Congress declare him president for life. This original tactic dealt with the reelection problem that had traditionally defeated his predecessors. The power of the army was checked in various ways; the army command was balanced off against the Palace Guard, the troops in the Dessalines Barracks next to the presidential palace, and the rural Volunteers of National Security, a sort of Duvalier partisan militia, all of which reported independently of the army command direct to the palace. Within the army, military commanders were played off against each other, and ammunition and explosives were kept by the president himself in the basement of the palace. An informal secret police of Duvalier militants, nicknamed the Tontons Macoutes, or bogeymen, carried guns and used them. "Papa Doc" also maintained good relations with the *houngans,* or Vodun priests. Duvalier's power was so absolute that before he died, in April 1971, he had his puppet Congress amend the constitution to lower the minimum age for president from forty to twenty and give Duvalier the right to name his own successor, his son Jean-Claude (who was apparently not even twenty when the old man died).

Jean-Claude Duvalier.   Under Jean-Claude, the system was at first eased. With the slogan "My father made the political revolution; I will make the economic revolution," Jean-Claude ended official prejudice against mulattoes, dropped charges against exiles and allowed most of them to return, and welcomed financial aid, advice, and guidance from United States and international agencies. At first, the more prominent members of the Duvalier old guard were eliminated, and the regime's leaders were no longer men who were known and hated under the François Duvalier administration, although they were often men who were equally implicated though less well known. Politics under Jean-Claude became a Byzantine affair of who was in favor and who was not, what cliques were forming around whom, and the like, so that it was impossible to gauge at any moment how decisions were being made or whose advice, among the members of the ruling group, was critical on this issue or that. In the terms used in Chapter 1, politics is conducted wholly in the private arena. However, this improbable regime, under which a nineteen-year-old boy became president for life, began to look quite plausible. The Tontons Macoutes dropped out of sight, and the rural Volunteers of National Security fell into disuse as a more conventional elite counterinsurgency force, the Leopards, was recruited and trained to deal with uprisings and domestic insurgency.

For a while it appeared that the personalist dictatorship of his father might be converted under Jean-Claude into an authoritarian modernizing regime, in which technocrats would replace torturers and the criteria of development would replace those of loyalty. Eventually, however, as the regime eased up, it came to a crossroads, as President Carter's human rights emphasis and the *aggiornamento* of the Catholic

Church encouraged the formation of Haitian human rights organizations and Christian Democratic parties. This proved too much for the government, and, after some initial hesitation and weighing the risks of the cut-off of foreign economic assistance, it decided to crack down, jailing dissidents and prohibiting opposition political activity. The assumption of power of the Reagan administration in the United States removed any inhibitions Jean-Claude had had about his new policy direction. The dictator's marriage to the daughter of a mulatto industrialist added her family to those entitled to plunder the national economy, and the millions accumulated in Swiss banks at an accelerated rate.

THE DOMINICAN REPUBLIC

General Description

Like the other countries of the Caribbean region, the Dominican Republic has historically been dominated by foreign powers. However, the relationship with Haiti, with which the Dominicans share the island of Hispaniola, has made that dependence of a special character.

Today the dependent relationship is, of course, with the United States. The Dominican Republic is the largest supplier of sugar to the United States, and sugar constitutes the republic's principal export. Agriculture, especially sugar, is the major factor in an economy where two-thirds of the population of five million live in rural areas. Social and economic levels tend to be below the Latin American average but are rising. Although worse off than its eastern neighbor, Puerto Rico, which is politically and economically part of the United States, the Dominican Republic is better off than its western neighbor and other point of comparison, Haiti.

History Before Trujillo

Nineteenth-century relations with Haiti.   Today, although the Dominican population is smaller than that of Haiti, the more advanced economy and society support a large and well-equipped armed forces for which the small Haitian army is no match. During the nineteenth century, however, the balance of power was the other way, and the Dominicans lived in continual fear of invasion and occupation by the Haitians. To defend themselves from attack from the west, the Dominicans repeatedly sought the protection of major foreign powers. But this only served to alarm the Haitians, who feared that the Dominican

Republic would be used as a base against them by a European power seeking to reestablish slavery, as, indeed, the French had done under Napoleon.

Invasions and occupations. As a result, the nineteenth century was for the Dominicans a series of disasters in which Haitian invasions alternated with European occupations, and national independence was feared and spurned by some as much as it was welcomed by others. A Spanish possession until 1795, Santo Domingo was occupied by the French from 1795 to 1801. The Dominicans freed themselves in 1809 from a Haitian occupation that lasted from 1801 to 1809 only to recall the Spaniards, who ruled the country again from 1809 to 1821. Regaining independence once more, the Dominicans attempted unsuccessfully to join the federation of Gran Colombia, which included present-day Venezuela, Colombia, Ecuador, and Panama, and in the following year the Haitians invaded again, imposing an occupation that lasted from 1822 to 1844, which was an unmitigated disaster for the country's economy and cultural life. Independence was regained in 1844 and maintained until 1860, when Spain was invited back, to rule the country until 1865. Independence lasted thereafter from 1865 to 1916 but only because a request to join the United States failed when Grover Cleveland vetoed the enabling act passed by Congress. But in 1916 the country was occupied by United States Marines, who stayed until 1924.

United States Influence and Class Structure

Subsequently, the country has been subject to United States influence. The United States Central Intelligence Agency was involved in the assassination of the country's strongman, Rafael Trujillo, in 1961;[4] the Marines were landed again in 1965, when the country was fighting a civil war; thereafter, the United States Agency for International Development, operating an aid program larger in per capita terms than it maintained in any country other than South Vietnam, was called "the parallel government."

This peculiar national history has left its mark on the country's social and political structure. Although a social elite developed comparable to what is generally called in Latin American countries "the oligarchy," this elite has not generally been in political control of the country, except for a period during the late nineteenth and early twen-

[4]"Alleged Assassination Plots Involving Foreign Leaders," *Reports of the Senate Select Committee on Intelligence Activities,* Washington, D.C.: U.S. Government Printing Office, November 20, 1975, pp. 191–216.

tieth centuries. Moreover, it has not dominated the economy, as is typically the case elsewhere in Latin America. The country's political and economic life have instead been dominated by foreign interests and by the armed forces working in collaboration with those interests.

The Trujillo Era

Origins.   For the period since the end of the Marine occupation in 1924, the dynamics of this process have been as follows. Before they withdrew from the Dominican Republic, the Marines organized and trained a constabulary force that was supposed to become the nonpolitical guarantor of law and order. Not long after the end of the occupation, the commander of this force, Rafael Leonidas Trujillo Molina, seized power. Thereafter, the army more or less stepped into the role of occupying force vacated by the United States Marines. Trujillo maintained good relations with the United States and favorable conditions for United States trade and investment, and in return, the United States tolerated his regime, which was a tightly controlled totalitarian system based on the arbitrary use of force, terror, and a comprehensive network of spies.

Interests served.   In economic terms, Trujillo ruled partly in the interests of the United States but principally in his own interest and that of the military, which became a privileged caste. By one means or another, he accumulated land and business interests until he all but owned the country. While some members of the oligarchy collaborated with Trujillo, and most tolerated him passively, he was not liked by the oligarchy, and the feeling was mutual. Trujillo himself was of non-elite antecedents, and the army was recruited from the lower and lower middle classes. Trujillo's rule was thus not the rule of a specific social class but a personal dictatorship based on a declassed military who served their own interests, that of their commander and his numerous family, and that of the United States.

The end of Trujillo.   Trujillo outlived his usefulness for the United States, however. Out of place in the new environment created by the Kennedy administration's espousal of democracy and progress in the hemisphere, he was also an obstacle to Kennedy's attempt to take action with collective Latin American support against Fidel Castro. How could the Latin Americans follow the United States' lead in acting against Castro, they asked, while doing nothing about the notorious Trujillo? Trujillo overplayed his hand in organizing an unsuccessful assassination attempt against his leading Latin American opponent, President

Rómulo Bétancourt of Venezuela, and, at the Venezuelans' insistence, the Organization of American States (OAS) imposed a partial economic boycott on the Dominican Republic, which put Trujillo on the defensive and encouraged internal opposition to his rule, which culminated in his assassination, apparently with United States connivance and aid.

The Post-Trujillo Period

The transition.   The lack of congruence between control of political power, social position, and wealth gave rise to the peculiar fluidity of Dominican politics in the post-Trujillo period.[5] At the time of Trujillo's assassination, Joaquín Balaguer, a literary figure and diplomat who had served the Trujillo regime without being implicated personally in its crimes, was serving as figurehead president. Balaguer attempted to assert himself politically and acquired popularity by distributing some of Trujillo's accumulated wealth; cab drivers, for example, were given the vehicles they drove. Nevertheless, the United States, acting through the OAS, maintained pressure for the dismantling of the Trujillo system, and Balaguer had to give way to a transitional Council of State, charged with preparing elections, which was dominated by members of the social elite. The oligarchy's candidate for president, Viriato Fiallo, ran on a platform of eliminating Trujilloism from Dominican life. However, the election was won by his major opponent, Juan Bosch, who took the position that Trujilloism was a question of the past and the real issue was that between oligarchy and masses. The appropriate lines of political cleavage, that is, were themselves in contention.

The Bosch government.   The role of the United States continued to be significant, as the Kennedy administration identified itself with Bosch's government. However, Bosch's rigidity and lack of political savoir-faire (he had spent many years in exile and had not held a responsible elective position before becoming president) made his tenure precarious. He also made enemies in the armed forces by refusing to countenance traditional practices of graft-taking and in the church by the adoption of a new constitution that separated church and state. He was finally removed by the military after only seven months in office, despite heroic efforts of the United States ambassador on his behalf.

The triumvirate and the Civil War.   Although the key figure in Bosch's removal was General Elías Wessín y Wessín, Wessín himself

---

[5]See Abraham Lowenthal, "The Dominican Republic: The Politics of Chaos," in Arpad von Lazar and Robert R. Kaufman, eds., *Reform and Revolution: Readings in Latin American Politics,* Boston: Allyn and Bacon, 1969.

chose to remain commander of the key San Isidro military base while the government was run by a triumvirate of the same general oligarchic complexion as the pre-Bosch Council of State. The downfall of the triumvirate came when its dominant figure, Donald Reid Cabral, began to maneuver himself into a position to win an election as president at a time when the economy was deteriorating and both Bosch and Balaguer were in enforced exile. A popular revolt broke out, led by Juan Bosch's PRD, or Dominican Revolutionary Party. It was tolerated by the military, who believed that it would lead to a military junta that would supervise elections in which Balaguer would defeat Bosch and would restore a neo-Trujilloist system. After the revolt was successful in overthrowing the triumvirate, however, the PRD and other elements that collaborated in the rebel "constitutionalist" forces instead took the position that Bosch was still the legitimate president, since his term of office had not yet expired. The military, led by Wessín, thereupon took up arms against the rebels, and a civil war began in which the United States, now under the more conservative Johnson administration, gave support to the military faction. When it appeared that the rebels might win, President Johnson sent in the United States Marines, ostensibly to protect American lives but actually to head off a rebel victory, which he was persuaded might turn the Dominican Republic into "another Cuba." The United States thus shares the responsibility for the killing of constitutionalists carried out by the military during this period and for some time afterward.

After a stalemate in the fighting was reached, the United States, acting through the OAS, negotiated a solution to the conflict. A provisional government was formed, headed by Héctor García Godoy, a former diplomat acceptable to both factions, and the military leaders of the two sides, Wessín and Francisco Caamaño Deñó, were sent into exile.

The Balaguer Era

In 1966, the provisional government supervised an election in which Balaguer defeated Bosch. Reelection was allowed under the restored pre-Bosch constitution, and Balaguer was reelected to the presidency in 1970 and 1974. His administration did not mean a simple restoration of Trujilloism, however. Although Balaguer tolerated a great deal of military autonomy, considerable political freedom was also allowed, marred by only intermittent acts of repression.

Character of Balaguer's government.   Balaguer's policies were eclectic. While he created a favorable climate for foreign investment and cooperated closely with the United States, he also resumed the land reform program that had begun under Bosch. This program has not presented the problem of expropriation faced in other countries that instituted an agrarian reform, since the Dominican state inherited vast expanses of land from Trujillo, along with a great many industrial and business holdings, so that the country accidentally acquired a "mixed economy" of the type common in Western Europe. Politically, the Balaguer regime represented a cross between authoritarianism and conservative democracy.

The party system.   The opposition to Balaguer was for a long time ineffective. The PRD suffered attrition and splits because of the erratic and autocratic conduct of Bosch, who also lost much popularity by his prudent but hardly heroic conduct in refraining from returning to the country during the 1965 civil war and who finally left the party himself in 1974 and formed the Partido de la Liberación Dominicana.

However, the PRD retained its support despite the defection of Bosch, and in 1978, elected its presidential candidate, Antonio Guzmán. The military resisted the political demise of Balaguer, who had allowed them virtually a free hand, however, and only strong pressures from the Carter administration, then stressing its human rights position, enabled Guzmán to take office. Guzmán, a wealthy landowner who had served as Bosch's Secretary of Agriculture, actually represented a more conservative position than the bulk of the PRD membership, whose loyalty was owed primarily to the party secretary-general, the charismatic José Francisco Peña Gómez; the party soon fell out with the president over policy questions and over Guzmán's desire to succeed himself despite the party's hostility to the principle of reelection. As it happened, Guzmán was able to secure the party's nomination neither for himself nor for his Vice-President, Jacobo Majluta, and Salvador Jorge Blanco became the party's victorious candidate in 1982.

The PRD and Balaguer's Partido Reformista, both multiclass and populist, remain the country's major parties. The Reformistas are generally more conservative and close to the military. The party of the oligarchy remains the Unión Cívica Nacional, under whose banner Fiallo had run against Bosch in 1963, but a host of other parties of vague political orientation and platform form and re-form around leading figures such as Wessín, Antonio Imbert and Luis Amiama, the two survivors of the group that assassinated Trujillo, and Francisco Lora, Balaguer's former vice-president. An ideologically coherent but small and multiclass party is the Revolutionary Social Christian Party, or PRSC. There are several parties on the far left, some illegal. One of these, the Dominican Communist Party, from time to time endorsed some of Balaguer's policies. Leftist revolutionary activity has been insignificant with one exception: in February 1973, Caamaño Deñó, the military leader of the rebels in the 1965 civil war, attempted an invasion from Cuba, which was quickly put down at the cost of his own life.

The peculiar fluidity of Dominican politics has led to continual splitting and re-formation of parties, with old antagonisms often forgotten in new and bizarre alliances. Thus the ideological and class content of politics is low. Personalism remains high, as does United States influence.

PRESIDENTS OF THE DOMINICAN REPUBLIC, 1961-82

1961	Joaquín Balaguer
1962-63	Council of State
1963	Juan Bosch
1963-65	Triumvirate
1965	Civil war:
	rival provisional presidents and juntas
1965-66	Héctor García Godoy
1966-1978	Joaquín Balaguer
1978-82	Antonio Guzmán
1982-	Salvador Jorge Blanco

CUBA

Cuba resembles the other Caribbean countries in the extent of foreign, especially United States, influence to which its has historically been subject. Foreign influence continues strong today, although it is now that of the Soviet Union.

Independence from Spain;
"Platt Amendment"

Cuba's independence from Spain came only in 1902, after the Cuban war for independence became absorbed into the Spanish-American War. But independence was not won directly from Spain; the United States assumed control over the island after defeating the Spaniards. Thus, instead of Cuba's gaining independence automatically with the Spanish defeat, it was granted by the Americans, and then only with conditions. The United States took a perpetual lease on Guantánamo Bay, on the eastern end of the island, which commanded the shortest sea route from Europe to Panama, for use as a naval base. Moreover, the Cuban constitution had to include the provisions of the "Platt Amendment," which gave the United States the right to intervene in Cuban affairs. In effect, the Amendment established a United States protectorate over the island, and American troops did, in fact, intervene when law and order was threatened, which was more or less every election time, when fighting broke out over the choice of a new government. Troops were sent in four years after independence, in 1906, remaining until 1908; on subsequent occasions, troops were landed and held in readiness without actually going into operation. The United States supervised some elections until 1920; however, the Republican administrations of the 1920s, whose policies prefigured the "Good Neighbor" policy, refrained from intervening, and Gerardo Machado was able to impose a dictatorship that lasted from 1924 to 1933. After the overthrow of Machado, the United States sent a "mediator" who made clear which factions were acceptable to the United States and which were not. From this situation, Fulgencio Batista emerged as military strongman and, from 1940 to 1944, as president. Although Cuban politics remained violent and corrupt, honest elections whose results were observed occurred in 1944 and 1948, the United States did not intervene, and Cubans believed their politics had attained a new maturity. However, Batista returned to the island and, believing that his presidential candidacy in the 1952 elections would not be successful, staged a coup that brought him again to power.[6]

Batista's Regime

In some respects, the Batista regime resembled that of Trujillo. That is, Batista, like Trujillo, had risen to power from humble antecedents. He did not represent the traditional social elite but only roughnecks like himself, who had become wealthy and powerful through their military positions. In maintaining good relations with the United States government and private American economic interests, Batista, again like Trujillo, in effect represented those interests.

Batista had staged his original coup in 1933 while still a sergeant. Holding power during the period of the New Deal and the Popular Front, he came, after an initial repressive phase, to a pro-labor and social welfare policy, developing good relations with organized labor and including two members of the Communist Party in the cabinet that served during his own 1940–44 presidential term.

Corruption.   After Batista returned to power in 1952, essentially because he had run through the money put aside during his early years in power, he followed no coherent social policy and was motivated almost exclusively by the desire to rebuild his private fortune. To that

[6]A good history is Jaime Suchlicki, *Cuba: From Columbus to Castro,* New York: Scribners, 1974.

end, he opened up Havana to large-scale gambling and other forms of "vice" illegal on the mainland. By the time he was forced out of power at the end of 1958, his cut of the proceeds of these activities could be reckoned in the hundreds of millions of dollars. At that time, the national per capita income was the third highest in Latin America and the highest of any country in the tropics, although wealth was concentrated in Havana. The rest of the island's economy was dependent on sugar, as it had always been.

Although sugar production was, in fact, the most profitable use of Cuban soil, it carried serious drawbacks. The agricultural force was unemployed or underemployed outside of the four months' cutting season. Little else was produced on the island; manufactured goods were imported from the mainland under a tariff preference system that inhibited the development of industry.

Opposition and repression.   Bastista's regime did not become repressive until the opposition to the dictator began to gather strength. A variety of groups of diverse orientation opposed the regime, but the majority of the population was at first passive and apathetic. As anti-Batista rebels, especially Fidel Castro's forces, had some successes, the repression became more severe, and the police resorted increasingly to torture and assassination, which alienated most of the middle class from the Batista government. Middle-class opposition to Batista was purely political, however; that is, it opposed primarily the repressive tactics and the undemocratic character of the regime. It hoped for a revolt against Batista that would restore democracy and would incidentally make possible some economic and social reform. But such a revolt would not necessarily change the character of Cuban society or bring a socialist economy.

The emergence of Fidel Castro.   The dominant figure in the opposition to Batista eventually became Fidel Castro, whose guerrilla movement eluded all of Batista's attempts at repression. Castro had become politically active as a student in the law faculty at the University of Havana. After receiving his law degree, he had been a candidate for Congress on a moderate left-of-center ticket in the elections that were cancelled after Batista seized power in 1952. His revolutionary activity grew out of his law school politics, and many of his companions in his first attempt at insurrection, the attack on the Moncada barracks, had been fellow students at the law school. Although his political position was still quite unformed, and he wisely avoided spelling out a revolutionary program that would alienate middle-class opposition to Batista, Fidel's ideas at this time were, in general, those typical of Latin American student revolutionaries. That is, he believed in land reform, improvement of the lot of the poor by labor and social welfare legislation, and the assertion of national independence from dominance by the United States. These ideas happen also to be those of the apostle of Cuban independence, José Martí, an idol of Fidel as of all Cubans.[7] However, such ideas can be given quite different specific implementations in policy, and governments that grow out of the ideas of leftist students may decide, like the governments of Acción Democrática in Venezuela, that in order to improve national standards of living it is necessary to maintain good relations with foreign companies and with the United States, and to introduce reform measures only gradually and with strictest adherence to constitutional forms so as not to provoke a military coup d'état. The actual direction taken by Castro's subsequent government, that is, grew out of the interaction between his attitudes and point of view and the circumstances he confronted; it was not determined ahead of time.

Fidel and the Communists.   There has been a lot of misconceived speculation about Castro's relations with the orthodox Communist parties. He did, of course, subsequently announce himself a Marxist-Leninist and organized a new Communist Party of Cuba, of which he became the First Secretary. Nevertheless, Fidel was always more radical than the Communists, and any influence from the orthodox Communist Party on Fidel was always influence in a more moderate direction.[8]

The relations of the Communists with Batista were rather ambivalent. They had collaborated in Batista's previous government and did not take the lead in anti-Batista activities under the dictatorship. The party's tacticians at first condemned Fidel Castro as a petit-bourgeois adventurist, and Communist-led unions refused to follow his call for a general strike against Batista. Later on, after Fidel had come to power and the orthodox Communists were supporting his government, they recommended moderation, urging him not to break with the United States and not to follow drastic revolutionary policies that would alienate middle-class businessmen and technicians and send them into exile. Fidel refused to listen, and the situation that the Communists had feared came about; that is, the country's development was retarded by shortages of trained technical and managerial personnel, as well as by

[7]Nelson P. Valdés, "Ideological Roots of the Cuban Revolutionary Movement," Occasional Paper no. 15, Institute for Latin American Studies, University of Glasgow, 1975.

[8]Helpful books in understanding Fidel Castro are Herbert Matthews, *Fidel Castro*, New York: Simon and Schuster, 1970, and Lee Lockwood, *Castro's Cuba, Cuba's Fidel*, New York: Random House Vintage, 1969.

the economic blockade imposed by the United States. The orthodox Communists continue today to take a moderate line, urging Fidel to a rapprochement with the United States. Fidel has never completely trusted what are called in Cuba the "old Communists," keeping them in a minority on the Central Committee of the Communist Party of Cuba, with the majority in the hands of the "new Communists," that is, followers of Fidel from his 26th of July Movement who only began to call themselves Communists after Fidel himself took that step.

Revolutionary Cuba

The instruments of power.   The political structure of revolutionary Cuba has changed over the years, as Fidel's political views have evolved, as he has shifted so as to ensure that various organizations do not come to have too much power, and as economic needs have caused manpower shortages. Originally, Fidel came to power representing the 26th of July Movement, named for the day of the assault on the Moncada barracks. Subsequently, he ruled largely through his comrades in the Rebel Army. However, as his policies crystallized in a socialist and anti-American direction, he could no longer rely on officers of the Rebel Army and increasingly used members of the old Communist party, the Popular Socialists. The arrest of Huber Matos, in October 1969, symbolized this shift away from the use of Rebel Army officers in favor of the Popular Socialists. Matos was a Rebel Army leader who resigned as military commander of Camagüey province over the increasing role being given to Communists in Cuba's government. The Rebel Army was then largely diverted to construction and other economic tasks, and a large militia force was created for defense purposes. However, the time consumed by members of the militia in training and drilling constituted a substantial economic drain. Fidel also drew back from heavy reliance on the old Communist party when he realized that its members were not unconditionally loyal to himself. In 1962, he denounced and suspended from his functions Aníbal Escalante, an "old Communist" charged with helping to organize the new ruling party, and in 1967 Escalante was imprisoned for "sectarian" activities, which involved passing information to the Soviet Union.

The political structure at the time of writing is dominated by a fairly elite Communist Party of Cuba, of about seventy thousand members, of which Fidel Castro is Secretary General, with Raúl Castro his deputy. A majority of members of the party's Political Bureau are "new Communists," that is, unconditional followers of Fidel rather than pre-revolutionary Communists. Agitation, propaganda, and surveillance are carried out by as many as two million revolutionary militants, organized as the Committees for the Defense of the Revolution in every residential block and place of work. A reorganized army, which has abandoned its previous egalitarianism and rough-and-ready character in favor of a fairly traditional rank structure and a high degree of professionalism and modern equipment, is about half a million strong, the largest army in the hemisphere as a percentage of national population. Raúl Castro is Minister of Defense, and Fidel Castro is commander-in-chief of the armed forces. An auxiliary labor force, the youth labor army, is under military control and discipline.

In addition to his positions as Secretary General of the party and commander-in-chief of the armed forces, Fidel Castro is president of the council of ministers, the "cabinet" of heads of government departments, and also president of the Council of State. The Council of State is in form elected by the national assembly and acts for it when it is not in session, which is most of the time. This is the governmental structure set up by the constitution adopted in 1976, under which Cubans elect legislative bodies at the local level. These bodies elect provincial assemblies, and it is the provincial assemblies that elect members of the national assembly. For the first seventeen years following the Revolution of 1959, there had been no elected legislature in Cuba (except for two years in the province of Matanzas, on an experimental basis).

Another key figure is Carlos Rafael Rodríguez, vice-president of the council of ministers, the only "old Communist" who had joined Fidel Castro while he was still in the Sierra Maestra. Ironically, Rodríguez had also been one of the two Communist ministers in Batista's 1940–44 cabinet.

The political system operated by this apparatus is a classic revolutionary regime. It attempts to rely on popular support and persuasion rather than repression; the repression is there if needed, however, complete with censorship of literature and cultural activities, and prosecution for economic crimes.

Economic and social performance.   An evaluation of the performance of the revolutionary government in the social and economic fields has to start by acknowledging the great improvement in the condition of the poorest Cubans, rural workers and marginal city residents, who did not participate in the affluence of pre-revolutionary Cuba. For them, the benefits represented by free health care, extensive housing construction and low rents, scholarships and new schools, are very real. These benefits apart, it is clear that the economic performance of the revolution has been poor. Production per capita has dropped substantially, and rationing of food is in effect. Many of these difficulties are due to the attempt to plan and manage the economy centrally in the face of a shortage of technical and managerial skills, the emigration of skilled people, and the United States' economic boycott.

There has been considerable expansion of the fishing industry, however, and tourism became a major hard currency earner as the island was opened up to tourism from Western countries in the late 1970s. The tourists from abroad included members of the Cuban exile community. Cubans ironically commented that from *gusanos* (worms —the term of abuse used for counter-revolutionaries) the exiles had blossomed into *mariposas* (butterflies).

However, many exiles were not prepared for reconciliation, and "action groups" continued campaigns of sabotage and terrorism. The poor economic performance of 1980–81 reflected in part the outbreak of hoof-and-mouth disease among cattle, rust disease in the coffee plantations, and various ailments that affected the sugar harvest, in circumstances suggestive of sabotage.

Poor economic performance also reflected confusion and naiveté in policy. Blaming dependence on sugar for the country's ills, the revolutionary government first attempted to diversify and industrialize the economy, only to find that Cuba lacked the raw materials, power sources, and export capacity to make industrialization a paying proposition. Reversing course and deciding again to concentrate on sugar, the government found that with new welfare programs and opportunities in the city, there was a shortage of cane cutters. This problem was only partly compensated for by the mobilization of voluntary cutting brigades of amateurs from city; a lot of cane was lost by unskilled cutting at the same time as the economic life of the cities was disrupted by the absence of so many people from their jobs there. Indifferent success has attended the introduction of a series of gimmicks, such as mechanized cutting and cane burning, to get around the problem of shortage of cutters, and the revolution failed to attain its goal of a ten-million-ton sugar harvest in 1970; in fact, post-revolutionary harvests do well if they match the amounts of cane cut before the revolution.

Economic policy in general has been bedeviled by the controversy over material versus moral incentives—that is, whether people should be motivated to work by the use of economic carrots and sticks or only by appeals to their conscience and public spirit. Che Guevara took a strong position in favor of moral incentives, arguing that to build a new socialist man uncontaminated by the selfishness and money-mania of capitalism, it was necessary to do without material incentives. However, the Cubans, like other revolutionaries, eventually discovered that while appeals to patriotism and public spirit can be effective in the short run, they cannot be used indefinitely to motivate people effectively. The return to material incentives has not been easy, however. Given the provision of basic necessities free or at low cost and the general scarcity of consumer goods, there is a shortage of material incentives to be offered. One of the economic problems that faces the country is, in fact, a high rate of absenteeism, as people find they have money that cannot be used to buy anything, so that there seems no reason to work diligently. The attempt is being made to increase the availability of consumer durable goods, such as refrigerators, precisely to provide material incentives. The Soviet Union and orthodox Soviet-oriented Communists have consistently urged the desirability of material incentives, together with strict economic planning and the integration of the Cuban economy into the "socialist division of labor" of the Eastern European countries.

The Soviet Union has had to subsidize the Cuban economy at a rate that reached a billion dollars a year by 1980. Ironically, in the effort to ease their burden, the Soviets are trying to persuade the Cubans to reestablish trade relations with the United States. The Cuban experience thus suggests that despite the problems that grow out of external economic dependence, there does not seem to be any alternative for a small country located in the Caribbean.

SUMMARY

The Caribbean countries face, in particularly acute form, the problem of external economic dependence, especially on the United States, in whose backyard they find themselves. Dependence is inevitable, but so is the resentment to which dependence gives rise.

Panama

In Panama, the central issue of control over the Panama Canal led to perpetual confrontation with the United States. For a long time it enabled the oligarchy to divert resentment away from itself, but the position of the traditional oligarchy has been challenged by a modernizing movement initially led by General Torrijos.

Haiti

In Haiti, the traditional struggle for power between the mulatto elite and the black masses, which differ not only in economic status but also in culture and religious practice, has led to an alternation between strong and often bizarre dictators and interludes of turbulence and chaos. Some hesitant economic development in the form of plantation agriculture and assembly plants has had little impact in an impoverished economy dominated by minifundia.

Dominican Republic

Not only is the Dominican Republic highly dependent on the United States for its well-being, through its sugar exports, but it has also seen persistent United States intervention and influence. The role of the military remains important, but the first hesitant steps to democracy have been taken.

Cuba

Cuba has emancipated itself from a long period of political, economic, and cultural dominance by the United States, only to find that dependence on a single export product, sugar, and therefore on foreign markets, remains economically rational. Distribution of the national product has become fairer to the masses, but the problems of producing the nation's wealth have not been solved.

5

The Andes I:
Gran Colombia,
or the Mountains
and the Sea

From *Political Forces in Latin America: Dimensions of the Quest for Stability* by Ben G. Burnett and Kenneth F. Johnson. © 1968 by Wadsworth Publishing Co., Inc., Belmont, California 94002. Reprinted by permission of the publisher, Duxbury Press.

THE ANDEAN PACT

In May 1969, in Cartagena, Colombia, the Andean Pact was signed. Under its terms, Colombia, Ecuador, Peru, Bolivia, and Chile pledged themselves to an economic alliance that would lead to a common market and a common policy toward foreign investment. After a great deal of internal debate, Venezuela joined the group in 1973.

At the time of the Cartagena agreement, elected civilian governments were in office in all six countries, and the agreement rode on a wave of political and economic optimism. Within five years of the signing of the agreement, however, the four southern countries had come under military dictatorship, and the Andes were no longer the backbone of Latin American democracy.

Although Ecuador and Peru were restored to elected civilian government in 1979 and 1980, respectively, and Bolivia was ruled briefly by civilians during the same period, the motive force had left the common market. The Chilean military government formally withdrew from the agreement in 1979 and the government of General García Meza that seized power in Bolivia in 1980 drifted in the same direction. The economic aspects of the agreement, which involved common policies toward foreign investment and a sharing-out of industrial production facilities, in addition to the mutual reduction of tariff barriers, proved difficult to maintain, and widespread deviation from the provisions of the agreement made it seem unlikely that the Pact would survive long into the 1980s.

The Mountains and the Coast

From another perspective, however, the "Andean" label might more strictly be confined to the central countries of the six: Colombia, Ecuador, Peru, and Bolivia. At the extremes of the region, in Venezuela to the north and Chile to the south, the Andean pattern does not dominate national geography and society the way it does in the other countries; a majority of the population in both Venezuela and Chile are coastal rather than mountain dwellers. Colombia does differ from Ecuador, Peru, and Bolivia in not having the large proportion of Indians in the population that they do. Yet in these countries, all four of which have substantial populations both in the mountain areas and on the coast, the contrast, and sometimes the opposition, between the two types of region and the two ways of life form one of the themes of national society, economy, and politics. In general, the mountain areas are the home of traditional agriculture, the dominance of the lower classes by an entrenched upper class, devout Catholicism, and political conservatism. The coastal areas, by contrast, depend more on foreign trade and export agriculture; there, class lines are less rigid, and political loyalties lie more to the left of center. On the coast, the lower classes are less Indian and more Afro-American; the better off are less likely to be of old Hispanic stock and more likely to derive from recent immigration from Europe and the Middle East.

This chapter will deal with the three northernmost Andean countries: Venezuela, Colombia, and Ecuador. These three are often grouped together, as they once formed (together with Panama, at that time a Colombian province) the federation of Gran Colombia, or Greater Colombia.

VENEZUELA

Regional Orientation

Although Venezuela has cast her lot with the Andean bloc, the country belongs in many ways to the Caribbean area rather than the Andes. The Andean influence was stronger in the country during the nineteenth century. Since then, the Andean region has been a reservoir of conservative and Catholic values, and the home of the country's military tradition, providing the country with a succession of military dictators—the last of whom, Marcos Pérez Jiménez, was removed from office only in 1958—but the population has shifted steadily from the Andes to the coastal area. By 1970, the coastal range of hills, including the capital city of Caracas, contained fifty-three percent of the national population, with another twelve percent in the coastal region around Maracaibo, the center of oil production. Only thirteen percent of the population remains in the Andean region, with eighteen percent in the rolling plains called *llanos* and another three percent in the Guyana highlands to the east.

The picture of Venezuela's as a dynamic, socially fluid population characteristic of the Caribbean region, rather than of the traditional stratified society of the mountains, is strengthened by other indicators.

The 1980 population of 15 million reflected a growth rate of 3.4 percent a year, one of the world's fastest; this means that two-thirds of the population is under the age of thirty. And over 80 percent of the population lives in urban areas. The literacy rate of ninety percent suggests the high degree of social mobilization of the population, which is confirmed by the relatively large proportion of the work force organized in trade unions—about forty-five percent in 1975, which is the highest figure in Latin America after Cuba and Argentina[1]—and the extremely high turnout of eligible voters, which sometimes exceeds ninety percent.

A Caribbean identity is also suggested by the fact that Venezuelans are very conscious of developments in the Caribbean area, especially those in Cuba. And, like the countries of the Caribbean, Venezuela has depended primarily on a single product exported primarily to the United States—in the Venezuelan case, oil. Manufactured goods have overwhelmingly been imported from the United States.

Entry into the Andean Pact

In the early 1970s, however,, the government of President Rafael Caldera, almost by an effort of will, reoriented the country in the direction of its continental neighbors to the west and south and led Venezuela into the Andean Pact. Venezuela had not been one of the original signers of the pact, and the country's entry into the regional community had been strongly opposed by business interests committed to the country's special economic relationship with the United States. These interests, centered in FEDECAMARAS, the National Federation of Chambers of Commerce, managed to block Venezuela's association with the Andean group for many years against the opposition of manufacturers attracted by the prospect of access to an Andean market protected by tariffs against manufactured imports from the United States.

The decision to throw Venezuela's lot in with the Andean group had always been indicated by ideological factors. President Caldera's party, the Social Christians (still known as COPEI, after the initials of its previous name), like other Christian Democratic parties in the hemisphere, has always had cooperation among the Latin American countries as one of its major principles. At the same time, the nationalism widespread among the parties of the center and left implied association with the Andean bloc. Venezuelan nationalism, like that of other Latin American countries, is not so much a passion for the fatherland above all other countries as it is an anti-Yankee sentiment that sees cooperation with other Latin American countries as the logical way

---

[1]Central Intelligence Agency, *National Basic Intelligence Factbook,* July 1975.

of strengthening national independence from the hegemonic power, the United States.

The Oil Industry

Nationalization. This nationalist sentiment, shared across the political spectrum, has dictated the gradual phasing out of North American dominance of the oil industry. At the beginning of 1976, the Venezuelan state oil corporation, CVP, assumed an exclusive position in petroleum exploration and production with foreign companies to operate in Venezuela only as contractors for the government oil company, on fixed fees and for fixed periods of time.

Economic importance. The oil industry has, of course, been the engine of economic change in Venezuela. In recent years, it has produced twenty percent of the country's gross national product, seventy percent of the government's budget revenues, and ninety percent of the country's foreign exchange. Income from oil has given the Venezuelans the highest per capita gross national product in the region and has simplified the government's problem of raising revenue. Yet, at the same time, it has brought its own characteristic set of problems, which contributed to producing the difficult and stormy period in Venezuelan history through which the country now seems to have successfully passed.

Problems it creates. The difficulty is that although oil produces a great deal of revenue, it employs very few people: less than three percent of the Venezuelan labor force. Thus it introduces a great deal of money into the country, which raises the incomes of those directly involved in the oil industry and also those in the bureaucracy whose salaries reflect the government's share of oil revenues. The increase in the amount of

PRESIDENTS OF VENEZUELA, 1945–81

1945–48	Rómulo Bétancourt (provisional)
1948	Rómulo Gallegos
1948–50	Carlos Delgado Chalbaud, as head of military triumvirate
1950–58	Marcos Pérez Jiménez
1958–59	Wolfgang Larrazábal (provisional)
1959–64	Rómulo Bétancourt
1964–69	Raúl Leoni
1969–74	Rafael Caldera
1974–79	Carlos Andrés Pérez
1979–	Luis Herrera Campins

money in the economy leads to an inflationary rise in the price level and thus contributes to a decline in the standard of living of those who do not benefit from the oil income.

Thus the affluence of some was accompanied by the impoverishment of a great many, and an economic polarization developed that was not only undesirable in itself but also highly dangerous politically.

Political System

The situation was particularly difficult because of the lack of any tradition of orderly political change. The country was ruled by military men until 1945. The revolutionary junta that then took power held a free election, the first with mass participation in Venezuelan history, in 1947, but the elected president, Rómulo Gallegos, served less than one year before he was removed by the military. The succeeding dictatorship, after 1950 under Marcos Pérez Jiménez, lasted until 1958.

Since then, the Venezuelans have learned the lessons of democracy the hard way. Pérez Jiménez had covered up the basic economic problem by employing a large number of people on public works projects in Caracas. Population in the capital city mushroomed, and many people moved into improvised shantytowns. Rómulo Bétancourt, the leader of the major party, Acción Democrática, won the elections held by the provisional government at the end of 1958 but had to confront not only the country's economic problems but also its expectation that political violence and military intervention would continue to be the normal features of national politics.

The Bétancourt administration.   Attempting to govern democratically from a center-left position, Bétancourt was faced not only with military conspiracies from the right (including an assassination attempt by agents of Rafael Trujillo, in which he was injured) but also with revolts and terrorism from the left, as young political militants, including a secession from Acción Democrática that called itself the Movement of the Revolutionary Left, or MIR, protested that he had sold out to imperialism by not nationalizing the oil companies and by breaking relations with Fidel Castro's Cuba. To some extent, Bétancourt was able to keep military leaders in line by pointing to this threat from the left. But he also took care not to tamper with the favored economic position of the military.

Bétancourt was also driven to adopting some of the techniques urged by the military for dealing with the insurrectionary left, including the arrest of left-wing congressmen involved in the insurrectionary attempts, although legislators had constitutional immunity from arrest. Acts such as this one enabled the left to protest that Bétancourt was no better than Pérez Jiménez, that he was also a dictator acting in the interest of foreign companies.

Especially with the hindsight of seeing so many governments fall under military rule as a result of the military's disaffection with what they feel is a weak response to left-wing terrorism, however, one can appreciate the magnitude of Bétancourt's achievement in keeping a hair-raising situation under control and becoming the first popularly elected civilian president of Venezuela to serve out his term of office.

The land reform.   Acción Democrática had added peasant support to its bulwark among the petroleum workers' unions as a result of the land reform programs. Venezuela was fortunate by comparison with other Latin American countries, not only in having sufficient funds to compensate landowners who were expropriated and provide newly settled farmers with equipment and loans, but also in holding most of the country's land area in public hands, thus minimizing the amount of expropriation necessary. The land reform program might better be called a settlement or colonization program, since most of it involved settling farmers on newly opened up land rather than subdividing existing estates, although that has occurred too. While the program has had mixed economic success—many farms have been abandoned as their owners moved to the cities—there has been a clear political payoff in the failure of Fidelista guerrillas to find any support in the countryside.

Political parties.   Over the years, Acción Democrática (AD) lost support in Caracas, however, both to more conservative parties that catered to the middle class and to more radical parties that appealed to the lower classes, and it narrowly lost power to the Social Christians (COPEI) for the presidential term 1969–74. This was the culmination of a process of decline that had seen the vote cast for AD presidential candidates go from eighty percent in 1948 (Gallegos) to forty-nine percent in 1958 (Bétancourt) to thirty-three percent in 1963 (Leoni) and finally to twenty-eight percent in 1968 (Barrios). The MIR broke away in 1960; a generational conflict led to a split-off of second-level leaders led by Raúl Ramos Giménez in 1962; and Luis B. Prieto Figueroa, a major party leader denied the presidential nomination in 1967, broke away to form the People's Electoral Movement (MEP), charging that the AD had grown too conservative, pro-United States, and favorable to business, a view that was widely shared. Nevertheless, the AD staged a strong comeback in electing its candidate, Carlos A. Pérez, for the 1974–79 term, and he proceeded to surprise those who thought the AD had grown conservative by implementing a strongly nationalist and progressive policy. The AD was weakened, however, by the struggle over the succession to Pérez, and by allegations of corruption in his administration, so that COPEI was narrowly able to elect Luis Herrera Campins to the presidency in the 1978 elections.

During the post-1958 period, Venezuelan democracy went from strength to strength. More than ninety percent of the electorate defied death threats from the extreme left to vote in the presidential elections of 1963. The transfer of power from Rómulo Bétancourt to Raúl Leoni in 1964 was the first such transfer from an elected president to his freely elected successor in Venezuelan history. The assumption of power of the Christian Democrat Rafael Caldera in 1969 marked the first time that a Venezuelan government had voluntarily relinquished power to the opposition. And, in the 1973 and 1978 elections, the voters seemed to be settling down comfortably with the two large center parties, as the host of personalist candidates and ideological movements that had hitherto complicated the political scene failed to draw significant support.

If this simplification of the Venezuelan party system into one of competition between the two large center parties, Acción Democrática and COPEI, continues, it will represent a real break with the past. Previously, a welter of parties competed in each election, very often divided not by any differences of program but only by the irreconcilable ambitions of their leaders. Except for the small groups of the far left, in fact, the parties had never differed much on questions of substance, and, indeed, all of the larger parties had been allied with each other in Congress and the cabinet at various times during the post-1958 period. There were differences among them on the question of how fast to move in nationalizing foreign oil companies or in resuming relations with Cuba. The former question, however, became moot when the nationalization took place, on January 1, 1976, although the Pérez Administration laid itself open to criticism over the amount of compensation the foreign companies received. At the same time, businessmen have been generally able to live with government policies with no more than a minimal amount of grumbling. This is due partly to the general health of the economy and partly to the fact that because of the necessity of rechanneling income from oil to other activities, no one can reasonably object to the large role government must play in the country's economy.

Social and Economic Cleavages

Thus, despite the high level of violent conflict the country has known in the recent past, social and economic cleavages are actually weaker in Venezuela than elsewhere. The country's wealth is created by the exploitation of a natural resource, not by the expoitation of one class by another; the highly paid petroleum workers, a fraction of the labor force, can hardly be considered expoited. Moreover, the fact that the government enjoys colossal revenues without having to extract them painfully from Venezuelans has given the political arena a degree of autonomy from the processes of class conflict not known elsewhere in the area. The major conflict of economic interest was between the foreign oil companies and everyone else; yet even there a counter-productive hostility was muted, on the one hand, by the fact that the country needed the oil companies, at least in the short run, and, on the other hand, by the fact that the government had learned to manage its relations with the companies to the national advantage. As with the other members of OPEC, the Organization of Petroleum Exporting Countries, rather than being expoited by the multinational oil produc-ers, the Venezuelan government was, in effect, using the companies as its agents in "expoiting" consumers of petroleum products.

With the increase in petroleum prices that took effect in 1973, government revenues rose so sharply that the surplus in the treasury became an embarrassment. The easy availability of money was clearly a factor in the corruption that afflicted government under Carlos Andrés Pérez. Perhaps the bigger tragedy, as Herrera Campins pointed out in his successful presidential campaign, was the way money was wasted without building up a sound and productive economy that could with-stand a possible collapse of the oil market. Agricultural production declined as farmers abandoned the countryside for the bright lights and easy money of the city, and Venezuela became dependent on imported food. Foreign exchange went to import not factory equipment but luxury consumer goods, and the streets of Caracas were jammed with expensive foreign cars. Bureaucratic employment mushroomed beyond all reason-able bounds and Pérez was driven to decreeing the creation of useless make-work jobs, such as elevator operator and washroom attendant, to try to reduce unemployment among unskilled workers.

While Herrera could denounce the problem, it became clear that, as president, he had no solutions to offer. Pockets of poverty remained amid affluence; but even comfortably-off Venezuelans shared the na-tional malaise, a diffuse anxiety about what would happen to a country that did not even produce its own food if tomorrow the world should discover a cheaper substitute for oil, or when, the day after tomorrow, the oil should all be used up.

Yet political prospects were good, and no one could deny the im-pressiveness of the achievement that had transformed Venezuela within one generation from a byword for military dictatorship and violence into one of the most solid democracies in the region with a reformist regime that had successfully surmounted the dangers that face that regime type: insurrection from the left and sabotage and military intervention from the right. The Venezuelan experience suggests that a stable democratic order is the political system appropriate to a developed society and that, after a period of strain, economic development does indeed lead to political development.

COLOMBIA

The Land and the People

In Colombia, the Andean element dominates over the coastal; of a 1982 population of twenty-eight million, more than twenty million lived in the Andes. The country has both Atlantic and Pacific coasts, on either side of the Isthmus of Panama, but the Atlantic coast is far more important, with 3.5 million people, compared with the one million on the Pacific side. Another million people are scattered through the plains and jungle that form the half of the country east of the Andes; this area is politically insignificant, although it has some economic importance, being the site of lumbering, cattle raising, and oil extraction.[2] The country's capital, Bogotá, is in the higher eastern Andes, on a cool and rainy plateau, far from the exuberance of the ports and the energy of the second city, Medellín, with its year-round spring climate, in the western Andes; and the climate of the capital imparts a sober, serious, businesslike tone to national life.

Colombia has now overtaken Argentina to rank third among Latin American countries in population. Its size and complexity, and the sophistication of its political class, make it unlike the smaller Latin American countries that can easily be dominated by a single individual or group, and the traditions of constitutionalism and democracy are well established. Colombian democracy has, nevertheless, been an oligarchic democracy, where the names of the leading families recur in the roster of the country's leaders. In 1974, in fact, the three leading presidential contenders—Alfonso López Michelsen, Alvaro Gómez Hurtado, and María Eugenia Rojas de Moreno Díaz—were all children of former presidents.

While socially conservative in the Andean fashion, with a strong Catholic Church, Colombia does not have a large Indian population like its southern neighbors. A few Indians are scattered in the jungle region, but the mass of the population is mestizo, with mulatto components on the coast. Not an Indian country like Mexico or Peru, or a country of

[2]A good source of economic data on Colombia is the newsletter *Colombia Today*, distributed by the Colombian Embassy in the United States.

tropical plantations like Cuba, or of Italian immigrants like Argentina, Colombia comes closest among the larger Latin American countries to the classic values and attitudes of traditional Spain, especially of Old Castile. Personal dignity, social deference, respect for intellectual achievement—plus refusal to acknowledge unpleasant realities—are the themes of Colombian life.

Crime and Banditry

There are, indeed, unpleasant realities of Colombian life, the dark side of the picture of a country led by hard-working, highly cultured aristocrats. If Colombia resembles nineteenth-century England in many ways, this is the England of Charles Dickens as much as of Queen Victoria and Anthony Trollope. Particularly noteworthy is the extent of the criminal underworld, which is legendary in Colombia. It even provides Colombians on occasion a sort of perverse pride, as when a visiting inspector from the French Sûreté, in Bogotá to consult with colleagues about crime prevention, had his wallet stolen before he had even left the airport. Colombian pickpockets ply their trade all over the Western Hemisphere and Western Europe, and Colombia is a major link in world narcotics traffic.

This urban crime has an archaic rural counterpart. The difficult mountainous terrain of the country makes communications and effective law enforcement difficult, and there are many regions of the country in which bandits have always operated with impunity. Bandits, like everyone else in Colombia, are either Liberals or Conservatives, and there are sometimes ties between bandit leaders and regional politicians.

Political Parties

In the dominance of the Liberal and Conservative parties, reinforced by provisions of electoral laws, Colombia again presents a traditional nineteenth-century aspect. Although on balance the Liberals are more progressive and secular than the Conservatives, a wide range of opinions can be found among the factions of both parties. In the traditional fashion, party allegiance cuts across class lines; peasants and the landowners they serve hold the same party loyalties. In recent years, a challenge to bi-partyism has been presented by the ANAPO, the National Popular Alliance of former dictator Gustavo Rojas Pinilla, whose demagoguery came close to returning the general to the presidency in the election of 1970, the results of which were so close as to raise a strong suspicion that Rojas was fraudulently deprived of the victory. The high point of the ANAPO's trajectory has passed, however, and despite the valiant efforts of María Eugenia Rojas, the old dictator's daughter and the party's presidential candidate in 1974, the ANAPO is no longer a serious contender for national power.

Rojas Pinilla. The ANAPO owed its appeal to the slow pace of social and economic change during the period that followed the overthrow of Rojas Pinilla in 1957. Rojas had been army chief of staff after his popular tour of duty as commander of the unit Colombia had sent to fight in the Korean War. He had seized power in 1953 to remove from office Laureano Gómez, a reactionary Conservative president, elected when a split Liberal party nominated two candidates. Riots following the assassination of the popular Liberal leader, Jorge Eliécer Gaitán, in Bogotá in 1948, led to fighting between Liberals and Conservatives that was aggravated by Gómez's extreme partisanship. This inter-party violence shaded into criminal banditry and later into Fidelista insurgency, so that its character was not always easy to define; nor was its scope, as government figures consistently underplayed its extent to try to maintain the country's public relations image. It is clear, nevertheless, that during "la violencia," many thousands died, and parts of the country were for considerable periods out of central government control.

Rojas's rule, after an initial honeymoon, contributed to the country's problems, including political violence, rather than resolving them, although in subsequent years the dictator managed to convince young people who had not known his regime, or those whose memories were short, that things had been better under his presidency; his presidency had coincided with a period of economic boom, no thanks to his policies. But, by 1957, his government was so repressive and unpopular that Liberals and Conservatives were able to bury their differences and unite to overthrow him.

The National Front

In the attempt to avoid the interparty hostilities that had brought the country so much grief and had provided the stimulus for Rojas to seize power, the two parties agreed to share equally in governing the country for a period subsequently extended to sixteen years. This bipartisan agreement, known as the National Front, provided that the two parties would alternate control of the presidency; that they would divide equally other public offices, from the cabinet and congress down to municipal councils; and that legislation would be passed only by a two-thirds vote, that is, that members of both parties would have to concur in it, since each party had only half of the legislators.

The National Front agreement was rightly hailed as an act of constructive statesmanship; nevertheless, during the sixteen years (1958–74) that the agreement was in effect, it encountered very substantial difficulties, which can be summarized as follows: 1) The necessity of securing bipartisan agreement led frequently to stalemate and inaction. 2) This inaction, together with the fact that bipartisan endorsement of presidential candidates guaranteed their election, contributed first to apathy and electoral absenteeism and then to support for the anti-National Front ANAPO; the percentage of those eligible who actually voted dropped from 72.7, in 1957, in the plebiscite to adopt the National Front agreement, to 59.9 in the presidential elections of 1958, 48 in 1962, and 35.2 in 1966. 3) Each of the parties split into factions as electoral competition revolved not around which party would win congressional seats, since that was settled by the National Front agreement, but around which faction would get the fifty percent of the seats earmarked for each party. 4) The Conservatives were guaranteed two presidential terms during the sixteen years, even though majority opinion in the country was to the left of the Conservatives and demanded social and economic change that the Conservatives were not interested in providing.

Conservative presidents under the National Front.   There were other difficulties, too; for example, the president chosen for the first Conservative term under the agreement, for the years 1962–66, Guillermo León Valencia, was chosen as the only leading Conservative acceptable to both major factions of the Conservative party and to the Liberals. On the basis of competence alone, Valencia should never have been chosen, however, as his subsequent conduct in office amply demonstrated. The do-nothing character of the Valencia administration helped to contribute to the growth of the ANAPO and the extreme left and also to negative evaluations of the National Front system. In fact, a widely reported and influential study produced by a United States Congressional committee at the end of Valencia's administration returned a negative verdict on the entire Alliance for Progress program on the basis of Colombia's economic and social progress at that time.[3] The second Conservative presidency, that of Misael Pastrana Borrero (1970–74), while not particularly dynamic or creative, did not show the bizarre incompetence of the Valencia period.

---

[3]*Survey of the Alliance for Progress: Colombia—A Case History of U.S. Aid.,* Washington, D.C.: Government Printing Office, February 1, 1969.

PRESIDENTS OF COLOMBIA, 1950–82

1950–53	Laureano Gómez
1953–57	Gustavo Rojas Pinilla
1957–58	Military junta
1958–62	Alberto Lleras Camargo
1962–66	Guillermo L. Valencia
1966–70	Carlos Lleras Restrepo
1970–74	Misael Pastrana Borrero
1974–78	Alfonso López Michelsen
1978–82	Julio César Turbay Ayala
1982–	Belisario Betancur

Liberal National Front presidents. The two Liberal presidencies under the National Front, however, those of the cousins Alberto Lleras Camargo (1958–62) and Carlo Lleras Restrepo (1966–70), must be accounted brilliant performances. Working within the constraints of the constitutional system and of the National Front Agreement, the two Lleras nevertheless managed to lay the groundwork for social and economic reform and for the diversification of the economy away from its dependence on coffee. Lleras Restrepo achieved the unification of the factions of the Liberal party, a modification of the two-thirds majority rule in the Congress that broke the legislative deadlock, and the creation of the Andean Pact, at the same time as he expanded the land reform program (which he had steered through the Congress as Lleras Camargo's legislative leader)[4]; he also stabilized the currency, improved tax collections, and inaugurated a system of government birth control clinics. By the end of Lleras Restrepo's term, the rate of growth of the country's gross national product was seven percent per year, which was one of the best figures in the region and one that has been more or less maintained since then. The country's nontraditional exports, that is, exports other than coffee, which were below $100 million in value when Lleras Restrepo became president, stood at more than $200 million when he left the presidency and have since climbed to more than $400 million, so that coffee constitutes less than half of the country's exports by value, instead of the eighty-five or ninety percent it had been when the Colombian economy was a case study in the dangers of dependence on a single product. And, as the National Front came to an end, Colombia stood with Venezuela as the only full-fledged democracies left on the South American continent.

López Michelsen. The first post-National Front president, Alfonso López Michelsen, a former left-wing dissident reintegrated into

[4]This story is recounted in Albert O. Hirschman, *Journeys Toward Progress: Studies of Economic Policy-Making in Latin America,* New York: Twentieth Century Fund, 1963.

the Liberal party by Lleras Restrepo[5], came to office in 1974 with a clear congressional majority and a popular mandate for a democratic reform program. Yet the National Front agreement provided for the continuation of bipartisanship in the cabinet for one more presidential term, and opposition to López by centrist Liberals and moderate Conservatives, who preferred his rival, Lleras Restrepo, led López to put together a cabinet out of left- and right-wing Liberals and right-wing Conservatives. This proved to be a recipe for stalemate and there was general dissatisfaction with the performance of the López government, especially on economic questions. As in the fable of the tortoise and the hare, however, it might still prove, in the perspective of history, that the achievements of the slow-moving Colombian constitutional democracy had been greater, on balance, than those of countries that attempted costly revolutionary shortcuts or that entrusted themselves to the benevolence of military dictators.

At any rate, the unimpressive performance of López Michelsen contributed to his defeat for reelection to the presidency in 1982 by the Conservative populist, Belisario Betancur.

To succeed López the Liberals passed over their most able figure, Lleras Restrepo, and chose a "safe," unimaginative, long-time party activist, Julio César Turbay Ayala, from the party's right wing. Turbay's only clear policy commitment, as president, was to "law and order." At least the military were given a free hand to fight "subversion," although the terrain of rural Colombia made it inconceivable that even the torture and other arbitrary violations of rights that the military reportedly engaged in could bring an end to the political banditry that has plagued the country throughout its history.

The law and order campaign was also supposed to be directed against drug production and traffic. Colombia's proximity to the largest market, the United States, and to the principal coca-growing areas of Peru and Bolivia, its extended unpatrollable coasts and its innumerable hidden airfields, and its huge professional criminal underworld made it the logical entrepôt of the drug traffic. Colombian peasants soon found they could make a lot more growing marijuana than wheat or corn, and it is generally believed that marijuana has overtaken coffee as Colombia's principal export, although it hardly shows as such in the official trade figures.

Meanwhile, the huge profits from the drug traffic have become a major economic factor as, reinvested, they have contributed to economic

---

[5]It is not clear to what extent López Michelsen's leftism was sincere and to what extent it was tactical and even opportunistic. His Liberal Revolutionary Movement was supported by the Bogotá station of the Central Intelligence Agency. See Philip Agee, *Inside the Company: A CIA Diary,* London: Penguin, 1975, p. 614.

growth. They have likewise become a major political factor, serving to buy off law enforcement officials, bribe administrators, and purchase influence with politicians. Politicians of national stature, including some close to Turbay Ayala, appear to enjoy income traceable to drug trafficking, which at one time raised questions about the sincerity of the president's drug enforcement efforts.

ECUADOR

The Regional Split

In Venezuela, the coastal element predominates over the Andean; in Colombia the mountainous regions are more important than those along the coast. In Ecuador, the third country of the group that once comprised the federation of Gran Colombia, the two elements have more or less equivalent weight in national life, and the contrast between them provides the basic conflict in national society and politics. The coastal region and the sierra each have slightly less than half of the eight million national population; the balance is composed of the inhabitants of the country's other two regions, the jungle area to the east of the Andes and the Galápagos Islands.

As in the other countries in the Andean group, in Ecuador the mountains are the home of traditional foodstuff agriculture for domestic consumption and of strong loyalty to the Catholic Church. The rigidity of social stratification is reinforced by the fact that the rural lower class is Indian in language, culture, and way of life, excluded from political participation by the provision that has recurred in the many constitutions Ecuador has had prior to the present one, that only the literate may vote. Thus the dominant interest in the sierra has long been the landholding oligarchy, who look with distaste at the coastal population, with its admixture of mulattoes, Lebanese, and other elements of non-Hispanic origin and the appalling slums and shantytowns of the principal coastal city, Guayaquil. They fear the concentrated economic power of the dominant interest on the coast, an interlocking clique of bankers and exporters.

For their part, the *costeños* (as the dwellers on the coast are called) despise what they think of as the old-fashioned ways and the religious fanaticism of the *serranos* and resent the political power given the sierra by the fact that the country's capital, Quito, is located in the mountains.

Economic versus political power. In some ways, the conflict between the coast and the sierra is a struggle of economic power against political power. *Serranos* dominate in the national bureaucracy and the army, which usually takes a hand in running the country. The *costeños* have retaliated by using their economic power for political purposes. For example, if sierra-dominated governments go too far in damaging coastal interests, Guayaquil business has traditionally retaliated by a general strike that closes up the country's principal port, thus denying the government revenue from customs duties, until recently its principal source of income, and forcing its collapse. Alternatively, or in conjunction with this tactic, accommodating student leaders are bribed to organize demonstrations that discredit the government and, if it represses them harshly, may result in its unpopularity and downfall. Guayaquil interests also acquire influence through their financing of successful presidential campaigns.

Economic changes and the regional balance.   The sierra-oriented military government that seized power in 1971 moved to reduce the political leverage given the coastal elite by its hold on the national economy. In the early 1970s, income from the substantial oil strikes in the Oriente, or jungle region of the country, started to flow in. Over Guayaquil opposition, the refinery and shipping facilities for the petroleum were located in the northern part of the coast, in an area more under Quito's influence than that of Guayaquil, and the revenue from oil royalties has freed the government from dependence on the customs revenues collected in the port city. These revenues are substantial; at its peak the oil flow reached one-quarter million barrels a day. The economic balance has also been shifted somewhat toward Quito by the development in the capital of manufacturing industries, operating under the protection of Andean Pact rules, to produce kitchen appliances and other durable goods, which have joined the textile factories that had been the major component of sierra manufacturing. A construction boom has also developed in Quito and threatens to change the face of what was long a quiet city of bureaucrats and small artisans.

Political Parties

Like everything else in Ecuador, the political party system long reflected the split between sierra and coast. While the two classic Ecuadorean parties, the Conservatives and the Radical Liberals, drew support from both sections of the country, the center of gravity of the Conservatives was clearly in the sierra, while that of the Liberals was on the coast. This could hardly be otherwise, given the different temper of the two areas. The Conservatives represented traditional Ecuador, stressing the values of religion, anti-communism, and the defense of the historical culture and institutions of the country. The Liberals espoused a mildly reformist position with a democratic and secularist flavor. A variety of other parties existed, with varying mixtures of ideologism and personalism, some much shorter-lived than others. The greatest of these, and the only one that could win votes equally well on the coast and in the sierra, was the Velasquista movement, which consisted of supporters of the extraordinary caudillo José María Velasco Ibarra, whose career spanned half a century and who was president of Ecuador five times (1933–35, 1944–47, 1952–56, 1960–61, and 1968–72). Velasco died in 1978.

PRESIDENTS OF ECUADOR, 1948–1982

1948–52	Galo Plaza Lasso
1952–56	José María Velasco Ibarra
1956–60	Camilo Ponce Enríquez
1960–61	José María Velasco Ibarra
1961–63	Carlos Julio Arosemena Monroy
1963–65	Military junta
1965–66	Clemente Yerovi Indaburu
1966–68	Otto Arosemena Gómez
1968–72	José María Velasco Ibarra
1972–76	Guillermo Rodríguez Lara
1976–79	Alfredo Poveda Burbano
1979–81	Jaime Roldós Aguilera
1981–	Osvaldo Hurtado

Velasco Ibarra. Velasco Ibarra was the Don Quixote of Ecuadorean politics. Tall and extremely thin, his idealistic forays into national politics invariably resulted in disaster. Expressing the noblest sentiments in stirring though abstract terms, his oratory, together with memories of the public works he constructed during previous terms of office, always mobilized the masses—which in Ecuadorean electoral politics meant the literate and semiliterate masses in the cities and towns predominantly—to vote for him. Naively trusting those who used his popularity for their own ends, Velasco ran administrations riddled with incompetence and corruption. Innocent of any understanding of economics, his idea of government was to spend money on public works until the treasury was bankrupt, whereupon his desperate attempts to raise more revenue led to chaos, escalating outbreaks of violence, and finally his overthrow. The only term of office Velasco was able to finish (1952–56) succeeded because it coincided with the prosperous period of Ecuador's banana boom. During this twelve-year period (1948–60), three successive presidents finished their terms, an unusual occurrence in Ecuadorean history. Unfortunately for him, Velasco's last term as president (1968–72) came too soon to benefit from the petroleum boom.

Military rule after 1972.   That privilege was reserved for the military officers that overthrew Velasco in 1972.

The seizure of power was partly motivated by the military's desire to be in a position to guide the country's petroleum policies, and incidentally to make sure that the military continued to receive the fifty percent of the government income from oil revenues that was earmarked for the armed forces by Velasco in his attempt to buy military acquiescence in his remaining in office. Guillermo Rodríguez Lara, the general who headed the government, managed for a period to develop a dominant position within the military and to maintain himself in the face of challenges from the civilian opposition. The military government also developed some expertise in dealing with the oil companies, joined the Organization of Petroleum Exporting Countries (OPEC), and raised the proportion of oil revenues going to the state to over eighty percent. However, the military were unable to avoid the same economic distortions that a huge oil income had brought to Venezuela: rapid inflation, social polarization, and increasing economic hardship among the poor, whose living conditions were already among the most miserable in the hemisphere. Moreover, a "prematurely nationalist" oil policy had expropriated—with compensation—Gulf Oil's holdings, which frightened away foreign firms before the expensive job of exploration had been completed (as it had been before nationalization in Venezuela) or anything close to it. The danger was that Ecuadorean oil production would peak at far too low a level, one that would barely suffice to cover domestic needs as these expanded during the 1980s.

The regional balance of power shifted in favor of the sierra as oil revenues freed the government from dependence on customs collected in Guayaquil, and as rural migrants from the sierra poured into Quito to work in the building trades, instead of moving to the coastal region, as had more commonly been the case in the past.

However, Rodríguez Lara was unable to heal the split among military officers between an economic nationalism and reformism along the lines laid down by the Peruvian military government and a conservative orientation to friendship with the United States and dependence on foreign capital like that of the Brazilian military. Emboldened by the split within the regime, civilian politicians united in inciting a military revolt against Rodríguez Lara in 1975, which he narrowly put down only to be overthrown finally at the beginning of 1976. The new military government under Admiral Alfredo Poveda Burbano announced its intention of serving only as a transitional government to prepare the way for elections.

The elections were finally held as promised, in 1978 and 1979, after a popular referendum had approved a new constitution, choosing the more radical one of two prepared by commissions appointed by the military. Some of the minor and more radical parties were overrepresented on these commissions, which had been boycotted by some of the larger parties. The referendum was thus the first national election that had been held in ten years; clearly the changes that had taken place in the country's economy and society—population growth, migration to the cities, the construction and industrial miniboom in Quito, the arrival of oil revenues and the growth of the middle class—had had their political effects. The constitution approved by the electorate gave the vote, for the first time, to illiterates, a change that will be far-reaching after it takes effect in 1983. As Ecuador's Indians gradually enter the electorate, politicians can be expected to appeal to their interests—the center of political gravity, that is, should shift steadily to the left.

But that process has, in fact, already begun, in response to the social and economic changes that took place during the 1970s. The presidential elections of 1978 and 1979 (there was a run-off, since no candidate had a clear majority on the first ballot) and the local elections of 1980 indicated a drastic shift in popular opinion. The major traditional parties shrank almost to insignificance, with Conservative strongholds limited to smaller towns in the sierra and the Liberals not doing much better. The Velasquistas and other personalist and minor ideological parties were virtually wiped out. The gainers were the newer parties of center-left orientation: Izquierda Democrática (Democratic Left) led by Rodrigo Borja; the Popular Democrats (Democracia Popular), a fusion of Christian Democrats and Progressive Conservatives, whose leading figure is Osvaldo Hurtado; the Partido Radical Alfarista (Alfaro was a Liberal hero of the early twentieth century), led by Cecilia Calderón; and the Concentración de Fuerzas Populares (Concentration of Popular Forces, or CFP).

The CFP has had an interesting career. A populist party centered on Guayaquil, it outlived the *caudillo* who had founded it, Carlos Guevara Moreno, and came under the domination of Asad Bucaram. An able but rather erratic demagogue, Bucaram was disdained by upper-class *serranos* and their military friends as uncouth, uneducated, and generally unacceptable because of his Lebanese parentage as well as his dangerous political tendencies; one of the motives of the 1971 coup was to forestall a presidential election which he appeared likely to win. The decree governing the 1978 presidential elections was worded so as to exclude candidates whose parents had not been born Ecuadorean (that is, Bucaram), whereupon the CFP nominated its intellectual leader, Bucaram's nephew-in-law, Jaime Roldós. Roldós and his running-mate, Hurtado, carried the CFP vote and more. Both men were in their thirties, and appealed to the young upwardly mobile profession-als, managers, and bureaucrats of Ecuador's developing middle class.

Of course the struggle for power between Roldós and his erstwhile mentor, Bucaram, installed as president of the Congress, was inevita-ble. Though it was finally won by Roldós, the struggle tore apart the CFP and absorbed so much of the young president's energies and forced him to make commitments to so many allies that the achievements of his administration fell far short of what his supporters had hoped. Nevertheless, he had served to break, at least for a time, with a past of oligarchic politics, military intervention, and lack of concern for the fate of the country's poor.

The young president's administration was cut tragically short by his death in a plane crash on May 24, 1981, which left Hurtado as his successor, and was followed within the year by the death of Bucaram. Although the rules governing oil exploration were revised in the at-tempt to attract foreign companies and expand Ecuador's reserves, economic and political prospects both remained obscure. The future seemed to lie with political movements of the center-left and a certain amount of modernization and economic growth; but it would be rash to assume that the years of economic stagnation, demagoguery, and mili-tary seizures of power were gone for good.

SUMMARY

Six countries of northern and western South America banded together in the Andean Pact to promote trade and industrialization by means of specialization and the removal of tariff barriers, with only limited success.

In most countries of the region the basic economic and social contrasts follow the cleavage between the mountains and the coast. The mountain areas of the Andes are more conservative and Catholic; they are the traditional region of large landholdings, where impoverished peasants produce for domestic consumption. The coasts, on the other hand, are the region of export agriculture, trade, and banking, more liberal and open to the outside world, usually with a heavy admixture of population of African stock.

Venezuela

During the twentieth century, Venezuela has made the transition from a predominantly Andean society to a predominantly coastal one, with population centers at the capital, Caracas, and in the oil-producing region around Lake Maracaibo. The country's oil wealth, which has given it the highest per capita national product of the Latin American countries, has also made it possible for the country's politics to transcend the traditional turbulence of dictatorship, insurrection, and military intervention and to pass to an era of peaceful competition among civilian political parties.

Colombia

Colombia's large population is not only divided between the highland and coastal regions but is also broken up in the mountains into isolated pockets in valleys and plateaus. The inaccessibility of so many regions has made possible the endemic banditry of Colombian life, which often has political overtones related to the split between the country's traditional Conservative and Liberal parties, and which fed into the extensive murderous violence, at its height during the 1950s, known as "la violencia." The two parties entered into a coalition agreement to attempt to moderate partisan violence and ruled in collaboration after 1958, the arrangement being phased out by 1978. While successful in reducing violence, diversifying the economy, and introducing some legal, political, and social reforms, governments of the National Front were hardly able to keep up with the massive social and economic problems that faced the country, which were later both alleviated and complicated by the growth of drug production and trafficking.

Ecuador

The cleavage between the mountains and the coast is the fundamental fact about Ecuadorean social, economic, and political life and contributes to the country's turbulent politics, in which moderate oligarchic governments long alternated with colorful demagogues and military regimes. The exploitation of the country's extensive petroleum deposits, which began in the early 1970s, began to transform an economy based on the traditional hacienda in the mountains and on export agriculture on the coast, but in the short run contributed only to inflation and military intervention. Social and economic changes have, however, led to an expansion of political participation and the growth of parties responding to the moderate progressivism of new middle-class elements.

6

The Andes II:
Revolution
and Reaction

PERU

An Archetypal Latin American Country

The problems of Peru, and the solutions to them that have been attempted, have significance far beyond the country's borders, for Peru is in many ways the archetypal Latin American country. When authors generalize about the whole of Latin America, the prototypical Latin American country they describe sounds rather like Peru. Miserable Indian workers living on haciendas of colossal size, surviving preconquest landholding communities, coastal plantations and sierra copper mines run by foreign corporations, an interlocking urban upper class of fabulous wealth, a mass revolutionary party of the center-left unfairly deprived of power at the polls, a powerful military that serves as guardian of the status quo on behalf of the oligarchy; all of these characterized Peru, or rather seemed at first glance to characterize the country, until only a few years ago. In fact, that picture has already changed substantially, and the realities of the situation were never quite what they seemed on the surface. While fishmeal, used primarily for livestock feed, has become in recent years the leading export, overtaking minerals, cotton, and sugar, Peru is not the classic monocultural economy by any means, and has developed a considerable industrial base. Nevertheless, Peru remains a classic case. While its political drama may not be enacted on behalf of all mankind, as Léon Blum said was true of France, developments in Peru are watched with great interest throughout Latin America and frequently provide models for occurrences elsewhere.

Regionalism. As in Ecuador and the other Andean countries discussed, the basic regional split in Peru is between coast and sierra. Of a population that by 1980 had passed twenty million, which makes it the fifth largest Latin American country in population terms, about one-third live on the coast, half in the sierra, and the rest in the selva, or lowland jungle area east of the Andes. While the sierra has more population than the coast, it dominates the country neither economically nor

113

politically. In this respect, Peru differs from the other Andean countries so far discussed, whose capitals are located in their most populous region: the coast in Venezuela and the mountains in Colombia and Ecuador.[1] The Spanish conquerors located their capital not on the site of the Inca capital at Cuzco but instead at Lima on the coast.

The ruling classes.   Lima itself, and coastal society in general, was always aloof from the life of the Indians of the sierra, who even today must be estimated at one-third of the national population. In Mexico, the nation identified itself through its symbolism with the Indians who had resisted the Spanish conquerors. In Lima, on the other hand, until recently the presidential palace was known after the conqueror of Peru as the Palace of Pizarro, and the body of Pizarro himself, enclosed in a glass coffin, could be viewed in the national cathedral. It would be an exaggeration to call the government of Peru a government of "white settlers" ruling, like the government of Rhodesia, over the members of a conquered race of aboriginal inhabitants of the country. But there was an underlying flavor of this kind.

Thus on the coast, and especially in Lima, were united both political and economic power. To some extent, there was a regional conflict like that in Ecuador, or at least a conflict between the ruling classes that dominated each of the major regions. As elsewhere, the ruling group in the sierra consisted of traditional landowners of conservative and pro-clerical type; on the coast were business interests based on export agriculture, banking and international commerce, manufacturing, and urban real estate. Not only did the greater size and wealth of the country make this coastal group more affluent than the coastal plutocracy of Ecuador, but the location of the capital on the coast also gave it access to bureaucratic influence, contracts and subsidies, government loans and tax-farming concessions, and guaranteed monopoly positions. In Peru, the oligarchs of the sierra were no match for this coastal plutocracy, which was not only economically strong but socially and politically resilient, coopting rising outsiders like immigrant entrepreneurs, ambitious politicians, and important generals.

Political Dynamics of Conservative Democracy

This was a powerful and well-entrenched system, and it is curious now to have to record that the system is being, if not completely ended,

---

[1]Today there are approximately equal numbers of people living on the coast and in the sierra in Ecuador, but the sierra had a large majority until the middle of the twentieth century.

at least fundamentally transformed. To explain what has happened, one has to look at recent Peruvian history in some detail.

During the second third of the twentieth century, the Peruvian political process fell into a predictable pattern, what might be called a conservative-democratic regime type. The competition among elite groups and cliques for power, which had characterized the system for a long time, was complicated by the development of a mass electorate, which, while it did not include the half of the adult population that consisted of illiterate Indians, and at first did not include the female half of the remainder, nevertheless extended down into the urban working class. The leading mass party was the APRA, originally the American Popular Revolutionary Alliance, founded in the 1920s and intended as a Pan-Latin American movement by its founder and leader, the ideologue Víctor Raúl Haya de la Torre. Haya's ideas, although expressed in a Marxist idiom, were essentially those common to the Latin American left and center-left, albeit with one or two distinctive features. They included protection of the rights of organized labor, social welfare legislation, improvement in the status of the Indian, land reform, university autonomy, the maintenance of political democracy, and the elimination of the political role of the military. The APRA program was "anti-imperialist" and espoused the inter-Americanization of the Panama Canal.

Repression of the APRA.   To the Peruvian upper classes, the program of the APRA of course represented a threat, especially since the party established itself as the leading one in popular favor, even of the restricted Peruvian electorate, and the party was repressed and decreed illegal with only occasional periods of toleration. Sometimes the charges against it were that it was "Communist," and it came under anti-Communist legislation; in fact, although the party had a certain ideological component of Marxism, and there were points of contact between its program and that of the Communists, the APRA soon became very strongly anti-Communist, viewing the Communists as its rivals for support of the masses, and it has remained strongly anti-Communist to this day. Sometimes the party was illegalized for its supposed international character, though it was not always clear whether the charges that the party was controlled from abroad were a reference again to supposed Communist connections or simply to the fact that Haya lived most of his life in exile; at any rate, the party's own claim, weak though it was, to be an international movement lent some color to this charge. The party was also suppressed on the grounds that it countenanced and encouraged the use of violent means, which was at times certainly the case, although it is not clear what other means it might have used, since it was usually forbidden to use its majority support among the population to come to power.

The APRA and the army.   Nevertheless, in the course of an *aprista* uprising in the northern town of Trujillo in 1932, a number of military officers were killed, allegedly after they had been taken prisoner. This the military never forgave, and annual ceremonies of remembrance provided the occasion for the renewal of military hostility to the party. At times, the APRA attempted to reenter the legal political arena by pledging its votes to candidates of oligarchic parties, such as the millionaire Manuel Prado, in return for the party's legalization. But the military, ever vigilant against the party, would predictably step in to annul elections that the party had won or to cancel them in advance.

Although the original hostility of the military to the Apristas derived from its playing its role of guardian of order, that is, objectively speaking, of defending the oligarchic status quo against violent change, the army's hostility to the party became an autonomous fact of life that persisted even after the APRA allied itself with oligarchic factions in its attempt to acquire respectability and become legalized.

The transformation of the APRA.   It should be added that the willingness of the APRA to ally itself with sections of the oligarchy was not only tactical but also reflected the growing conservatism of the party's aging leaders, especially of Haya himself. The party's anticommunist stance made it, in the 1950s and 1960s, an acceptable candidate for right-wing alliances. Its anti-imperialism by then had shifted away from the United States toward the Soviet Union, which Haya regarded during the cold war, and especially during the era of the Alliance for Progress and Soviet emplacement of missiles in Cuba, as a greater threat to the Latin Americans than was the United States. The APRA had become so used to an illegal or semi-legal existence in which its principal mission was to maintain its popular support intact against the day when legalization would make possible the capture of the national government through elections that it opposed not only the Communists but also any other movement whose success in implementing a program of reforms might result in the loss by the APRA of its supporters' loyalties. Thus, again in tune with its oligarchic allies, it opposed both the reformism of President Fernando Belaúnde Terry (1963–68 and 1980–   ) and spontaneous movements for land reform on the part of peasants. In all respects, except in oratory, by the middle of the 1960s the party was for practical purposes on the right side of the political spectrum.

Political ferment in the early 1960s.   Belaúnde's vaguely reformist Acción Popular and the personalist following of former dictator Manuel

Odría (1948–56) constituted the APRA's chief rivals in the presidential elections of 1962 and 1963 (the 1962 election was annulled by the military for supposed fraud), although the small Christian Democratic and Social Progressive parties were its rivals in the area of devising creative solutions for the country's problems and were of influence in intellectual circles. Further to the left, Fidelista-inspired guerrillas found Peru a logical place to attempt to reproduce the Cuban experience, and the army had to put down a left-wing insurgency in the Cuzco-Puno area. The Trotskyite intellectual Hugo Blanco had some success in organizing peasant syndicates in La Convención district.

The transformation of the military role.   But the major change of the 1960s occurred in the thinking of military officers. Concluding that there must be something wrong with a political system that required military intervention at every election time to maintain itself, and becoming disgusted with an oligarchy that allied itself with the military's old enemies in the APRA, many in the military were impressed by the grievances against the system expressed by the guerrillas against whom they had to fight in the sierra.

The system was moving toward the crisis of another election time when military intervention was catalyzed by what the military considered the weak and equivocal actions taken by the Belaúnde government with respect to the International Petroleum Company, a Standard Oil of New Jersey affiliate that had long been regarded in Peru as enjoying an unreasonably favored position. The seizure of power in 1968 was a joint action of all three services, led by army commander Juan Velasco Alvarado.

The Post-1968 Military Regime

Once again, the significance of events in Peru transcended national frontiers as people in other Latin American countries began to wonder if the progressive measures taken by the Peruvian military junta implied a model applicable elsewhere. However, experience with military governments elsewhere, which typically prove conservative, repressive, and/or highly incompetent, is not encouraging, to say the least, and the spectacle of a military regime in Peru that actually put through social reforms and that seemed as competent as, and not much more repressive than, previous civilian regimes seems a very unusual case from which it would be foolish, and perhaps fatal, to generalize. This is especially true since the government of Francisco Morales Bermúdez, who overthrew Velasco Alvarado in 1975, shifted to a much more moderate position.

Economic and social policies.   Nevertheless, there seems no basis to doubt the genuineness of the military's reforms in Peru. In its industrial policy and its attitude to foreign companies, the Velasco Alvarado regime opted for a middle-of-the-road approach that accepted foreign private enterprise but, at the same time, sought safeguards for national and popular interests, an approach that was not too distinct from the general policy line of the other Andean countries or that of Mexico. Thus, there were attempts to promote majority Peruvian ownership and to limit the volume of profits that could be repatriated. At the same time, the Peruvians went further than other governments in promoting workers' participation in ownership of firms through the provision that a percentage of the profits be set aside to buy stocks in the enterprise in the name of the company's workers each year. This "participationist" approach, which is neither socialist nor individual capitalist, resembles some of the ideas of the Christian Democratic movement, and the Peruvian Christian Democrats, though not happy about the absence of political democracy under military rule, supported the regime's policies. The left divided, with some leftists preferring a more conventional socialist approach and others lamenting the lack of political freedoms, but a considerable number, including the members of the Moscow-line Communist party, supported the regime, and some even took service with it, like the former organizer of guerrilla activity, Héctor Bejar. In agriculture, the agrarian reform program involved the expropriation of both traditional sierra haciendas and coastal plantations producing for export. The cynic is entitled to point out that the land reform gave the military government some leverage in trying, on the whole without success, to break the power of Aprista sugar workers' unions in northern coastal Peru. The expropriated farms were set up as cooperatives but were more or less under the control of government agents who were supposed to be advisers.

The country's military rulers attempted to improve the status of the Indian. This is easier to attempt than to accomplish, but some striking symbolic acts included the change of name of the presidential palace from "the House of Pizarro" to "the House of Tupac Amaru," after the Inca emperor, and the commitment to use Quechua as the language of instruction in primary schools in the rural sierra.

Political participation.   The APRA found itself in an awkward position vis-à-vis Velasco Alvarado. It was reduced to claiming credit for much of the junta's program on the premise that the government's measures were advocated by the APRA long ago. At the same time, it objected to the lack of political democracy (from which, as probably still the largest party in popular support, it could hope to benefit) by arguing that it was not possible to talk of a revolution from which popular participation was excluded. This was a sore point with the junta, which tried to organize popular support through SINAMOS (which translates awkwardly as The National Movement in Support of Social Mobilization but whose acronym means "without masters"), a vehicle for agitation and propaganda for the government's program which was led by a curious combination of leftists, ex-Apristas, and generals. SINAMOS, which was presumably intended as the forerunner of a revolutionary single party on the Mexican model, tried uneasily to reconcile its role as, at the same time, a vehicle for mass mobilization and a government agency, and had little success. Popular participation controlled by bureaucrats seems to be a contradiction in terms, but, in any case, attempts at organizing genuine participation, as in elections for workers' representatives on agricultural cooperatives, often had the undesirable consequence (from the government's point of view) of resulting in Aprista representatives. These and other paradoxes of a revolution run by military bureaucrats resulted in a great deal of dissatisfaction.

After Morales took power in 1975, he moved the "Peruvian Revolution" back to a much more moderate line of policy. The profit-sharing and workers' participation programs were eliminated; the fishing industry was de-nationalized; the rules against foreign capital were softened.

Politically, the Morales regime was at once more and less repressive than that of Velasco. Morales allowed back in the country those exiled by his predecessor and relaxed government control of the media. Nevertheless, he took strong, even brutal, action against the strikes which grew out of his government's stringently deflationary policies. Those policies, urged on the government by the International Monetary Fund, were designed to restore an economy weakened by adverse conditions in the fishing industry and heavily mortgaged abroad to finance the extravagant arms purchases of the Velasco years.

The moderate policy line followed by Morales represented the views of senior officers more faithfully than had the radicalism of Velasco Alvarado, which seemed in retrospect due to Velasco's personal views rather than to the army's counter-insurgency experiences or to the teachings of allegedly leftist professors at the Center for Higher Military Studies (Centro de Altos Estudios Militares, or CAEM), as had been suggested.

After the modifications of the Morales period—indeed of Velasco's later years, for he then took a more favorable attitude to foreign investment and even settled up with IPC in order to satisfy the international banks—the net effect of the "Peruvian Revolution" seemed to be a more modernized Peru, with a stronger labor sector, the beginnings of participation in national society by Indians, a somewhat more equitable distribution of wealth, and the reduction, if not the elimination, of the power of the old landed oligarchies.

Some of these effects were already visible in the Constituent Assembly elected under Morales to restore the country to democracy. Presided over by the aged Haya de la Torre, who was to die before the presidential elections he might finally have won took place, the Assembly produced a constitution which at last gave illiterates, that is, Indians, the right to vote. Although the left was of course splintered among a welter of parties, its total vote in 1980 was greater than it had been in pre-1968 elections. The APRA split over the succession to Haya: the left wing of the party took the nomination, but it divided and weakened the party in the process. Victory went to Fernando Belaúnde, the president Velasco had overthrown, who had spent the intervening years in an exile in which he had apparently learned nothing, to judge from his campaign and the first year of his administration, which merely reiterated themes that had seemed novel twenty years before but which failed to face the issues of the new Peru.

Belaúnde was helped over the unpopular deflationary policies forced on him, as on Morales, by the IMF, by patriotic sentiment stimulated by the outbreak of fighting with Ecuador early in 1981 over a border dispute. The border in question had been demarcated forty years before after a forcible Peruvian occupation of a vast disputed area in the Amazon thought to contain oil. Ecuador has never accepted the legitimacy of that loss of territory, although fortunately for her the oil that has been found has been on indisputably Ecuadorean soil.

Peru has about enough oil to meet domestic demand, with a small exportable surplus in some years, which is a considerable strength in the years of OPEC's price manipulations. The economy retains other long-term strengths despite short-term financial problems, the urban crises of various kinds afflicting Lima, and the vast unmet needs of the country's Indian population. In its strengths and its potential for development, as well as in its problems, Peru remains the archetype of the Latin American state.

PRESIDENTS OF PERU, 1945–82

1945–48	José Luis Bustamante y Rivero
1948–56	Manuel Odría
1956–62	Manuel Prado
1962–63	Military junta
1963–68	Fernando Belaúnde Terry
1968–75	Juan Velasco Alvarado
1975–80	Francisco Morales Bermúdez
1980–	Fernando Belaúnde Terry

BOLIVIA

Geography and Population

Bolivia differs from the other Andean countries discussed thus far in not having a coastline. The coastal province of Antofagasta, together with its rich nitrate deposits, was lost to Chile as a result of Bolivia's defeat in the War of the Pacific in 1883, although the Bolivians have not reconciled themselves to the loss and campaign continually to regain access to the sea, the *"salida al mar."* The principal geographic regions are thus the west, which consists of an extremely high mountainous area, with the capital, La Paz, on a high plateau in the center of the region and the major mining centers of Oruro and Potosí to the south; the lower-lying valleys of the south central region, the most important of which is Cochabamba, which produces most of the country's food; and the lowland regions of the north and east, a great deal of which is sparsely inhabited forest and jungle, but which also contain, in the southeast portion, the country's deposits of oil and natural gas and a rapidly developing agricultural center at Santa Cruz. Of the national population of five million, about four-sevenths live in the western region, two-sevenths in the south center, and one-seventh in the north and east.

With the exhaustion of the silver mines at Potosí and the loss of the nitrate fields of Antofagasta, Bolivia became one of the poorest of the Latin American countries. About forty percent of the population is literate, roughly the same proportion as live in the city. Somewhere between sixty and eighty-five percent of the country's population can be considered Indian, depending on the criteria of definition used, with Quechua speakers, who dominate in the south central valleys, outnumbering the Aymará speakers of the western mountains and high plateau.

Chronic Political Instability

Traditionally, Bolivian political life has been very unstable. The country enjoyed a period of political stability between 1952 and 1964 but has since returned to the traditional pattern, and since 1964 governments, mostly led by rival military figures, have averaged a little more than one year in office.

The country's political instability grows out of the interaction of two problems. One is the generally poor performance of the country's economy; Bolivia has one of Latin America's lowest per capita standards of living, and, until very recently, the economy was in disastrous condition. The other problem is that the population is fragmented into a variety of different contenders for power, none of which can dominate the system by itself, but each of which can make it almost impossible for the others to rule. Alliances among these groups do not last because of the incompatibility of their interests, especially of labor and the middle class, and the rival ambitions of their leaders.

MNR Rule, 1952–64

The period of stability from 1952–64 was made possible by the maintenance of a coalition among elements of four of the five major power factors by the ruling party, the National Revolutionary Movement, or MNR; these power factors were the peasants, the miners, the armed forces, and part of the middle class, which left only students and some middle-class elements outside the ruling coalition. However, the MNR regime fell apart over the secession of the miners from the dominant consensus and the fragmentation of the movement's political leadership over the attempt of the president to perpetuate himself in power. Thereafter, the miners, who are the dominant element in organized labor, have been, except briefly, in permanent opposition, subject to violent and brutal repression.

Antecedents of the 1952 revolution. The MNR was founded in 1940 as a revolutionary and nationalist movement influenced by both fascism and communism, as well as by the ideas of various democratic tendencies. The party shared power with radical younger officers in the government of Major Gualberto Villarroel (1943–46), which itself followed in the footsteps of the nationalist governments of Colonel Toro and Major Busch that had held power in 1936–39. The radicalization of these officers grew out of the country's defeat by Paraguay in the Chaco War (1932–36), which they ascribed to the self-interest, incompetence, and corruption of the politicians of the oligarchic parties that had ruled Bolivia before and during the war.

In addition to radicalizing some elements of the military, the war also had the effect of mobilizing and politicizing many of the country's Indians, who had been drafted to fight in the Chaco. Taught the value of organization and the use of modern weapons, they acquired self-confidence along with wider horizons and some knowledge of the world. It was veterans of the Chaco who began the organization, in south-central Bolivia, of the peasants' syndicates that played the major role in the land reform of 1952.

The leadership group. Coming to power in 1952 in a revolution that vindicated the party's claim that its leader, Víctor Paz Estenssoro, had been defrauded of his 1951 election victory, the MNR included a wide variety of loosely affiliated elements led by an assortment of barely compatible personalities. Paz Estenssoro himself, whose outlook on policy questions was flexible and pragmatic, had authoritarian tendencies and dealt harshly with the opposition. His vice-president and successor as president for the 1956–60 term, Hernán Siles Zuazo, was a political moderate of democratic persuasion. Of the party's other major figures, Walter Guevara Arze was a fairly conservative intellectual, while Juan Lechín Oquendo, leader of the mineworkers' union and thus of the country's labor movement, had generally Trotskyite views.

Revolutionary policies. On its accession to power, the MNR put through a revolutionary program; or perhaps it might be said more accurately that the MNR government ratified the revolutionary actions already taken by the mass organizations that were loosely affiliated with the party. The peasant syndicates, that is, seized the haciendas and divided them among their members, while the mineworkers' union seized control of the tin mines. The government legalized these acts post facto with a land reform law and a law that nationalized the mines and gave the workers' union joint control with the government in the new state mining corporation, COMIBOL.

The third principal act that completed the revolutionary transformation of Bolivian society was the reorganization of the armed forces. Those elements of the army that had stayed loyal to the previous government were defeated in the 1952 street fighting, in which MNR loyalists were joined by the national police. A much reduced army whose officers pledged loyalty to the MNR was allowed to exist, although alongside a variety of armed workers', peasants', and party militias.

Economic problems and attempted solutions. The Indians (now referred to as "peasants," since *campesino* does not have the pejorative connotations that *indio* had come to have) who had come into possession of land were better off than they were, or at least they ate better than they had, before the revolution. But the disorganization of production and the supply of foodstuffs to the cities led to severe shortages. Labor discipline declined at the mines as political hiring and featherbedding grew. Even with the miserable subsistence wages paid to miners, Bolivian tin cost more to produce than the tin coming onto the world market from the revived mines of Malaysia.

The Bolivian economy was finally rescued by aid from the United States, which had decided to support the MNR regime after puzzling over its character and intentions, over the possibility that a government hostile to the United States might come to power if the MNR fell, and over the fact that the nationalization of the mines had expropriated only

Bolivian and not American interests. Nevertheless, the United States insisted as a condition of aid that an attempt be made to turn the Bolivian economy into a viable proposition, so the Siles administration became a period of agony as austerity measures were instituted to try to break the runaway inflation that had grown out of the government's attempts to solve the economic problem by means of the printing press.[2] The United States also insisted on the rehabilitation of the tin mines, a program that took the form of the so-called Triangular Plan, under which West German capital and management were brought in, workers were taken off the payroll, wages were cut, and subsidies were withdrawn from the miners' commissaries. The miners' reaction to all of this was, of course, predictable and violent, but their protests were somehow contained by the agile maneuvering of Juan Lechín, who was given the vice-presidency for Paz's second term (1960–64) and clearly saw himself as the heir apparent to Paz if he could keep the miners in line. However, Paz saw that the day of reckoning was coming and obtained United States aid, now available in substantial amounts due to President Kennedy's counterinsurgency orientation, to build up the regular armed forces.

The overthrow of the MNR. The strengthened military were brought into play when Paz moved to have the constitution, which included the standard Latin American prohibition of presidential reelection, amended as a preparation to succeeding himself in the presidency. He had been egged on to this decision by individuals in the United States government and the international financial institutions, who feared the leftism of a Lechín government. A disgusted Lechín threw in his hand and put himself at the head of the miners in the actions they took against the government, which then had to be repressed forcibly by the military. Conscious of the critical role they were now playing in the maintenance of the regime, the armed forces insisted against Paz's wishes on being assigned the vice-presidential nomination in the 1964 elections, which went to the popular air force general, René Barrientos Ortuño. Although Paz survived the election, he was abandoned by many in the MNR, including Siles, and there was general resentment at the elections, in which Paz was the only candidate. The other major MNR leader, Guevara Arze, had taken his followers out of the party four years before when his own ambitions had been thwarted by Paz's decision to return to the presidency. The new vice-president, drawing not only on his military support but also on his popularity

[2]Richard W. Patch, "Bolivia: U.S. Assistance in a Revolutionary Setting," in Richard N. Adams, *et al., Social Change in Latin America Today*, New York: Random House, 1960.

among the peasants (he had been raised in Cochabamba and spoke Quechua) and appearing to sympathize with the complaints of the miners and the dissident sectors of the MNR, overthrew Paz without difficulty. The army was not altogether sure about this primacy of a representative of the air force, and Barrientos was forced to share power with the army commander, Alfredo Ovando, finally conceding the provisional presidency to Ovando while he himself campaigned for the presidency, to which he was elected in July 1966.

Government Since 1966

René Barrientos.   Barrientos did not tamper with the agrarian reform or the nationalization of the tin mines, although he encouraged foreign investment and proved extremely harsh on the miners, cutting their pay and repressing protests at the cost of the lives of many miners and their families. But the country began to prosper, relatively speaking, as the rehabilitation of the mines began to pay off, petroleum was discovered in the eastern lowlands, and foreign investment began to trickle in. Barrientos apparently shared personally in this new prosperity, and his visit to Switzerland "for medical attention" may also have had private banking purposes.

One of the reasons why Barrientos was able to stay in office as long as he did, apart from his personal popularity and the relatively good performance of the economy, was the fact that it was his government that was able to track down and capture (and assassinate) the legendary Che Guevara. Why Che chose Bolivia as the site of his new guerrilla campaign needs some explaining, as the country seems totally unsuitable for the application of the tactical lessons Che had learned from his Cuban campaign. Far from being disaffected, the Bolivian peasants were contented with owning their own land (although it must be pointed out that there has been some revival of latifundism in Bolivia, especially in the newly developed lands around Santa Cruz, but also elsewhere). Che and his men could not speak the peasants' language (Guaraní in most of the area where they operated), and the guerrillas had little urban support, partly because the Communist party had refused to cooperate.

The death of Barrientos and renewed turmoil.   When Barrientos was killed in a helicopter crash in 1969, the official version was that the craft had struck a power line. Most Bolivians appear to believe the story

[3]A sympathetic account, by a "participant observer," is Régis Debray, *Che's Guerrilla War,* translated by Rosemary Sheed, London: Penguin, 1975.

that emerged several years later, to the effect that the helicopter had, in fact, been shot down on the orders of the army commander. General Ovando, so the story went on, was enraged that Barrientos had double-crossed him in withholding Ovando's share of the commission of more than two million dollars due for their part in arranging for French jet planes and spare parts, ostensibly purchased for the use of the Bolivian armed forces, to be reshipped to Israel in defiance of General de Gaulle's veto on weapons sales to the Jewish state. Although corroborating details have accumulated, it has proved difficult to establish the truth of this story beyond a doubt.

But all this was far in the future when in 1969 Ovando allowed Barrientos's vice-president, Luis Adolfo Siles Salinas, to succeed the dead general while Ovando prepared his own campaign for the coming presidential elections. It transpired, however, that the popular mayor of La Paz also decided to become a candidate, so Ovando determined not to await the uncertain outcome of the polls and instead seized power in a coup.

Alfredo Ovando Candia.   Unsure of support outside the armed forces, Ovando made a bid for popularity among leftist miners and students by expropriating Gulf Oil's Bolivian properties. However, he became trapped by his ineptness as the country began to lose millions when the international oil companies refused to purchase petroleum from the expropriated fields. When Ovando finally announced that the oil would be bought by an independent Spanish firm, it did not take long for it to become public knowledge that the Spanish firm was, in fact, a subsidiary of Gulf, and Ovando had in effect been forced to capitulate to the corporation. This succeeded in alienating the left, which had never trusted the leftist credentials of the man who had been army com-mander when the military, under the tutelage of covert United States "advisors," had tracked down and assassinated Che Guevara. His leftist demagoguery had already alienated the right, so that Ovando no longer had a leg to stand on. In October 1970, he was overthrown by a right-wing coup led by General Rogelio Miranda; but the left refused to accept the coup and found a leader in a disgruntled army chief of staff who had been removed shortly before by Ovando, Juan José Torres. Torres emerged victorious in the fighting after a day in which the Bolivians say they established a new record, having had five presidents within twenty-four hours: Ovando, then Miranda and the two other service commanders who had announced themselves as "co-presidents" with him, and finally Torres.

Juan José Torres. Although Torres had been the actual field commander of the troops that tracked down Guevara, his leftism seemed rather more sincere than that of Ovando, although the students and miners did not trust him completely either. However, the ten months of Torres's presidency saw a resurgence of the left, as the miners seized the administration of COMIBOL and the students seized university offices and police stations and went on to destroy the office of the United States Information Agency. Although he tried to sabotage this threat to his authority, Torres was not able to prevent the meeting of a "popular assembly" of miners, students, and some peasant representatives, which elected Juan Lechín its presiding officer. The assembly spent its time in oratory and passing resolutions rather than in seizing power, however.

Hugo Bánzer Suárez. Meanwhile, the right wing was preparing its comeback, and a broad coalition was organized that included the various disparate elements of the now reunited MNR, together with the center-right Falange Socialista Boliviano and elements of the military, encouraged by the business interests of booming Santa Cruz and, it is said, financed by funds of the right-wing Brazilian government. The revolt was led by a prestigious colonel from Santa Cruz who had been prematurely retired for plotting, Hugo Bánzer Suárez. Bánzer took power backed by a wide coalition, which not only included the MNR and the Falange, the country's two major parties, and the bulk of the armed forces, but could also count on peasant neutrality, if not active support.

However, this combination proved incompatible, and gradually MNR support dwindled as one sector of the party after another left the government in protest over Bánzer's conservative policies. Paz Estenssoro himself was the last to give up on Bánzer, thus alienating himself again from the temporarily reunited party. Bánzer's moderate conservatism had left him enemies on the right as well as the left, and he was able to stay in power only by dint of extremely agile maneuvering, promises (later withdrawn) of early elections, intermittent repression, promises to secure from Chile a Pacific port and control of land access to it, and favorable developments in raw materials exports. Prices rose, even of tin, and advantageous arrangements were made for oil and natural gas development and sales with Argentina and Brazil, each eager to check the influence of the other.

Although Bánzer's agility enabled him to remain in office longer than any other twentieth-century president of Bolivia, finally his time ran out and he was unable to secure armed forces support in the elections he scheduled for 1978, finally agreeing to back an air force general,

PRESIDENTS OF BOLIVIA, 1952–82

1952–56	Víctor Paz Estenssoro
1956–60	Hernán Siles Zuazo
1960–64	Víctor Paz Estenssoro
1964–66	René Barrientos and Alfredo Ovando
1966–69	René Barrientos Ortuño
1969	Luis Adolfo Siles Salinas
1969–70	Alfredo Ovando Candia
1970–71	Juan José Torres
1971–78	Hugo Bánzer Suárez
1978	Juan Pereda Asbún
1978–79	David Padilla Arancibia
1979	Walter Guevara Arze
(1979	Alberto Natusch Busch)*
1979–80	Lidia Gueiler
1980–81	Luis García Meza
1981–	Celso Torrelio

*Natusch claimed to be president for a two-week period, but was never fully in control.

Juan Pereda Asbún. Left-wing and progressive opinion rallied behind former President Hernán Siles Zuazo, perhaps the leading Bolivian politician to have survived the country's long political wars with his honor most intact. When it appeared that the government's intervention in the elections had not been enough to win them for Pereda, they were annulled, ironically, as fraudulent, leaving Pereda to seize power on the well-grounded suspicion that Bánzer planned to use the confusion to perpetuate himself in office. Younger officers, some resenting Pereda's transparent use of the military for personal ends, and others uneasy at being ruled by an air force general, overthrew Pereda four months later, replacing him with the popular army chief of staff, David Padilla.

In the elections that were then held in 1979, Siles again received the most votes, though not an absolute majority, so that Congress had to choose from among the leading candidates.

However, there was no majority in Congress either. The balloting continued right up to the day scheduled for the inauguration of the new president, when Congress finally chose its presiding officer, Walter Guevara, to serve as provisional president for one year. In Bolivian politics, however, one year is a long time. In fact, Guevara was overthrown within four months in a bloodbath organized by Colonel Alberto Natusch Busch, the nephew of a former president. The great loss of life attendant on Natusch's coup, and the wave of democratic sentiment then running high in Latin America, led to the mounting of a formidable resistance of labor unions and popular organizations, backed by a

United States government committed to a strong stand in favor of human rights. After two weeks Natusch gave up, and a face-saving formula was adopted under which Guevara would not return to the presidency but would be replaced by another former associate of Paz Estenssoro, Lidia Gueiler, Bolivia's first woman president and Latin America's second. Again elections were held, the following summer, for the third successive year; again they were won by Siles Zuazo; and again they were annulled by the military.

Again the takeover was bloody, and several major political figures, including the Socialist candidate for president, Marcelo Quiroga Santa Cruz, were killed. The new president, General Luis García Meza, quickly established a brutal and repressive regime; however, it was not these qualities that aroused international opposition to him, perhaps, as much as the fact that García was involved with drug traffickers and growers in the Santa Cruz area. Initially, the García Meza regime was ostracized by the other Andean countries and condemned in United Nations resolutions. No invitation went to the government to be represented at the Reagan inauguration. Eventually García Meza stepped down, being replaced by a provisional junta headed by the army commander, Celso Torrelio, in a move that did nothing to bring an end to the perpetual plotting, the grafting and dope dealing, and the indifference to the general welfare that characterized Bolivia's uniformed politicians.

CHILE

The Land and the People

Chile's distinctiveness begins with its geography. As the Andes go south, the distance between the foot of the mountains and the Pacific coast to the west diminishes; as a result, Chile, which occupies the territory between the Andes and the Pacific Ocean, is a narrow strip of land barely more than one hundred miles wide at its widest point, although it extends twenty-five hundred miles in length. Thus this geographic curiosity includes a variety of climatic zones from north to south whose European equivalent would involve passing from North Africa to northern Scandinavia.

The center of Chile's eleven million population, in the Central Valley in the middle of the country, contains the bulk of the country's manufacturing and commerce and, of course, its political and bureaucratic activity. The good agricultural land of the Central Valley was until recently occupied by latifundia; geographically, this was Chile's equivalent of Mediterranean Europe. North and south of this central region the farms became smaller, of family size; while the landowners of the Central Valley are Conservatives and their workers Christian Democrats or leftists, the independent family farmers are Liberal or Radical in views. In the cold far south, cattle and sheep raising coexist with fishing and the extraction of coal, iron, and petroleum. In the hot far north are the copper mines and the nitrate fields.

The Political Tradition

Political stability.   Chile's geography has kept it apart from the rest of Latin America. For much of the country's history it has been isolated from the Andean countries to the north by the Atacama desert and from Argentina to the east by the Andes, which at that latitude are snow-covered and inhospitable. Chile has at the same time been united by her lengthy coastline with the world's dominant naval power, Great Britain. Preferring to think of themselves as "the English of South America," Chileans developed a respect for the rule of law and constitutional government, reinforced perhaps by the fact that the country's economy in most of the years after independence was prosperous, in contrast to the experience of the other countries of Latin America.[4] Immigrants came not only from Latin Europe but also from temperate northwest Europe, settling in the familiar temperate woodlands of south central Chile. The small Indian population, unconquered and unenslaved, retreated to the south, eventually becoming small-scale farmers. Defeat of Peru and Bolivia in the War of the Pacific (1879–83) led to the acquisition of the nitrate fields of Antofagasta, which enabled the government to finance itself without imposing onerous taxes.

Political turmoil.   This idyllic picture should not be overdrawn. When President Balmaceda tried to reassert the presidential powers that had been allowed by his predecessors to drift into the hands of the legislature, a civil war was fought (in 1891) that ended in the defeat of the president's forces, his suicide, and the beginning of a period of weak parliamentary governments on the contemporary French model. With the development of synthetic nitrates in the 1920s, the economy went into a depression that anticipated many of the features of the world-wide depression of the 1930s. Eight years of political turbulence, of coups, counter-coups, popular revolts, military dictatorship, and the growth of left and right extremism, ended in 1932 with the imposition of a new constitution that provided for a strong president.

The need for reform.   For most of the succeeding period, the center, especially the Radical party, which represented middle-class profes-

[4]Régis Debray, *Conversations with Allende,* New York: Random House-Vintage Books, 1971.

sionals, technicians, small businessmen, and bureaucrats, held the balance of power, but the economy continued to be weak and dependent on copper exports. Low wages and low standards of housing, social welfare, and public health contrasted with the country's high levels of literacy and political sophistication. Landholding was highly concentrated, with eighty-seven percent of all farmland held in estates larger than two hundred hectares (approximately five hundred acres).[5] Demands for fundamental reform gradually accumulated as mass participation in politics developed, with a corresponding growth of the left-wing parties and of the center-left Christian Democrats as shantytowns mushroomed and electoral law changes guaranteed secrecy of the ballot to the rural worker wanting to vote differently from his patrón. Rallying to the Christian Democrats to prevent a victory for the left-wing presidential candidate, the voters of the right finally gave the victory to the Christian Democrat Eduardo Frei in 1964, and the process of reforming the Chilean economy and society began.

The Frei administration, 1964–70.   With some difficulty, the Frei administration maneuvered through the Congress a land reform program under which cooperative farms were established on expropriated land for a transitional period until the peasants voted whether to continue with the cooperative or divide up the land in individual holdings. (They have almost invariably opted for the latter alternative where the votes have been held.) Government participation in the ownership of the copper mines was voted. The tax system was reorganized, and low-cost housing was built.

It is true that the achievements of the Frei era did not live up to the exorbitant expectations that the Christian Democrats' oratory had aroused; the inflation, reduced during the early years of the Frei administration, began again to grow, the government's "Chileanization" of the copper industry proved more advantageous to the foreign companies than to the Chileans, and the extent of the land reform was limited. Nevertheless, the process of overhauling Chilian society had begun, and the economy started to grow after a long period of stagnation.

The Popular Unity Government

The 1970 elections.   For the 1970 elections, the Christian Democrats nominated a presidential candidate further to the left than Frei, and rather than again endorsing the Christian Democrat, the right wing decided to go into the presidential election with its own candidate,

[5]Ben G. Burnett, *Political Groups in Chile,* Austin: University of Texas Press, 1970, p. 15.

the popular former president (1958–64) Jorge Alessandri. The split in the anti-socialist forces made possible a very narrow electoral victory for the candidate of the left, Salvador Allende. Failing to win a clear majority of the vote, Allende had to be voted into office by the Congress, which occurred after the Christian Democrats had exacted his agreement to a series of constitutional reforms designed to prevent the establishment of a left-wing dictatorship, and after desperate attempts by the right, by foreign business interests, and by the United States Central Intelligence Agency[6] had failed to produce another solution.

PRESIDENTS OF CHILE, 1952–82

1952–58	Carlos Ibáñez del Campo
1958–64	Jorge Alessandri Rodríguez
1964–70	Eduardo Frei Montalva
1970–73	Salvador Allende Gossens
1973–	Augusto Pinochet Ugarte

Allende's political situation.   Although a long-time militant in a socialist party more radical and less committed to constitutional procedures than the democratic socialists of Western Europe, Allende himself believed in constitutional and democratic processes and honestly attempted to govern within the law. This was good tactics as well as a question of belief, since it was clear that the Chilean armed forces would remove him if he overstepped constitutional limits. In fact, the Allende presidency did end in his overthrow by the military halfway through his six-year term. It is worth examining the Allende period in some detail, because it constitutes a classic study in the difficulties of attempting to put through a revolutionary program within a constitutional framework.

Allende found himself in an extremely difficult political position. He was elected to the presidency in 1970 with a percentage of the vote lower than he had received as the runner-up in 1964, when the anti-socialist forces were united behind Eduardo Frei. Moreover, he lacked a majority in the Congress, although his supporters held more than the one-third of the seats necessary to block constitutional amendments or presidential impeachment. At the same time, he presided over a coalition internally split. The Communists and some of the Socialists took a moderate and gradualist position. The sector of the centrist Radical party that had joined Allende's Popular Unity coalition was also moder-

[6]"Alleged Assassination Plots Involving Foreign Leaders," *Report of the Senate Committee on Intelligence Activities,* Washington, D.C.: U.S. Government Printing Office, November 20, 1975, pp. 225–245.

TABLE II   Chilean Presidential Elections, 1958–70 (percentages of votes cast)

	1958		1964		1970	
Right	Alessandri*	31.18			Alessandri	35.19
Christian Democrats	Frei	20.46	Frei*	55.58	Tomic	28.01
Radicals	Bossay	15.36	Durán	4.94		
Left	Allende	28.51	Allende	38.58	Allende*	36.53
Minor Left	Zamorano	3.31				

*Denotes winner; blank and null votes omitted.

Source: Kenneth Ruddle and Philip Gillette, eds., *Latin American Political Statistics* (supplement to the *Statistical Abstract of Latin America*) Los Angeles: UCLA Latin American Center, September 1972, p. 75.

Some curious conclusions emerge from these figures:
1. Allende was elected in 1970 with a lower percentage of the vote than he received when he was defeated in 1964.
2. Alessandri was defeated in 1970 with a greater percentage of the vote than he received when he won in 1958.
3. If Zamorano had not run in 1958 and his votes had gone to Allende, Allende would have edged past Alessandri in 1958, as he later did in 1970.
4. This suggests the striking persistence of the share of the vote going left, right, and center, despite the far-reaching events that had occurred in the meantime and the formidable changes in the composition of the electorate, which more than doubled during the period.

ate in its views. A substantial element of the Socialist party and some of the Christian left elements in the coalition were, however, more sympathetic to the violent line of the Movement of the Revolutionary Left, or MIR, which stayed outside the coalition and persisted in pursuing a line of direct action, including land occupations, in defiance of the Popular Unity government.

Thus Allende was faced with problems on his right: the difficulty of getting legislation through a Congress where his supporters were in the minority; on his left: violence and direct action on the part of the MIR; and behind him: dissension within the coalition. Because he placed first priority on the necessity of keeping his fragile coalition together, Allende was not a free agent in determining his strategy with respect to the challenges from left and right. The Communists urged the advisability of coming to an understanding with the Christian Democrats. This strategy would have provided a solid government majority in the legislature, would have undermined the attempts to organize a right-wing revolt against the regime, and need not have meant much modification in Allende's legislative program, in that the Christian Democrats were prepared to contemplate a great deal of social and economic reform. There would have been difficulty in reaching such an agreement, and it might have resulted in a split among the Christian Democrats, just as it would have led to a split among the elements of the Popular Unity coalition, but it was probably a feasible and constructive strategy. However, such a right-wing policy on Allende's part would have meant, sooner or later, a crackdown on the MIR, whose strategy was to force the government to the left by taking radical action itself, in the shape of land occupations in the countryside, for example, which the government would then not dare to repudiate. And a crackdown on the MIR would probably have meant deaths among the *miristas,* who were very often the sons and daughters of the leaders of the left and even of the center (including Allende's own nephew). Nevertheless, that strategy would have been the logical one in the light of Chilean history, for it would have resembled the policies followed by the Radical presidents elected with left-wing support in the 1930s and 1940s (the so-called violin presidents—"put up by the left but played by the right").

The alternative left-wing strategy, urged on Allende by the left wing of the Socialist party, was to abandon insistence on constitutionality, resort to the use of the plebiscite, and arm the workers for the violent clash between the social classes that the far left believed was inevitable. Needless to say, the adoption of such a strategy would itself have made that clash inevitable, apart from having only the slimmest chances of success.

Allende's strategy and tactics.   Allende chose instead a third, centrist strategy. Attempting to remain scrupulously within the constitution, he tried to discourage the direct action of the MIR by persuasion. When such tactics were not successful, however, he refrained from using force against the MIR, thus passively acquiescing in the land occupations and other illegal acts they engaged in. He was careful to cultivate the armed forces, showing them every courtesy and appointing military officers to his cabinet in times of crisis.

Neither enjoying a legislative majority nor relying on mass violence, how did Allende manage to get so much of his program through? On the nationalization of the copper mines, the congressional vote was unanimous, but majorities could not be found for other reforms. Allende thus came to rely on the powers of the executive, and not legislative action, for the institution of most of his programs. A revolutionary socialist government that had held office briefly during the turbulent 1930s had put on the statute books several measures that had never been repealed, such as one that allowed the government to take control of industries that had ceased to supply the public some essential service. Using this and similar statutes, Allende was able to enact much of his program by executive decree.

In fact, however, his program was hardly as extreme as it was made out to be by the Chilean right; it rather resembled the policies of the British Labour government that had taken office in 1945, with its strategy of seizing only "the commanding heights" of the economy rather than socializing it completely. Nevertheless, the center and right detested Allende's manner of proceeding, of acting on the basis of executive orders and thus circumventing Congress, especially since his less-than-majority election hardly gave him a mandate for his program. Some acts of this kind were, in fact, declared unconstitutional by the courts and the independent Controller's office, although the court decisions and Controller's rulings were ignored by the government. To the regime's opponents, this was evidence that the regime had overstepped the bounds of legality and could thus properly be resisted, and even overthrown. To government supporters, such judicial decisions simply constituted evidence that the notoriously conservative judiciary was abandoning its proper role and involving itself in political questions.

The economic situation.   What proved to be the fatal problem for the Allende government, however, was the catastrophic economic situation. The causes for this situation were multiple. Copper prices on the world market were in decline. Business confidence was low, and foreign credits were difficult or impossible to obtain. A great deal of dislocation was due to the nationalizations. Moreover, many businessmen and technicians had left the country out of fear that the Popular Unity government would transform Chile into an Eastern European totalitarian state; qualified people were also removed from posts in the nationalized industries to make way for less qualified people with the correct political credentials. Administration of some of the businesses taken over by the state was incompetent and even corrupt.

The major underlying cause of the economic debacle, however, was the economic strategy adopted in the first days of the Allende government. The brainchild of economy minister Pedro Vuskovic, this strategy started from the premise that what was wrong with the Chilean economy was that the effective market was too small. There were idle plant and idle people, the argument ran, who could be put to gainful use if the purchasing power of the population were raised so that they could buy the products of a more productive industry. Thus the country could develop, in effect, on the basis of raising everybody's wages. As can be imagined, this was a doctrine welcome to government ministers and their supporters alike, and, indeed, the policy worked well enough for the first year. Wages were doubled, consumers went on a buying spree, and, although prices were held down by government decree, businessmen found that they were making as much as before because the volume of their sales had increased so greatly.

As it turned out, however, the policy of expansion through consumption overlooked several things. There was a limit to the amount of idle plant that could be brought into production, and when the limit had been reached, the increased amount of purchasing power found itself pursuing a restricted number of goods, thus creating a classic inflationary situation. Moreover, plant expansion and the purchase of increased supplies of raw material were dependent on the availability of foreign exchange. Yet the availability of foreign credit was reduced by both foreign suspicion of Chilean socialism and the decline in copper prices, so that foreign exchange soon became unobtainable. Together with the flight of businessmen and technicians, and the administrative problems that resulted from the nationalizations, the economy soon found itself subject to acute distortions in production and supply because of runaway inflation and raw materials shortages. Refusing to acknowledge the weaknesses in its policies, the government took the position that the shortages were due to deliberate economic sabotage and hoarding by the middle classes and to economic warfare by the United States. This view, which contained much truth, was accepted as the whole truth by the masses, whose support for Popular Unity, as measured in municipal and congressional elections, remained high until the end.

The overthrow of Allende.   As the coup that was to overthrow Allende was being prepared, large sections of the armed forces remained faithful to the government. The army and navy commanders had to be maneuvered into retirement, and the revolt opened with the shooting of armed forces officers who opposed the uprising. Yet the very ferocity of the revolt, which included the bombardment of the presidential palace, the massacre of militant workers, and the shooting of Allende himself (officially called suicide), was in a paradoxical way a testimony to Chile's high level of political development. It would not have been necessary, that is, to use such violence in seizing the government of an underdeveloped Central American country where the population was apathetic and the government lacked popular support.

Chile After the Coup

In the aftermath of the coup, all of the parties that had participated in the Popular Unity government were declared illegal, along with the MIR, and the Christian Democrats and right-wing Nationalists were placed "in recess," while the military government, under General Pinochet, made it clear that it intended to stay in power indefinitely, although its imprisonment, assassination, and torture of people who were only suspected of holding left-wing opinions soon cost it much of the sympathy it had enjoyed in the center and right. The regime's economic policies hardly won it any mass popularity although it impressed many foreign observers as a sincere attempt to create the conditions for a textbook free-market economy. A savage deflationary policy reduced economic activity and imposed real hunger and privation on the masses; inflation rates responded only slowly and partially. After some years, a gradual resumption in economic growth occurred whose benefits were concentrated in the upper levels of the income distribution.

The only threat to Pinochet's power came after the assassination, in September 1976, in Washington, of Orlando Letelier, who had been Ambassador to Washington and Minister of Defense and Interior under Allende. DINA, Pinochet's feared secret police, targeted a prominent exile for assassination each year on the anniversary of the coup: General Carlos Prats, the former commander of the armed forces who had served as Allende's Interior Minister and provided a rallying point for moderate and military opposition to Pinochet, was killed in Buenos Aires in 1974; Bernardo Leighton, the chairman of the Christian Democratic party, still the largest single party and the natural pivot of Chilean politics, escaped with serious injuries the attempt made on his life in Rome in 1975. Letelier, who was coordinating exile opposition activities from Washington, correctly believed he would be next on the DINA hit list.

DINA agents contracted Cuban exiles to do the actual killing; Letelier's research assistant, an American citizen, was also killed in the attack, which took place on Massachusetts Avenue, Washington's "Embassy Row." The FBI finally tracked down the assassins, and the Cubans were tried and sentenced. After its request to extradite the head of the DINA was turned down (the head of the DINA had made clear to Pinochet that, if extradited, he would reveal Pinochet's complicity), the Carter administration shrank from using serious pressure on the Chilean regime and the matter was left in limbo until the Reagan administration, despite its strictures against "international terrorism," swept the affair under the rug, even resuming the military assistance to Pinochet that had been suspended by Carter.

In 1980 Pinochet went through the motions of constitutionalizing his rule; his appointees produced a bizarre document, approved by a cowed and dispirited electorate, under which he could stay in power, unchecked by effective constitutional restraints, for another ten years. Chile, which had once been a byword for peaceful, civilized, and democratic politics, had now become a synonym for brutal repression.

SUMMARY

Peru

Peru long presented a classic picture of a highland oligarchy ruling, in its haciendas, over impoverished Indian serfs; a coastal plutocracy involved in foreign commerce, banking, some manufacturing, and export agriculture; and foreign interests, chiefly in petroleum and mining. Oligarchic factions succeeded each other in a formally democratic system, with military intervention being called into play to prevent the coming to power of the APRA, a mass reformist party. However, resentment over this role and concern about the possibility of insurrectionary guerrilla warfare led a section of the military finally to assume a progressive modernizing role and introduce fundamental changes that improved the status of the Indian and weakened the position of the oligarchies.

Bolivia

A barren mountainous country, landlocked and of harsh climate, Bolivia is one of the poorest states of Latin America. The revolution of 1952 eliminated the oligarchy, gave land and status to the country's Indians, and drastically reduced the army in size and influence, but it could not alter the basic facts of the country's poverty. Resorting to United States economic assistance, the revolutionary leadership tried to rehabilitate the uneconomic tin mines that produced the country's principal export, at the cost of reducing miners' incomes and forcing them into rebellion. The army, which had been built up to use against the miners, finally assumed power but provided only intermittent stability, together with a great deal of corruption, as personalist left-wing and right-wing army factions battled for control.

Chile

Chile constitutes essentially one long thin coastal strip. Separated from the rest of South America by the peaks of the Andes and the Atacama desert, Chile has depended on the sea and has been heavily influenced by the power that ruled the sea during most of its history as an independent nation, Great Britain. This influence, and the geographic separation from its Latin American neighbors, contributed to making Chilean society peaceful and democratic though traditional and nonegalitarian in its economic and social structure. Attempts to change archaic social and economic structures, long unsuccessful, finally met with some success during the twentieth century, culminating in the Popular Unity government of Salvador Allende. Meeting with mixed success in a very difficult economic and political situation, the Allende administration provoked extreme right-wing opposition, abetted by elements in the United States government, and it was finally drowned in blood by a right-wing military coup that imposed a dictatorship unprecedented in Chile's democratic history.

7

The Argentine
Sphere of Influence

PARAGUAY

Population

No other country in Latin America is quite like Paraguay. Its aboriginal Indian population consisted neither of nomads roaming the plains, as in Argentina, nor of settled mountain dwellers of high cultural development, as in the Andes, Mexico, and Guatemala, but of dwellers in riverside forests earning their living in a fishing and gathering economy. Their confrontation with the Europeans also followed a distinct pattern. Neither chased away, wiped out, or rounded up on reservations, like the plains Indians, nor conquered and subjugated like the mountain civilizations, the Guaraní inhabitants of Paraguay received the Europeans as friends. The few Spaniards, other than priests, who bothered to go into Paraguay intermarried with the Indians, creating a mestizo race that maintains the use of both mother tongues, employing Spanish for formal and public occasions and Guaraní in more domestic and personal contexts.

Early Leaders

The process of racial fusion was promoted by the first ruler of independent Paraguay, the extraordinary Dr. Francia, who cut off all contact with the outside world, believing that no good could come from the imitation of foreign models. The history of his successor's son suggests that perhaps Francia had a point; after returning from an extended stay in France and succeeding his father, Carlos Antonio López, as dictator, Francisco Solano López modeled himself on Napoleon III, leading his country into a series of diplomatic and military adventures that ended in 1870 with the virtual annihilation of the country's population in a war against the Triple Alliance of Argentina, Brazil, and Uruguay.

Wars, Revolts, and Political Parties

To this day, the dominant position of the conservative Colorados[1] owes something to the "antipatriotic" stigma attached to the Liberals, some of whom had collaborated with the Brazilians in the government that followed the death and defeat of Francisco Solano López, now regarded as a great national hero. The country's third major political force, the Febrerista party (there is also a small Christian Democratic group), owes its origins to the revolt of February 1936, which made Colonel Rafael Franco president. Franco was the hero of Paraguay's victorious campaign against Bolivia in the Chaco War (1932–35). Precipitated by Bolivian politicians expecting an easy conquest of the disputed Chaco area, thought to contain petroleum, the war was costly to both sides.

The Febreristas' brief period of rule was followed by dictatorship and then turmoil, which lasted until 1954, when General Alfredo Stroessner staged the coup that was to place him, and the Colorado party, in power for more than a quarter-century. The Paraguayan constitution limits the president to two consecutive five-year terms, which made it necessary for President Stroessner to have a new constitution drafted in 1967 and then amended in 1977.

Exiles and the Economy

In their exile, the Febrerista leaders are among the almost one million Paraguayans that live abroad, mainly in Argentina, where most of them, together with Bolivian immigrants, form an urban underclass.

More Paraguayans have economic than political reasons for living outside the country. Paraguay itself has a relatively low standard of living; exactly how low cannot be determined, since so much of the country's economy is, in fact, based on smuggling, a logical activity in a poor country placed next to two giant and wealthy neighbors. However, Paraguayan statistics are probably in any case the most unreliable in Latin America. It is even impossible to ascertain such things as the percentage of illiterates, which the government gives as one fifth of the adult population, whereas unofficial observers estimate the figure at over twice that amount. Apart from agriculture and fishing, the country's legitimate, non-smuggling economy involves cattle raising and lumbering. Few businesses are in Paraguayan hands; perhaps eighty percent, including the large cattle ranches, are owned by Brazilians and Argentines.

[1]Not to be confused with the Uruguayan Colorados, who are Liberals.

The Foreign Presence

The presence of two giant neighbors rather than one, however, has enabled General Stroessner to achieve some freedom of action by playing one off against the other. For most of its history, however, Paraguay has been an economic colony of Argentina, dependent on transport down the Paraguay-Paraná river system to Buenos Aires for its contact with the outside world. But Paraguay is now strengthening ties with Brazil through joint road-building and hydro-electric projects, and through Brazilian investment and tourism.

Apart from Brazilian tourists, Argentine cattle ranchers, and members of American technical assistance missions, other foreigners have appeared in Paraguay, especially German settlers. Some of these were businessmen who contemplated prospects in Latin America only to find that the British and the Americans had already taken hold of the economic opportunities in the wealthier countries, and only Bolivia and Paraguay remained. Others coming later, to both countries, were political refugees of both anti-Nazi and pro-Nazi varieties. To most of these recent arrivals, the population shows the same easy-going friendliness with which their ancestors welcomed the Spaniards.

The Stroessner Regime

Politically naive and apathetic, most Paraguayans appear to accept the Stroessner dictatorship more or less willingly. The dictatorship's harshness is partly mitigated by its inefficiency and by conflicts of authority among government bureaucrats, Colorado party officials, and military officers of different services and branches. President Stroessner governs the country under permanent "state of siege" powers but sometimes goes easy on the opposition to accommodate the strange ideas of the people at the American Embassy; the opposition is in any case weak and presents no real threat. However, opponents of the regime, and even only suspected dissidents, who lack influential foreign contacts or family connections in high places, can find themselves in jail indefinitely, and conditions in a Paraguayan jail might make even an Arkansas deputy sheriff shudder.

The only real threat to Stroessner's rule might have come from within the military, perhaps from officers disappointed at their cut of the income from the country's largest industry, contraband. But for most people, Paraguay has been a peaceful, not unpleasant, up-river backwater where the troubles of the rest of the world seem far away.

Yet change is bound to come, even to Paraguay. The building of roads to Brazil has opened up hitherto unsettled areas in the eastern part of the country. The boom based on dam-building and contraband has led to the rapid expansion of an urban middle class. Politicians have begun to maneuver for position in the post-Stroessner era, which cannot be far off. And the completion of the dams now under construction assure the country of a comfortable, even affluent, future as the exporter of electric power to Brazil, and perhaps to Argentina.

PRESIDENTS OF PARAGUAY, 1936–82

1936–37	Rafael Franco
1937–39	Felix Pavia
1939–40	José F. Estigarribia
1940–48	Higinio Morínigo
1948	Manuel Frutos
1948–49	Natalicio González
1949	Raimundo Rolón
1949	Molás López
1949–54	Federico Chaves
1954–	Alfredo Stroessner

ARGENTINA

General Description

In Argentina, we have left behind the Latin America of Indians living on mountain haciendas and of blacks working on coastal plantations. Argentina reflects another vision of Latin America, a vision in which development signified Europeanization, that is, the implantation of European standards and style of behavior in the economy, in education, and in cultural and social life.

Supplier of cattle and wheat to Europe.   During the colonial period, when wealth meant gold and silver mines, tropical plantations, and docile Indian labor, Argentina was a neglected backwater overshadowed by the magnificence of Lima. As the Western European countries, especially England, industrialized and grew in population, they became no longer able to feed themselves and had to look elsewhere for the meat and bread to sustain their populations. The enormous expanse of the highly fertile Argentine land thus acquired new value as the pampas began to supply the cattle and wheat that Europe needed. The *estancieros* that owned the land became fabulously wealthy, and the rich Argentine became a stock character in the street scenes of Paris.

Nineteenth- and Early Twentieth-Century Argentina

Statecraft in late nineteenth-century Argentina meant finding people to work the land, with a modern attitude to work and the capability of being educated to a level appropriate to the citizens of a wealthy and important country—European people, that is, whose numbers would swamp the uncouth mestizo gauchos who set the tone of the Argentine interior.

European immigrants. This new population came in the shape of Italian and Spanish migrants, sometimes commuting as seasonal workers, but finally settling in Argentina. Rather than populating the interior and developing its agriculture, however, many, if not most, of the immigrants remained in the port city of Buenos Aires, whose population continued to grow until it became one of the great world capitals, comparable in size to London, New York, and Tokyo. Evoking the immigrants' homeland capitals of Madrid and Rome, Buenos Aires is in some ways also reminiscent of London, which ruled the economy of Argentina, and Paris, which set its cultural standards. Today no less than one third of the country's population of twenty-eight million lives in the capital and its surrounding area.

Political system; Radicals versus Conservatives. As Argentina differs in social and economic structure from the neighboring countries among which the Argentines sometimes seem surprised to find themselves, so it differs in political profile. Although the immigrants remained largely apolitical, the growth of Buenos Aires and other cities expanded the numbers of the native middle classes, who were represented principally by the Radical party, the Union Cívica Radical. The Radical program called for good government and honest elections, some very mild anti-clerical measures, and some modest social reforms. The estancieros, represented politically by a variety of provincial parties known collectively as the Conservatives, were riding high on the crest of the income from meat and wheat exports, however, and were unwilling to yield power to this rising middle class.

Thus the Conservatives hung on to power, rigging elections where necessary, while the Radicals talked to sympathetic military officers and staged unsuccessful revolts. By the time electoral reform made possible the victory of the Radicals, in 1916, a pattern had been set of class antagonism and exclusiveness, and the politicization of the officer corps, which has continued to the present.

Accustomed to a life of conspiracy in an undemocratic system rather than the give and take of democratic politics, the autocratic Radical leader, Hipólito Irigoyen, was unable to hold together a party based on the heterogeneous elements of the middle class, when the necessities of governing made it no longer possible to paper over differences of view. In his second term, beginning in 1928, the senescent Irigoyen could not deal with the problems arising out of the depression, and was removed by a military coup in 1930. The ideas of the fascist sympathizer who led the coup, General Uriburu, were too extreme for his colleagues and civilian collaborators, however, and control of the country was returned, again via rigged elections, to Conservative hands.

World War II and the Rise of Juan Perón

Wartime sympathies.   Conservative rule was unable to withstand the strains of World War II, however. By virtue of its economic ties with Great Britain, the ranching oligarchy was pro-Allied. Some of the population sympathized with Spain and Italy, with which so many had ancestral ties; among the military, many authoritarian-minded officers, some of whom had had training from German missions or in German schools, were pro-Axis. Resentment at the military aid and equipment furnished to the pro-Allied Brazilians by the United States helped this authoritarian group to put together the support necessary to overthrow the acting president, Ramón Castillo, in 1943. Conflict between pro-British and authoritarian elements led to turmoil in the ruling group that was finally resolved in favor of the authoritarians and their key figure, Colonel Juan D. Perón.

Perón and fascism.   Perón emerged from the matrix of Argentine authoritarianism. Initially, his policies continued to be those of the military government, in which he had served as Secretary of Labor, Minister of War, and Vice-President. A key element in these policies was nationalism. Since the main foreign influences in Argentina at the time were those of Britain and the United States, nationalism connoted opposition to the English-speaking countries, which, in turn, meant sympathy with their enemies in World War II. By the time Perón himself became president, in 1946, the Axis powers had been defeated, and there was clearly no point in proclaiming sympathy with them. Nevertheless, there can be no doubt about Perón's fascist sympathies. He had been an admirer of Mussolini as military attaché in Italy, and his supporters were militantly anti-Semitic, staging attacks on synagogues and desecrating Jewish cemeteries.[2]

In the tradition of the Argentine right, the military government, and, in its initial phase, the government of Perón, were pro-clerical, and religious instruction was made mandatory in the public schools. Like the European fascist governments, the Argentine military government of 1943–46 was also repressive and dictatorial, gagging the press and taking over the administration of the universities through political appointments to rectorships and professorships.

Perón's popular appeal.   Perón continued these policies but with certain important differences. First, he was an elected president, winning clear victories in the presidential elections of 1946 and 1952. It is true that the campaigns against the opposition candidates exceeded the bounds of democratic propriety; violence was used against individuals, the offices of newspapers supporting the opposition were wrecked, and so on. There seems no doubt, however, that Perón did receive a majority of the vote in both presidential elections.

Thus, although Perón had emerged as a political leader through intrigue within the military, he became a popular leader. In fact, his popular base soon became more secure than his base within the military; when in 1945 a military faction fearful of his growing personal power managed to secure his removal from office and imprisonment, it was the mass demonstrations of his civilian followers that forced his release and adoption as the regime's presidential candidate. From that point on, Perón was regarded by most military officers as a threat to the military institution rather than a loyal son.

Perón had all the attributes necessary for a charismatic popular leader (as well as some that are not necessary, such as a doctorate in history). Handsome and athletic (he had won army championships in boxing, fencing, and skiing), he became a stirring orator.

Support of organized labor.   The core of the popular support which Perón sought in the attempt to free himself from dependence on the outcome of factional struggles within the military was organized labor. Industrial labor was a new force on the Argentine political scene. Cut off from supplies of industrial finished products by World War II, Argentina started to develop its own industry, or rather it continued to develop an industry that had begun early in the twentieth century but

[2]For Perón's ideas, see George I. Blanksten, *Perón's Argentina*, Chicago: University of Chicago Press, 1953.

had been held back by capital, raw materials, and transport shortages caused by World War I and the depression. The supply of European immigrants, except for a few refugees, had, however, also been cut off, and to supply the needs of the new industrial plants a migration of lower-class Argentines began from the rural areas to the new industries of Rosario, Córdoba, and especially Buenos Aires. Perceiving the political potential of this growing urban working class, Perón had himself appointed to the minor post in charge of labor affairs, made it into a full ministry, and transformed a poor and weakly organized incipient proletariat into a strong political machine committed to him personally. The weak Radical or Socialist identification of some segments of labor was easily brushed aside as Perón replaced trade union leaders unwilling to play ball with him and rewarded favored unions and union leaders with raises and fringe benefits.

Perón's success with organized labor created one of the paradoxes, or at least difficulties, in the interpretation of the Peronist phenomenon. Observers familiar with European experience generally assume that labor movements have socialist sympathies and can be counted "on the left." As Perón showed, however, labor could just as easily be nationalist and authoritarian, if its economic needs were taken care of. Socialist ideology, that is, does not naturally grow out of the objective economic situation of the industrial working class; it has been adopted in Western Europe for certain specific historical reasons that may not exist elsewhere.

The Perón Era, 1946–55

Eva Perón's role. After he became president, Perón adopted the dignified stance of "president of all the people" and delegated the handling of labor politics and the delivering of rabble-rousing speeches against the oligarchy to his striking blonde wife, Evita. Eva Duarte, an actress who was something of a star on Argentine radio, had a background of poverty and social unacceptability that enabled her to identify with the aspirations and resentments of the urban poor. Living with Perón before his 1945 arrest, she had been one of those responsible for organizing the mass demonstrations of support on "Loyalty Day" that led to his triumphant comeback, and they were subsequently married. Developing into a powerful demagogue in her own right, Eva took over the handling of the labor movement and the mobilization of the masses behind the Peronist regime. By means of "voluntary" contributions from business, Eva also financed the Eva Duarte de Perón Foundation, which provided mass charity and also went to help build a personal fortune for the Peróns abroad. The cult of Evita grew to such an extent that one distinguished sociologist has identified Evita rather than Perón himself as the charismatic leader of the regime.[3] She was hated and feared by the more conservative elements within the regime, and her nomination for the vice presidency for Perón's second term was blocked by military opposition.

The totalitarian impulse.   If the first paradox of Peronism was that of a "right-wing" regime based on the support of organized labor, the second was that of a constitutionally elected president who was also a would-be totalitarian dictator. Totalitarianism has to be understood in this sense not as a fixed and static system of rule, but as a process in which a political leader attempts steadily to expand his absolute power until it extends throughout the society. In this perspective, it is not possible to achieve perfect totalitarianism; some areas of life manage to escape control, in the nature of things. Nevertheless, the totalitarian impulse was clearly at work, and the totalitarian process was going forward under Perón. The leader tried to bring the armed forces under control not only through the regular chain of command, but also through oaths of loyalty to Perón personally and courses of indoctrination in Peronist principles in the military schools. Such courses were also given in the public schools and, indeed, in the universities, whose rectors were Peronist appointees and whose student associations were taken over by the regime. The press was brought under control by the establishment and political use of a government monopoly on the supply of newsprint. His election victories gave Perón control of the legislature, and he used that control to take over the judiciary; members of the supreme court were impeached, removed, and replaced by Perón's appointees. In this respect, as in others, the dictator worked through the legal forms as much as possible.

The Catholic church and the regime.   Like other would-be totalitarians, however, Perón met his match when he tried to break the power of the church. Initially, the regime had good relations with the church, which was delighted with the introduction of compulsory religious classes in the public schools. However, around 1950, Perón became worried that the growing Christian Democratic movement might provide a threat to his power, and he saw in the lay movement Catholic Action the nucleus of a powerful future Christian Democratic Party. Reversing his field in an attempt to weaken the church, Perón had compulsory religious education discontinued and divorce and prostitu-

[3]Jose Luís de Imaz, *Los que mandan,* translated by Carlos A. Astiz, Albany: State University of New York Press, 1970, pp. 45–47.

tion legalized. The conflict escalated to the point where Peronist supporters were attacking churches and worshippers leaving church after mass, and Perón was finally excommunicated. His personal life had meanwhile become a cause of scandal to the faithful after Evita's death from cancer in 1952. Perón's excommunication was the catalyst for the first, unsuccessful, military uprising against him, and the successful uprising that followed was led by a conservative general of devout Catholic belief.

Economic policies.   Perón's reversal of policy with respect to the church was paralleled by a shift in his economic policy. His original economic nationalism had entailed buying out foreign businesses, especially the railroads, public utilities, and meat-packing plants. He had been able to expropriate foreign-owned businesses and pay compensation because of the huge sterling balances that Argentina had accumulated during the war, when the country had continued to sell beef and wheat to Britain but was unable to buy consumer goods since British production was directed to war industry. This inherited affluence enabled Perón to expropriate with compensation at the same time as he was raising workers' standards of living. Of course, there came a time when the money ran out and the substantial wage increases had to stop.

To some extent, the regime's programs could still be financed by the monopoly on agricultural exports Perón had established. Farmers and ranchers were supposed to sell their products for export to a government agency that paid them less than the export sales produced and used the difference to finance welfare benefits and subsidies to urban industry. Nevertheless, this source proved inadequate, as a steady deterioration in the performance of the industries that had been taken over by the government set in. The railroads were particularly notable in this respect; labor costs rose as maintenance was neglected and quality of service deteriorated. Eventually, in desperation, Perón was forced to go back on his nationalist policies, to make peace with the United States, and to reopen the country to foreign investment. Just as proclerical supporters abandoned him over his clash with the church, at the same time economic nationalists passed over to the opposition when Perón invited foreign oil companies to enter Argentina on very favorable terms. This reversal of policy in the religious and economic fields added new ambiguities to the meaning of "Peronism," or "justicialism," an elusive ideology that had, in any case, always stressed the need for flexibility and pragmatism.

Peronism as a sectoral movement.   One further ambiguity should be noted. Although the core of Perón's support clearly lay in organized labor and the urban poor, Perón did not represent the working class exclusively. In fact, some observers have tried to interpret Peronism, at least as represented by the general's policies in office, as a sectoral, rather than a class, movement.[4] That is, Perón's economic and political hostility to the cattle-ranching oligarchy that controlled wealth and social position in Argentina was shared not only by the working class but also by a new class of urban industrialists, who were as nationalist as Perón because they wanted to keep out foreign goods that competed with their own products, and who supported the raising of workers' standards of living, which created a larger market for sales of those products. The evidence is rather mixed on this point, and industrialists who supported the government's policy of favoring industry over agriculture could also oppose it when it was a question of raising the wages of workers in their own plants. Nevertheless, it seems clear that there was at least intermittent support for Perón from some elements in the business community. In political terms, however, these businessmen should be considered allies of the Peronists rather than as hardcore Peronists themselves. Most of them did not remain loyal to the dictator after he was overthrown, when the hard core of Peronism was reduced, essentially, to organized labor.

The Aftermath

Ambiguities in the opposition to Perón.   The ambiguities in Peronism appear clearly from the character of the coalition that opposed Perón's reelection in 1952, ranging as it did from Conservatives to Communists, from wealthy oligarchs embittered that he had encroached on their wealth and privileges to democrats dismayed at his strong-arm methods of governing. These ambiguities persisted after Perón's overthrow and contributed to the turmoil of the eighteen years that elapsed before Perón again assumed power in October 1973. During those chaotic eighteen years, Argentina had ten presidents.

The fundamental dilemma that rendered political stability impossible until the return of Perón was the question of what to do about the Peronists. The dilemma had its roots in the paradox of a president who had won a majority of votes but yet was a dictator. The victorious anti-Perón forces wanted to reestablish democracy in Argentina, yet democracy meant elections. And if elections were held, the Peronists would win and proceed to reestablish the dictatorship. How was one to escape from this vicious circle? What attitude should be taken toward

[4]Marcos Mamalakis, "The Theory of Sectoral Clashes," *Latin American Research Review*, vol. 4, no. 3, Fall 1969; and Gilbert W. Merkx, "Sectoral Clashes and Political Change: The Argentine Experience," *ibid.*

the Peronists? Should one try to eliminate them from Argentine political life, and if so, how? Or should one attempt to reintegrate them and hope that they would behave democratically? This dilemma split all the Argentine parties, and the armed forces as well, and provided the fundamental political dynamic of two decades of Argentine political life.

Splits among the non-Peronist forces. The dilemma was posed immediately after the "Liberating Revolution." The leader of the first post-Perón government, General Eduardo Lonardi, was a nationalist Catholic who opposed essentially only the about-faces in policy of Perón's last years, not the dictator's early policies, and he took a "soft" line toward the Peronists. He was thus unacceptable to the more fundamentalist anti-Peronists and was replaced in a coup by General Pedro Aramburu. Aramburu outlawed the Peronist party and eliminated Peronists from public life preparatory to the holding of elections and the returning of the government to non-Peronist civilian hands.

But the problem of what attitude to take toward the Peronists split the civilian parties just as it had split the military. With the Peronists barred from competing, the majority political party was clearly the Radicals. Indeed, the Radicals might have been able to defeat the Peronists in a free election in which Perón himself was neither president nor presidential candidate. However, the Radicals split over the question of what attitude to take toward the Peronists, with the nationalist

TABLE III   Percentage Distribution of Votes in Argentine Elections During Period of Exclusion of Peronists from Office, 1957–65

Occupant of Presidency	1957	1958*	1960	1962	1963†	1965
	Aramburu		Frondizi		Guido	Illia
UCRP	24	25	23	20	24	29
UCRI	21	41	20	24	17	4
MID (Frondizi)						6
FNPC (Conservatives)	6	3	8	6	5	5
PDC (Christian Democrats)	5	4	4	2	5	3
PSA (Socialists)	6	6	4	2	3	2
PSD (Socialists)			4	3	3	2
UDELPA (Aramburu)					14	
Peronists				32	7	35
Blank (Peronists)	25	9	24	3	19	2
Other (mainly Conservatives)	14	11	9	8	4	11

*Presidential election; winner, Frondizi (UCRI).
†Presidential election; winner, Illia (UCRP).

wing of the party, the one more sympathetic with the original Peronist policies, breaking away to form the new UCRI, or Intransigent Radicals, while the majority of the party, under the party's leader Ricardo Balbín, called itself the UCRP, or People's Radicals. The leader of the Intransigents, Arturo Frondizi, was a nationalist who had attacked Perón over his agreement with the foreign oil companies. Now he sent emissaries to Perón, in exile in Madrid, who agreed that Frondizi would legalize the party and allow Peronists gradually back into public life in return for their votes in the 1958 presidential elections. The arrangement had to be kept secret because of the strong anti-Peronism of the Aramburu regime and the military. The margin of Frondizi's victory over Balbín in the presidential election, however, indicated fairly clearly what had happened, and, although Frondizi was allowed to take office, he was kept under close and suspicious watch by the anti-Peronist military.

Arturo Frondizi; A Delicate Balance

Between the suspicions of the military and his commitments to the Peronists, Frondizi was in a difficult position. But he thought he knew the way out of the problem; he would allow Peronist re-entry into politics gradually, in stages, which was made possible by the Argentine practice of staggered elections for provincial governorships and the partial renewal of the Congress. However, his own closeness to Peronist policies would at the same time wean Peronist voters away from their allegiance to the exiled dictator and gradually enlist them as supporters of the UCRI. When the Peronists were finally allowed to run their own candidates, in this scenario, they would only lose. In this way, Frondizi would build his party and his own position while at the same time honoring his commitment to the Peronists and still keeping the military under control.

Economic problems.   Unfortunately for Frondizi, a further difficulty was introduced into this already delicate situation. Because of Peronist mismanagement and high-consumption policies, and a decline in commodity prices, the Argentine economy was in desperate straits. To attempt to reduce inflation and get the economy going again, Frondizi, like Perón before him, made an about-face on his original economic nationalism, trying to secure foreign investment and taking out a loan from the International Monetary Fund (IMF). As is its practice, however, the IMF conditioned its aid on the adoption by Argentina of a monetary stabilization program that would break out of the inflationary cycle through budgetary stringency and the avoidance of wage increases. Frondizi was therefore presented with the problem of how to secure the support of Peronist voters, who were mostly industrial workers, while he was holding down their wages in a time of rising prices.

Economics and politics.   For almost four years, Argentina was presented with an extraordinary balancing act as Frondizi made his own deal with foreign oil companies and solicited United States investments while making symbolic nationalist and anti-Yankee gestures (such as having a friendly chat with Che Guevara). After beginning his presidential term by granting a general sixty percent wage increase, he soon clamped on wage controls. Astonishingly enough, the balancing act seemed to be working. Inflation dropped from one hundred percent per year in 1959 to twenty-seven percent in 1960 and eighteen percent in 1961. Argentina became self-sufficient in petroleum, and foreign investment began to flow in. And immediately before the partial elections of 1960 and 1961, Frondizi made gestures to the Peronists by allowing Peronist union leaders to resume their union offices and by decreeing wage increases. The UCRI candidates received substantial majorities, and economic controls were clamped on again after the election.

The Overthrow of Frondizi and the Interregnum

Convinced of the success of his strategy, and having won a grudging freedom of action from the impressed military, Frondizi allowed Peronists to be candidates for provincial governorships in the elections of 1962. This was to have been the final demonstration of the success of his strategy, as the Peronist candidates would be beaten by Intransigent Radicals. Unfortunately for Frondizi, things did not turn out that way, and the Peronist candidates won resounding victories. That was all the military needed to arrest Frondizi and remove him from office. The president of the Senate, José María Guido, then became president in what the military maintained was a constitutional fashion, Frondizi having allegedly violated the constitution by leaving the capital city without securing the permission of Congress (since, after his arrest, his captors had taken him to Martín García Island). Guido's succession was clouded not only by this dubious piece of constitutional interpretation, but also by the fact that he had previously promised Frondizi that he would refuse to accept the presidency if Frondizi were overthrown. The Intransigent Radicals promptly split, half of the party staying with Guido and the other half remaining loyal to Frondizi.

The Guido administration.   The eighteen months of the Guido administration were an extraordinary period in Argentine history. The

Frondizi solution of the problem of what to do with the Peronists had collapsed, and the military didn't know where to turn next. One faction, the so-called *colorados,* or reds, the more fundamental anti-Peronists, espoused the thesis of "democratic dictatorship." This would be outright military rule for an indefinite period to prevent the reemergence of the Peronists. The *azules,* or blues, also known as the legalists, favored a return to constitutional civilian rule. Tanks rolled through the streets as coup and countercoup were staged over which faction controlled the ministry of war. Guido meanwhile stayed as figurehead president, eventually going over to the *azules,* who finally emerged victorious with the appointment of General Juan Carlos Onganía as military commander. Meanwhile, the country was run by senior civil servants and technocrats, who look back to the Guido era today as their finest hour.

The 1963 elections.   The position with respect to political activity that finally won out among the military was that elections would be held but that any candidate who received Peronist support would not be allowed to run. This position led to an extraordinary tragicomedy as the army vetoed one candidate after another, an independent, a Christian Democrat, and a Conservative, as each, in turn, was designated to be the recipient of Peronist votes. Amid general disbelief that the elections would actually take place, Balbín decided not to bother to run himself, and the People's Radicals nominated a little-known provincial politician named Arturo Illia. At the last minute, the Peronists received instructions to cast blank ballots, the elections were held, and, to everyone's surprise, Illia was the winner with twenty-four percent of the votes, defeating both General Aramburu and the UCRI candidate.

The Illia Administration

The relief that was generally felt at this more or less democratic outcome of the situation soon paled as Argentines were introduced to Illia's style of government. Very much an old-fashioned politician, Illia gave jobs to deserving People's Radicals, many of them, like him, little-known provincial politicians from the days before Perón. The foreign oil contracts were again cancelled. The government dawdled in the face of urgent problems.

Illia and the Peronists.   With respect to the Peronists, Illia's approach was quite different from that of Frondizi. Rather than attempting to capture the Peronist voters for his own party, Illia instead tried to rally all of the anti-Peronist votes to the People's Radicals, at the same time allowing the Peronists to participate in political life. The idea was that the Peronists would be reintegrated into political life as a loyal opposition and would gradually remodel themselves along the lines of the British Labour Party. The People's Radicals would become the only viable alternative to the Peronists, managing to attract the more than half of the electorate who were not Peronist, and would thus block the Peronist way to power quite democratically. This at least was the theory of the so-called option strategy, although the military were not convinced of its feasibility. Nevertheless, partial elections suggested that the strategy might be successful, as the People's Radicals began to pick up votes from the other non-Peronist parties.

Illia and the military.   General Ongania remained as chief of staff and held the military united under civilian control, reorganizing commands and retiring the most politically minded generals. Unfortunately for Illia, however, the president decided that Ongania was becoming too powerful altogether, and the chief of staff was dismissed. Military men offended by Ongania's dismissal, those suspicious that Illia's strategy would only lead to a comeback by the Peronists, technocrats who had tasted power under Guido, and various other disgruntled elements then combined to stage the most unnecessary and unjustified coup in recent Argentine history, removing Illia from office in June 1966 and replacing him with Ongania.

Ongania

Paradoxically, the leader of the legalist officers in promoting military obedience to civilian authority was now president by virtue of having overthrown the elected constitutional president he had loyally served previously.

General strategy.   Appropriately, Ongania made the about-face complete by adopting the former *colorado* program of a "democratic dictatorship." He would rule, he announced, for at least ten years. During this period, the activity of the government would be divided into three phases. The first phase would be devoted to solving the country's economic problems. When those were solved, the government would tackle the country's social problems. There would be no politics during the first and second phases. In the third phase, the regime would restructure Argentine political life preparatory to allowing a revival of party politics. In this purified political system, there would presumably be no Peronism, since once the country's economic and social problems had been solved, there would be no grounds for dissatisfaction and extremism.

Even for the military mind, this program was extraordinarily naive. One doesn't know which was more preposterous, the idea that politics could simply be excluded from national life while economic and social problems were being solved, or the idea that economic and social problems could be "solved" once and for all, after which there would be no need to bother with them.

Economic problems.   The country's economic problems were, indeed, severe. The economy was stagnant, so that even with an extremely low rate of population growth, barely more than one percent a year, deterioration took place in the standard of living. This was to be sure an extremely high standard, one that had been in the early twentieth century perhaps the highest standard of living in the world. Even during those hard times, Argentines were consuming an average of five pounds of beef and two liters of wine per capita per week. But these high consumption levels were borne on the back of a weak agricultural sector, not only subject to the vagaries of weather but also inefficiently organized and run. Nevertheless, agriculture provided ninety percent of the country's exports and bore the major weight of the tax system. Industry provided hardly any exports, not being competitive with the products of Western Europe and the United States, and surviving in Argentina only by virtue of tariff protection and subsidy. The nationalized industries were notoriously inefficient and had to be subsidized at considerable expense to the government's budget. When revenue was inadequate, the government, of course, resorted to deficit financing, with inflationary effect. By the end of Onganía's term of office, the cost of living was seven times what it had been at the overthrow of Perón.

Repression of the unions.   In this situation, unions had cause to demand wage increases; however, since the unions were Peronist, Onganía chose to regard wage claims and strikes as Peronist political activity and tried to repress them by force. Argentines were thus treated to the paradox that under a military government supposed to provide a strong hand, disorder and violence increased, leading finally to the *cordobazo,* an outbreak of violence in the automobile manufacturing city of Córdoba, always the spearhead of labor militancy in Argentina, which almost became civil war. Thus it was brought home to General Onganía that politics could not be held in suspension while one "solved" the country's economic problems, especially when the solution to those problems adopted required the freezing of wages.

Levingston

Perceiving that Onganía's economic policies had failed, the junta of armed forces commanders, led by the military commander, Alejandro Lanusse, removed Onganía and picked a new president, a little-known general named Roberto Levingston, to reverse economic course. Onganía had followed a so-called liberal economic policy; that is, he had taken a favorable attitude to foreign investment and followed a conservative fiscal and monetary policy designed to hold down inflation. Levingston opted for the alternative "nationalist" policy, that is, to attempt to do without foreign investment, expanding Argentine industry and developing a national market that would encourage production for domestic consumption. This strategy proved in short order even more disastrous than Onganía's. Wages went up, but, instead of rising, production dropped in the face of lack of business confidence. Inflation went from the 6.6 percent that Onganía had brought it down to in 1969 to 22 percent in 1970. Signs that Levingston was trying to build a political position independent of control by the joint chiefs proved the last straw and the military removed him in March 1971, after less than one year in office, and Lanusse took over the presidency himself.

Lanusse: Accommodation with Perón

Just as Onganía had switched position from being a supporter of civilian control of the military to being the leader of a "democratic dictatorship," Lanusse had changed positions in a different direction. Originally a strong anti-Peronist who had, in fact, been jailed by the dictator in 1951, Lanusse took the position that some kind of accommodation had to be worked out with Perón. The main task was to pacify the political scene, and Lanusse reversed Onganía's priorities, attempting to deal with the political problems and ignore the economic ones.

The political scene was, indeed, disheartening. The violence that had developed under Onganía had now become widespread. Urban guerrilla movements of various political shades had been organized, principal among them the left-wing Peronist Montoneros, and were actively robbing banks and kidnapping leading figures. Major labor leaders and military officers were assassinated, among them General Aramburu. Since many of the terrorist groups called themselves Peronist, Lanusse hoped that a deal with Perón would enable him to bring them under control. The People's Radicals also saw no other way out and made an alliance with the Peronists to urge a return to constitutional rule.

Like Frondizi, however, Lanusse was playing something of a double game, trying to forge an alliance of all political forces, including the Peronists, but behind his own presidential candidacy. He was thus in a position of trying to conciliate Perón without, at the same time, allowing him to run for office. In furtherance of this strategy, he made various personal gestures to Perón; the former dictator's military rank and pension were restored, together with his Argentine passport, and the embalmed body of Evita Perón, hidden away in Italy in fear that it might become the object of a Peronist cult, was shipped to Perón's home in Madrid. Although Lanusse maintained his veto of Perón's candidacy, he was not able to promote his own successfully, and when elections were finally held in 1973, the winner was the Peronist candidate, Héctor Cámpora, who defeated several candidates, Balbín among them.

Héctor Cámpora

With the return of Peronism to power, its latent contradictions became manifest. As long as General Perón remained in Madrid issuing ambiguous statements, it was possible for those holding a wide range of opinions to consider themselves Peronists. This ambiguous Peronist identification was shared by unreconstructed fascist sympathizers, right-wing Catholics, socialist union leaders, labor racketeers and gangsters, extreme-left intellectuals, and student followers of Che Guevara. Cámpora took a left position, hoping thus to make peace with the violently inclined militant Peronist youth movement. Cámpora's administration lasted only two months, however. Loyal to Perón's instructions, he resigned in July 1973, together with his vice-president, to make way for elections in which Perón would at last be allowed to run. The Speaker of the Chamber of Deputies, Raúl Lastiri, became provisional president and organized elections which Perón did indeed win, with wide support and a substantial majority. In October 1973, the former dictator, now an old man, again assumed power.

The Return of Perón

Perón's vice-president was his third wife (Evita had been the second), María Estela (Isabel) Martínez. Lacking Evita's leadership gifts, the new vice-president had been a dancer before Perón met her and made her his secretary. Perhaps Perón picked her for the vice-presidency, as most observers thought, so he could have a deputy unconditionally loyal to him, without an independent political position and identified with none of the sectors within the Peronist movement. However, he .may also have wanted to demonstrate how his authority was now at its maximum, greater even than in 1952, when he had been prevented from imposing Evita as his vice-presidential candidate.

Economic policies.   The old man seemed to have retained his political skill and his luck. Wheat was in demand on the world market, and its price was rising. He had always maintained good relations with the Arabs, whose oil resources gave them new economic power; no one could suspect Perón of pro-Jewish sympathies. The economic nationalism that had been Perón's platform twenty-five years before was now the common ground of Latin American governments, and Perón's return was hailed by Fidel Castro, by Omar Torrijos in Panama, by the Peruvian military junta, even by Salvador Allende, who had been bitterly anti-Peronist in the 1940s and 1950s.

Abandonment of the left.   After a brief attempt to harmonize the distinctive tendencies within the Peronist movement, it became clear that the old man's sympathies were with the conservative elements in the movement, and not with the young militants and left-wing ideologues, even though the left refused to believe that the government's conservative line came from Perón himself, blaming instead Isabel Perón and José López Rega, the president's secretary and Minister of Social Welfare. But even that ground for hope was taken from them when, in July 1974, the old man's heart finally gave out, and Isabel Martínez de Perón became the first woman president of a Latin American country.

Isabel Perón

All the military and the Radicals could do was to keep their fingers crossed and hope for the best. The kidnappings and assassinations continued as, without even loyalty to the old general's person to keep them together, the sectors of Peronism flew apart and at each other's throats.

Isabel ran a weak and corrupt administration, being caught herself embezzling social welfare funds. López Rega, a former police corporal and amateur astrologer, organized a right-wing terrorist organization, the AAA, or Argentine Anti-Communist Alliance, which kidnapped, tortured, and assassinated left-wing figures, even after López Rega was forced out of office. Isabel managed to hang on until April 1976, although she twice took a leave of absence from the presidency "for reasons of health."

The Coup of 1976

A reluctant military, painfully aware of the failure of the military regimes of 1966 to 1973, finally took power in a long-awaited coup. The military junta was headed by the army commander, General Jorge Videla, a devout Catholic of right-wing views, but who seemed eager not to follow the brutally repressive policies that had made his Chilean colleague, General Pinochet, so notorious. Yet the prospect that faced

Videla was discouraging. Left-wing terrorism had become virtual insurrectionary warfare in Tucumán province. Agricultural production
was down, in response to the Peronist policy of obligatory sales, at
one-third world market prices, to the government purchasing agency.
Inflation was running over three hundred percent annually, the highest
rate in the world. Union leaders were unhappy and workers were bitter.
The Peronists resented the overthrow of Isabel, and the second largest
party, the Radicals, opposed military government on principle. Argentina had clearly not broken out of the economic and political vicious
circles in which it had been trapped for a quarter of a century. Nevertheless, economic difficulties were ameliorated somewhat under Videla's
Economics Minister, José Martínez de Hoz. Martínez de Hoz followed in
general a pre-Peronist line of policy favorable to the *estancieros*. The
distribution of income became more regressive, but beef production and
export increased. The peso strengthened, though inflation continued to
run around one hundred percent annually. Finally, a wave of bank-
ruptcies and collapses of banks led to the replacement of Martínez de
Hoz. Videla's successor, General Robert Viola, was chosen by ranking
military officers for a three-year "term," after which, it was hinted,
political parties might be allowed to play a role in choosing the president.

    Videla and Viola were fairly successful in convincing middle-class
opinion at home and abroad that they represented a "moderate" line of
policy that found rather uncouth the "disappearances," that is, the
kidnapping, torture, and killing of suspected oppositionists. Nevertheless those activities occurred, especially in the earlier years of the
regime, serving to remind observers of Argentina's distinctive recent
history. Fascism was never defeated in Argentina; it remains a live
option, and its crazy, conspiratorial, anti-Semitic ideology permeates
elements of the armed forces, which remain the major power factor in
Argentina today.

    As it happened, Viola's term of office proved much shorter than the
scheduled three years. The economic policies adopted to replace those of
Martínez de Hoz proved to contribute to an even more rapid inflation,
and the peso had to be devalued. Viola suffered a heart attack and was
temporarily replaced by General Horacio Liendo. Over Viola's protests,
he was not allowed to resume office on his recovery, and the army
commander, General Leopoldo Galtieri, was picked by the military
commanders to replace him.

    The sequence Videla-Viola-Galtieri seemed to parallel that of
Onganía-Levingston-Lanusse ten years before. A military president
whose economic policies were not working well was replaced by another
whose policies proved worse yet; after a few months, the army com-

mander himself took power. To complete the analogy, Galtieri, like Lanusse, indicated he wished to lead a new non-Peronist political movement.

The Falkland Islands War

Trying to rally popular support in the face of Argentina's unsatisfactory and deteriorating economic and political situation, and honoring the pledge with which he had secured navy support for his seizure of power, on April 2, 1982, Galtieri ordered Argentine troops to occupy the Falkland Islands, called by Argentines the Malvinas. Long claimed by Argentina, the rainy and windswept islands lie some 300 miles east of the Strait of Magellan. After changing hands among European powers various times, they were seized finally by the British, who claimed them, in 1832 (incidentally, in apparent violation of the Monroe Doctrine). By 1982 they had an English-speaking population of about 1800, mostly shepherds and others of Scottish ancestry.

Argentines are brought up to regard the Malvinas as rightfully theirs, and British rule there as a survival of colonialism. Recent British governments had been prepared to transfer the islands to Argentina, a logical supplier of the islands' needs, but felt they should not ignore the preference of the inhabitants to remain British.

In seizing the islands, Galtieri had expected no opposition from the "decadent" British, support from the "anticolonial" Third World, and at least favorable neutrality from the United States, eager to have Argentina act as United States surrogate in the wars of Central America, and the Soviet Union, hungry for Argentine grain. Along with enthusiastic support from Argentines across the political spectrum, he received some Latin American, Third World, and Soviet backing, with different degrees of enthusiasm, but he had not anticipated United States and Western European objection on principle to the first use of force, apart from distaste for the unsavory character of his government. When the British chose to fight, Galtieri found himself faced with a military defeat and hundreds of casualties, not to mention the economic costs of the fighting and of a European trade and financial boycott.

Analysts and commentators of all varieties rushed to draw conclusions from the Falklands crisis—conclusions about modern armaments, about the nature of war, about the fighting quality of armies that get mixed up in politics, about international relations. For the Argentines, two conclusions stood out: that they had lost touch with the values and ways of thinking of the rest of the world; and that the decision-making processes of democratic governments, with all their defects, are preferable in the long run to the arbitrariness, the lack of judgment, and the political naïveté demonstrated by nonresponsible military regimes.

PRESIDENTS OF ARGENTINA, 1946–82

1946–55	Juan D. Perón
1955	Eduardo Lonardi
1955–58	Pedro Aramburu
1958–62	Arturo Frondizi
1962–63	José María Guido
1963–66	Arturo Illia
1966–70	Juan Carlos Onganía
1970–71	Roberto M. Levingston
1971–73	Alejandro Lanusse
1973	Héctor Cámpora
1973	Raúl Lastiri
1973–74	Juan D. Perón
1974–76	María Estela (Isabel) Martínez de Perón
1976–81	Jorge R. Videla
1981	Roberto Viola
1981–	Leopoldo Galtieri

URUGUAY

General Character

Uruguay, like Paraguay, is a small country of three million inhabitants whose place in the Argentine sphere of influence is now being challenged by influence from Brazil. In other respects, the contrasts between the two countries could hardly be greater. Paraguay is economically and socially underdeveloped, a mestizo country with a strong Indian flavor, a perpetual military-dominated dictatorship. Uruguay is a modern country of European population which until recently was one of Latin America's strongest democracies.

Like the other countries of Latin America, Uruguay traces its independence to the armed struggle of a band of patriots led by the national hero, in the case of Uruguay, José Artigas. Nevertheless, Uruguay's independence is, from another perspective, due to British support for a buffer state between Argentina and Brazil that would end the perpetual fighting between the two over control of the disputed area. Today, Uruguay is again caught between conflicting pressures from Argentina, whose influence, while waning, remains strong, and a developing Brazil beginning to realize its potential. For most of its history, however, Uruguay could clearly be considered in the Argentine sphere of influence.

Social and Economic Characteristics

In its major social characteristics, Uruguay much resembles Argentina. A country of European ancestry, with no Indians and only a handful of blacks, most of Uruguay's population derives from Spanish and Italian immigration of the late nineteenth century. Universal literacy and high educational standards accompanied what was for the first half of the twentieth century one of Latin America's highest standards of living. Like Argentina an exporter of animal products—in the case of Uruguay, mutton and wool more than beef—the country is nevertheless highly urbanized, with perhaps half of the population living in Montevideo and the surrounding area. Montevideo is very much under the influence of Buenos Aires, which is only a few hours by boat across the estuary of the Río de la Plata; natives of both cities pronounce their Spanish in ways that would be considered bizarre in Lima or Bogotá. Again like Argentina, Uruguay's pastoral exports support the commercial, industrial, and bureaucratic growth of the capital city. But if industrial development in Argentina is uneconomic and must be protected by tariffs and encouraged by subsidies, industry in Uruguay is breathtakingly uneconomic. The domestic market for which Argentina produces consists, after all, of twenty-eight million people; in Uruguay there are three million who live, moreover, in a land deficient in raw materials or fossil fuels. Yet what is the solution, if a country's economic potential lies in farming and everyone wants to live in the city? This fundamental weakness of the Uruguayan economy, brutally exposed when world commodity prices dropped after the Korean War, was rendered much worse by a government structure and policies that, while well intentioned in themselves, had disastrous effects. Thus year after year, despite a low birthrate like that of Argentina, Uruguay annually experienced an actual lowering of its per capita gross national product.

The Heritage of Batlle

Political and economic weakness reinforced each other. The story goes back to the dominant figure of twentieth-century Uruguay, the twice president (1903–07 and 1911–15) José Batlle y Ordoñez. A middle-class Radical more or less resembling Irogoyen in Argentina and Arturo Alessandri in Chile, Batlle led the liberal Colorado party in establishing stability, democratic government, and an end to the fighting with the more proclerical and rural Blanco, or Nationalist, party. In contrast to Alessandri and Irigoyen, however, Batlle became more radical during his second term of office than during his first. He propounded fundamental constitutional reforms, brought basic industries into public ownership, and enacted an extensive social welfare program.

The fate of social reforms.   Enlightened as they seemed at the time, these reforms sowed the seeds for later disaster. The nationalized industries became bureaucratized and featherbedded over the years to the point where their inefficiency and costliness constituted a major drain on government resources. Social welfare costs, similarly, expanded as a large proportion of the adult population became entitled to government pensions. Rents were controlled in the interest of tenants, but as inflation proceeded and fixed rents became nominal, landlords abandoned maintenance of their deteriorating properties.

The collegial executive.   Batlle's major constitutional reform, which he was not able to put through during his presidential term, was also well intentioned and enlightened in appearance but disastrous in its effects. To avoid the typical Latin American problem of presidential dictatorship, Batlle urged the adoption of a collegial executive, in which executive powers would be shared by a council that represented all political forces. A compromise version of this plan was adopted by a constitutional convention in 1917 but was abolished in 1933.

In 1951, the system of the collegial executive was reintroduced by popular vote: Colorados voted for it out of loyalty to the memory of Batlle, Blancos voted for it because even a minority of the seats on the council would get them closer to executive power than they had been in one hundred years of being defeated for national office at the hands of the majority Colorados.[5] So the *colegiado* was restored, with a four-year term, beginning in 1954–58. Seats on the nine-man council were divided, six to the majority party, three to the minority party. In Uruguay, however, as in all countries with a strong two-party tradition, each of the parties consisted of people with a range of divergent views, often organized into permanent factions. To take account of this, the six majority seats were to be subdivided, four to the majority and two to the runner-up faction within the major party. As the politicians wheeled and dealed, however, trying to avoid being totally excluded from the executive council, the lists of candidates for the council on which Uruguayans voted became not merely factional lists but coalitions of factional lists. The result was that when the nine members of the

[5]Ironically, however, in 1958 the Blancos managed to get a majority of the vote for the first time in a century, narrowly repeating the feat in 1962.

executive council assembled, they represented several different factions of each of the two parties with quite divergent attitudes, and as a result no majority could be found for any particular policy. Uruguayan delegations at international meetings soon had to keep running to the phone to find out if Montevideo had managed to decide on a policy yet, returning glumly to their seats only to abstain from voting.

Deterioration of the Economy

Unfortunately, this weakness in the executive coincided with a period of economic decline after the Korean War in which decisive action was necessary, and it continued until 1966, into an era of urban guerrilla warfare when government weakness could be fatal. As economic conditions deteriorated, the government met its problems by inflating the currency; as inflation grew, workers struck for higher wages. In the fairly socialist Uruguayan economy, many of these workers were government employees, and their wage demands called for some government response, but the national council was unable to decide what to do. Strikes became endemic as every sector of the economy tried to protect itself from inflation; the weak government eventually yielded to all demands, financing its costs by printing money, which led to further inflation. Cattle ranchers smuggled their herds across the border into Brazil rather than sell them to the government monopoly for the low prices it paid in the attempt to finance the public sector of the economy with export profits.

In this Alice-in-Wonderland situation, people held several jobs in the attempt to make ends meet. This did not necessarily entail a great deal of work. Many government jobs were sinecures in which the employee turned up only to receive his paycheck. In some cases, people holding several jobs were on strike at one or more of them at any given time. In fact, life was not as desperate as an outsider might have thought. The average work week was twenty-five hours, and there were always the miles of beautiful beaches close to Montevideo. Also, as the Uruguayan peso weakened, floods of Argentines poured in to spend money on inexpensive vacations, so that sometimes there were literally more Argentines than Uruguayans on the streets of Montevideo.

The Restored Presidential System

Gestido, Pacheco, and the Tupamaros.   But enough was enough, and in 1966 a plebiscite restored the presidential system. The Colorados returned to power, electing a retired general with a reputation as a good administrator, Oscar Gestido. However, the high hopes riding on Gestido's election were soon defrauded as the old general died within months of taking office, leaving in the presidency a nonentity from a minor conservative faction of the Colorado party who had been picked as vice-presidential candidate to balance the ticket, Jorge Pacheco Areco. Pacheco Areco proceeded to run a fumbling and corrupt right-wing administration that proved to be a sitting duck for the growing Tupamaro urban guerrilla movement. The economy deteriorated, inflation soared, and the government was eventually reduced to making secret sales from its gold reserves on the world market. The repression of the Tupamaros, even though it violated constitutional norms and guarantees, still proved ineffective. After failing to secure support for his reelection, which would have needed a constitutional amendment, Pacheco gave his support to a young rancher more conservative than himself, also from a minor and unrepresentative faction of the Colorado party, named Juan Bordaberry.

The elections of 1972. By this time, matters had gone so far that Wilson Ferreira, the Blancos' leading candidate, was more progressive than the principal Colorado candidate, and a variety of smaller groups, including some splinter factions from the two main parties, together with the Christian Democrats, the Communists, and the Socialists, combined in the "Broad Front" to nominate a respected general and former chief of staff, Liber Seregni. Seregni received eighteen percent of the vote, and Bordaberry edged out Ferreira by forty-one to forty percent. Under the Uruguayan system, which combines a primary and the general election, several candidates from each party compete, with the leading one being credited with all votes cast for his party's candidates. In fact, only about one-fourth of the votes were cast for Bordaberry personally. Moreover, it later transpired that the Colorado's margin of victory had been provided by falsified ballot papers.

Military Intervention

The Tupamaros had called off their activities during the election campaign so as not to prejudice voters against Seregni, although they themselves did not believe in electoral and constitutional means of coming to power. After the election, however, they resumed a guerrilla campaign in which they robbed banks, kidnapped government figures, and escaped from jail with apparent impunity, often securing and publishing information on political corruption. Disgusted both with this government corruption and with the ineffectiveness of the government's repression of the Tupamaros, the military intervened in 1973, first assuming a veto power over government acts, in Februrary, and finally in June establishing a dictatorship. It was at least a measure of Uruguay's democratic tradition that the military only intervened when the situation had deteriorated far beyond what it would have taken to bring military intervention in any other Latin American country. Bordaberry remained as a willing figurehead president for the military regime, providing continuity and avoiding the internal dissension that the military would have faced if they had taken over the government completely. Legislative elections scheduled for 1976 were canceled. Bordaberry's views were such that he was just as happy as president in a military dictatorship as he would have been in a constitutional regime.

Using drastic measures, including torture, the military regime succeeded in crushing the Tupamaros, thus demonstrating two things: one, that even the best organized and most skillful urban guerrilla movement, facing the weakest of governments, still does not provide a road to power; two, that violence from the left only succeeds in making the political situation worse than it was before.

Finally bored with Bordaberry's political maneuvering in the attempt to stay in office, the military removed him in 1976; after a brief interregnum they turned the presidency over to an extreme right-wing lawyer, Aparicio Méndez, who eagerly played the role of figurehead. At first the military politicans appeared to have no policy beyond stealing government funds and arresting and mistreating anyone who complained. Under the leadership of the Minister of Economy, Alejandro Vegh Villegas, they then adopted a modified neo-liberal policy, which aimed to reduce tariffs and promote investment. Some new industry developed on the basis of elaborating Uruguayan raw materials, in clothing manufacture and leather goods production. Something of a construction boom took place, especially of luxury apartments, as Argentines found Uruguay a convenient place for the money they wanted to send out of Argentina.

In 1980 the country's military rulers yielded to pressures from the Carter administration to return the country to constitutionality to the extent of holding a plebiscite to ratify a constitution that would, in effect, have given the military perpetual supervision of the political system. To their and the world's surprise, the electorate defeated the new constitution, showing Uruguayans' independence and democratic loyalties, even under dictatorship, and leaving the political future of the country a question mark. In the following year, the military ruling group chose a retired general, Gregorio Alvarez, as president. General Alvarez was reputed to be from the military "soft line," more democratic and more nationalist, and the possibility of a moderate "opening" of the regime to more democratic practices, such as was happening in Brazil, and even to some extent in Paraguay, emerged. Meanwhile, however, Liber Seregni remained in jail, and Wilson Ferreira in exile.

PRESIDENTS OF URUGUAY, 1948–82

1948–51	Luis Batlle Berres
1951–52	Andrés Martínez Trueba
1952–54	Collegial Council of Government, Colorado Party majority
1954–58	Council of Government, Colorado majority
1958–62	Council of Government, Blanco Party majority
1962–66	Council of Government, Blanco majority
1966–67	Oscar D. Gestido
1967–72	Jorge Pacheco Areco
1972–76	Juan María Bordaberry
1976	Military junta
1976–81	Aparicio Méndez
1981–	Gregorio Alvarez

SUMMARY

Paraguay

Argentine influence has long been dominant in Paraguay and Uruguay, although it is now being challenged by the influence of a resurgent Brazil. Paraguay presents an unusual blend of Spanish and native Guaraní populations and cultures, with an admixture of European, especially German, immigrants of recent vintage. Long isolated in a stagnant backwater, its population depleted by major wars, Paraguay is typically governed by the dictatorship of a ranking military officer, who shares power with the conservative Colorado party, the bureaucracy, and the army. Small-scale industry and much agricultural land are owned by Argentine and Brazilian interests, and Argentina and Brazil are the destination of the smuggling that may be Paraguay's chief economic activity.

Argentina

Argentina's rich pampa lands form the economic base for an oligarchy of beef- and wheat-producing estancieros, whose power has been challenged, but not broken, by an urban industrial and professional class formed largely from the sons of recent European immigrants. These classes have, in turn, been challenged by the rise of an urban work force politically organized by Juan Perón and committed to

Peronism, which has sometimes found allies, in its authoritarianism and economic nationalism, among industrialists producing for the domestic market and the middle classes of provincial towns. Saddled with an uneconomic industry, fluctuating prices for agricultural products, and a militant labor force, the country has been in a long-term economic decline. For some time, the military tried to keep the Peronists out of power by repeated interventions and finally by assuming power themselves. Returned to power, the Peronists split, and left-wing extremists within the movement resorted to guerrilla warfare, while the extreme right mounted campaigns of assassination. The military reassumed power in 1976.

Uruguay

Traditionally peaceful and democratic Uruguay has been unable to withstand the deterioration of its agriculture-based economy as the population has become increasingly urban and dependent on government employment and the extensive welfare system. Corrupt and ineffectual government gave rise to the strongest urban guerrilla movement in Latin America, the Tupamaros, whose successes led, in turn, to a military seizure of power, at first behind the façade of a conservative civilian government.

8

Brazil

INTRODUCTION: COMPARATIVE PERSPECTIVE

Brazil is different. Of course, all countries are different from each other—but some are more different than others.

Brazil's difference begins with its language. The national language is Portuguese, and Brazilian culture and traditions derive from the Portuguese variant of the Iberian cultural complex. Brazil's difference begins with language but doesn't end there. While Spanish America split, forming new nations along old colonial administrative lines, Portuguese America held together in a country of tremendous size; in area, Brazil is the fifth largest country in the world, after the United States, Canada, the Soviet Union, and China. In population, Brazil is seventh largest in the world, reaching about 130 million in 1981.

A country of Brazil's size and variety is difficult to generalize about. As Roger Bastide has put it, "Brazil, land of contrasts, is also and at the same time the land of nuances, such that one no longer knows what dominates, the rules or the exceptions to the rules."[1]

The People

Brazilian character. Brazilian character is clearly different from that found in Hispanic America, paralleling the differences in character between Spaniards and Portuguese, but with an additional African flavor. Brazilians are much less formal than Spanish Americans, more relaxed, more direct, more easy-going. They take life, including politics, less seriously.

[1]Cited in Richard M. Morse, "Some Themes of Brazilian History," *South Atlantic Quarterly,* Spring 1972.

Race relations. The easy-going character of the Brazilians is reflected in a generally relaxed attitude on race relations. While color
prejudice exists (this is one of the nuances Bastide referred to), it is mild,
and Brazil is a long way from the caste-like social rigidities and hostilities that used to characterize the United States and to some extent
still do. It may also be true, as Marvin Harris has argued[2] that fundamental demographic and geographic facts share responsibility for
Brazil's amicable race relations. Portugal was a small country that
attempted to rule half a continent. There were simply not enough
Portuguese available to take up the intermediate positions on the social
scale, so mulatto freedmen, and even slaves, held occupations that
called for the exercise of skill and responsibility. It remains true,
nevertheless, that skin color lightens as one goes up the social scale and
that the people with the darker faces generally hold the humbler jobs.

Social and economic characteristics. According to the statistics,
Brazil places slightly above the middle among the Latin American
countries on indicators of social and economic development, such as
gross national product per capita, literacy, and so on. However, aggre-
gate national statistics conceal the tremendous variations that exist
among the Brazilian regions; some areas have the living standards and
the way of life of Switzerland or the United States, while others look
more like Indonesia or Nigeria.

Cities, States, and Regions

Center-south. Two-thirds of the population is concentrated in the
center-south of the country, where Rio de Janeiro, the former capital,
remains a center of commerce and tourism, and the city of São Paulo is
the home of manufacturing and banking. Hard-working São Paulo has
long since overtaken the more frivolous Rio in size and is now one of the
world's great cities, with about twelve million inhabitants. Belo
Horizonte is the capital of conservative Minas Gerais state, still important for mining but also now for manufacturing and agriculture as well.
The state of São Paulo is more important economically, however, not
only because of the manufacturing activities of São Paulo city but also
because the rural part of the state produces a great deal of Brazil's
principal exports, coffee and soybeans.

South. The major state of the region further south than the Rio-
São Paulo-Minas triangle, Rio Grande do Sul, has cattle raising as its
principal activity, though coffee is grown elsewhere in the southern

[2]In *Patterns of Race in the Americas,* New York: Columbia University Press, 1964.

region. The population here is primarily European, with many family farms in the hands of German and Italian immigrants, but also includes many Japanese. The *gaúchos* of Rio Grande do Sul, natural cavalrymen, have a strong military tradition. The state provided Brazil's most active military frontier in the days when Brazil and Argentina fought over control of Uruguay. The headquarters of the important Third Army are today in Pôrto Alegre, Rio Grande's capital, and the state contributes a disproportionate share of all Brazilian army officers. When the armed forces commanders tried to prevent the accession to the presidency of the *riograndense* vice-president, João Goulart, in 1961,they were forced to back down because of the opposition of the governor of Rio Grande and the Third Army commander.

Northeast.   More than twenty percent of the national population lives in the northeast, the "bulge" of Brazil. Like the southern United States of the early twentieth century, this is a region of plantations, farmed by impoverished black tenant farmers and sharecroppers. Sugar is grown along the coast, cotton inland; further inland in the highlands, there are cattle ranches. In recent years, some industry has come to the northeast, taking advantage of cheap labor and tax waivers, again as in the southern United States. Nevertheless, the northeast remains over-populated and underemployed, and there is continual migration to the richer opportunities of the center-south. This migration increases drastically during the droughts, which come on the average every six or seven years, inflicting great hardship on a population already living at a bare subsistence level. A special government program for development of the northeast has had only limited success, and in the early 1960s radical peasant leagues were formed to press for land reform and other structural changes.

North and west-center.   The populations of the two remaining regions, the north and the west-center, are small. Much of the northern region, the area around the Amazon, is an underdeveloped tropical area where a few Indians and mestizos sell forest products, such as lumber, rubber, and nuts, to trading boats that come up the river. However, Manaus, the major town in the region, has the status of a duty-free port of entry and is experiencing a boom that recalls its great days as the center of the rubber trade in the early twentieth century. Each Brazilian government has a pet project whose success is intended to reflect credit on the regime, and the development of the Amazon has been the show-case project for the military governments in power in Brazil since 1964. This program has entailed a colossal road-building effort to try to link the north to the rest of the country. Rushed through with inadequate preparation, like many Brazilian projects, the building of the Amazon road has contributed to severe erosion and other ecological problems and has led to the depriving of hitherto undisturbed Indian tribes of their way of life, their land, and sometimes their lives.

The west-center has a small population, mostly white, whose economic activities include agriculture, mining, and cattle raising. However, the region is most notable as the location of the federal capital of Brasília, constructed as the pet project of President Juscelino Kubitschek (1955–60), which was designed to serve as a pole of development to open up the western region.

Brazil's strong regionalism has always constituted a centrifugal force that must be combatted by the central government and especially by the president, who has assumed the emperor's old role of integrator of the fragmented political system. Yet the complexity and diversity of the country give the president, as they gave the emperor, room to maneuver. The pressures to act in one direction are usually counterbalanced by pressures to act in another, leaving the president great freedom of action.[3]

HISTORICAL BACKGROUND

The Empire

Unlike the countries of Spanish America, Brazil won its independence peacefully and without overthrowing the monarchy. Becoming the seat of the Portuguese royal house of Braganza after Napoleon's invasion of the peninsula, Brazil achieved independence when the prince who was its viceroy decided to make himself emperor of an independent Brazil rather than obey the command to return home to Portugal. The emperor ruled by playing off the various factions against each other. Slavery lasted until 1889 and was then abolished by the emperor's daughter, acting as regent in his absence. The large landowners, feeling betrayed, thereupon lost their interest in defending the monarchy against the republican middle class, and some active republicans took advantage of military grievances to get the army to go along with the proclamation of a republic.

The "Old Republic"

During the period known generally as the "old republic," from 1890 to 1933, the withdrawal of the emperor as the integrator of the political system weakened the central authority and left the state gov-

[3]Nathaniel H. Leff, *Economic Policy-Making and Development in Brazil, 1947–1964,* New York: Wiley, 1968.

ernments the strongest elements. Power at the national level depended on a coalition of state party machines, and the presidency more or less alternated between the outgoing governors of the two major states of São Paulo and Minas Gerais. (The city of Rio de Janeiro constituted a federal district.) However, the other states' representatives, especially those of Rio Grande do Sul, the third largest state, often played critical roles in the Congress. Elections were generally rigged in favor of the dominant faction in each state, although sometimes when the dominant state political machine was out of favor with the forces that controlled the national government, dissident local leaders or opposition factions secured federal troops to guard the polling stations and permit an opposition victory. The local bosses in the system, usually well-to-do leaders in the community's economic and political life, were known generically as *coroneis,* or "colonels," after the courtesy titles in the state militia that many had.

In social and economic terms, the system represented a coalition of "coffee with milk," the coffee-raising interests of São Paulo and the dairy farmers of Minas. Through the interpenetration of agricultural and industrial interests in São Paulo, however, part of Brazil's nascent manufacturing industry, and associated middle-class elements, were also included in the alliance. The principal elements excluded from this alliance, therefore, most of which were to coalesce behind the Vargas administration, were urban labor, the plantation agriculture of the northeast, and cattle ranchers of the southern states.

Getúlio Vargas

The reigning system broke down in 1930 when a candidate from Rio Grande do Sul challenged his state's exclusion from the presidency in a situation where there was general dissatisfaction, outside São Paulo, that a *paulista* president was attempting to have another paulista succeed him. Alleging that the election was rigged against him, the *gaúcho*[4] candidate, Getúlio Vargas, led the forces of Rio Grande in a successful revolt that installed him as provisional president.

Provisional, constitutional, and dictatorial phases.   A shrewd and flexible politician who had specialized in financial policy, Vargas managed to hang onto the presidency for fifteen years, during which time the country underwent extensive modernization. The provisional presidency lasted until 1934, when Vargas was elected constitutional president. In 1937, before the end of his constitutional term, he staged a coup and converted himself into a dictator. The dictatorship was extended on

[4]That is, from Rio Grande do Sul.

the excuse of the wartime emergency. When that pretext could no longer be used, at the end of the war in 1945, Getúlio[5] scheduled elections but began to manipulate the situation so that he would be "drafted" as a candidate, whereupon the military stepped in and forced his resignation. Nevertheless, he retained his popularity, and returned as elected president in 1950.

Vargas' programs.   Reflecting the heterogeneity of the forces that supported him, as well as his own pragmatic bent, Vargas was politically even more ambiguous than Perón. Like Perón he fostered labor organization and introduced welfare legislation of a general "New Deal" stamp. Although at the beginning of his dictatorial period, in 1937, he decreed a fascist-style constitution and talked of a "new order," Getúlio was totally pragmatic and unideological. Despite the dictatorship, he was a close and warm ally of the United States during World War II; in fact, it was the contradiction between the democratic ideals of the Allies and the undemocratic Brazilian reality that prepared the way for his downfall. Without an ideology, Vargas also lacked a political party, ruling personally by means of maneuver and equivocation rather than force. State autonomy was abolished, and the Vargas era helped to create a national consciousness in Brazil.

DEMOCRACY, 1945–64

Political Parties: A Vargas Legacy

As well as labor organization, welfare legislation, nationalism, and friendly relations with the United States, Getúlio's legacy included the party system that dominated the next twenty years of Brazilian politics. Although he ruled without a party, Vargas decided to organize a party to support him during the democratic era that was to begin in 1945. He eventually organized two parties, rather than a single party, however, since the elements in his support were contradictory. One party, the Brazilian Labor Party, or PTB, was led by Getúlio's ex-minister of labor and owner of a ranch neighboring Getúlio's in Rio Grande, João Goulart. It enlisted the support not only of organized labor but also of Vargas's supporters among the unorganized masses. The other party, the Social Democratic Party, or PSD, consisted of the government officials at the federal, state, and local levels who had

[5]Brazilian politicans, like other Brazilians, are usually known by their first names or nicknames.

worked for the Vargas administration, and politicians who had collaborated with him. It was more moderate in orientation than the PTB, but the two parties were often allied with each other in the succeeding years. The third major party of the post-Vargas period, the National Democratic Union, or UDN, was formed by the various elements that had opposed Vargas. Like the opposition to Perón, it was therefore very heterogeneous in character, including both democratic progressives who opposed the dictatorship and right-wing oligarchs who opposed Getúlio's welfare and labor policies. Since Vargas's rule had been milder, less strident, and less totalitarian than that of Perón, the opposition to the Brazilian leader was rather narrower and more right-wing than the opposition to Perón. Based primarily on business and agribusiness elements, the UDN was thus an eminently middle-class party with a posture of classic liberalism, rather like the Free Democrats in West Germany.

Formation of coalitions.   Although these were the three major national parties, a variety of others, of regional, personalist, or ideological character, did compete during the twenty years after Vargas left office in 1945. The PSD was the largest party in popular support during this period, although the PTB steadily grew in numbers. In presidential elections, the two parties founded by Vargas generally formed a coalition, which was successful in two of four of the presidential elections during the period, electing Marshall Enrique Dutra in 1945 and Juscelino Kubitschek in 1955. Vargas himself was elected on the PTB ticket in 1950, the PSD endorsing another candidate.

Electoral System

The parties were of minimal importance, however, in part because of the extraordinary electoral system adopted during the Second Republic period. For elections in which only a single post was at stake, such as those for president or governor, coalitions of parties were generally formed. These coalitions were of all varieties, except that it was rare for the UDN to be found in alliance with the PTB. In legislative elections, however, the candidates for state and federal legislatures did not run in individual districts but at large over the whole state. Thus, if there were two hundred seats in the state legislature and four parties nominated candidates for each seat, then the voter could choose one of eight hundred candidates to vote for. While the number of seats won by a party depended on the total won by the party's candidates, which of the candidates took those seats depended on their individual vote. This meant, in effect, that a candidate was running against candidates of his own party as well as those of other parties. It also placed a large premium on wealth, since it was expensive for a candidate to try to get his own name across to the voters when there were seven hundred and ninety-nine others trying to do the same thing. Finally, it meant, in effect, that the voter supported a single individual, not a party. This gave great bargaining power to individual politicians who had either wealth or large popular support, vis-à-vis the parties. A wealthy or popular individual could switch parties quite readily in an attempt to secure the nomination for a post he wanted. Party allegiance was nebulous, campaigns were chaotic, and, once elected, candidates tried to recoup by fair means or foul the huge quantities of money they had spent during the campaign.

Vargas: Reelection and Suicide

Vargas was easily reelected to the presidency in 1950 as the candidate of the PTB. Toward the end of his term in 1954, an unsuccessful assassination attempt on an opposition journalist, Carlos Lacerda, in which an air force officer was killed, turned out to have been ordered by the head of the president's bodyguard. Instead of acceding to the resultant military ultimatum that he resign, Vargas committed suicide. His suicide note, placing responsibility on ill-defined "reactionary forces," was addressed to João Goulart, head of the PTB.

Juscelino Kubitschek

By the time Getúlio Vargas wrote "I leave life to enter history," the armed forces were more or less committed to an attitude of opposition to Vargas, and subsequently to his successors, "the widows," as they were known, his associates in the PSD and the PTB. The military felt responsible for constitutional continuity; it had been the armed forces that secured the abdication of the emperor and had enforced the return to democracy in 1945, military presidents succeeding to office on both occasions. The fact that an air force officer was killed in the assassination attempt of 1954 was added to other grievances against Vargas of an institutional kind, such as that fact that he had played down the role of the Brazilian expeditionary force that fought alongside the Allies in Italy during World War II in fear that some military hero might become his political rival.[6] At the same time, the leftism of some of Vargas's protégés in the PTB threatened good relations with the United States, a source of substantial military assistance, and also might have led to a

---

[6]This point is discussed in Alfred Stepan, *The Military in Politics: Changing Patterns in Brazil,* Princeton, N.J.: Princeton University Press, 1971.

threat to law and order. This antagonism to Vargas did not, at least at first, become the settled hostility the Argentine military developed for Perón, which led to the veto of any party or candidate owing loyalty to the ex-dictator. To be sure, there were some, both inside and outside the army, who took this view toward the heirs of Vargas, and a movement developed to prevent the inauguration of the Getulistas elected in 1955, President Juscelino Kubitschek of the PSD and Vice President João Goulart of the PTB. However, the army commander, Henrique Teixeira Lott, staged a "preemptive" coup, which permitted the inauguration of Kubitschek in January 1956.

Construction of Brasília.   Kubitschek was understandably careful not to offend the army during his term of office and he concentrated on relatively noncontroversial policies, the most notable of which was the building of the capital, Brasília, in the center-west region in a new federal district carved out of the state of Goiás. Unwilling to impose new taxes or raise old ones, and drawn into very heavy expenses in a crash program to complete the building of Brasília before he left office, Kubitschek resorted to deficit financing, that is, the printing press. This policy he justified on the basis of a plausible but unfortunately flawed financial theory, which later made its appearance in a somewhat different form during the Allende period in Chile, which held that in underdeveloped countries an increase in the money supply need not lead to inflation but, instead, brings into economic activity unused people, resources, and productive capacity. Kubitschek left office extremely popular, although with inflation hitting the one-hundred percent per year mark.

Jânio Quadros

Juscelino was succeeded in office by a candidate supported by the UDN, although he was a politically independent former Christian Democrat, an ex-governor of São Paulo state called Jânio Quadros. A rare case of someone reaching the highest position in Brazil without either wealth or military rank, Quadros owed his tremendous popularity to a combination of ruthless administrative efficiency and honesty, and crowd-pleasing oratory and public relations stunts. Quadros's platform style put one jaundiced observer in mind of "a second-rate Brazilian actor doing an impression of Charlie Chaplin playing Hitler." A Brazilian nationalist, Quadros broke the tradition of automatically following the United States lead in international affairs, and even awarded Che Guevara Brazil's highest decoration when Guevara stopped over in Rio on a flying visit. The United States swallowed its chagrin at these acts in its delight at having someone with the will, capacity, and popularity to restore Brazil to financial health.

Austerity program.   Despite his verbal "anti-imperialism" Quadros was impeccably orthodox in his financial views, and he proposed a drastic program of ferocious budget cutting and tax raising in the attempt to end the inflation. This approach was, of course, hugely unpopular with the Congress, which refused to enact the part of his program which needed legislative action (some measures Quadros could implement on his own authority as president) and Quadros resigned, in a confusing incident never satisfactorily explained, after only seven months in office.

João Goulart

The vice president in line to succeed was "Jango" Goulart, whose reputation as a rabble-rousing radical led to a movement, spearheaded by the chiefs of the three branches of the armed services, to prevent his assumption of power. However, a mobilization of pro-Goulart forces, led by his brother-in-law Leonel Brizola, who was governor of Rio Grande do Sul, was widely supported within the armed forces, especially by the great number of officers who were gaúchos. To avoid further division in the armed forces and perhaps a repeat of the 1930 revolt, the service chiefs backed down and accepted Goulart as president, securing a face-saving compromise in the form of a constitutional amendment under which the president was reduced to a figurehead, with the direction of government policy to be in the hands of a prime minister responsible to congress.

Failure of the parliamentary system.   Predictably, the parliamentary system failed to provide strong leadership, as cabinet coalitions came and went and the nation's economic problems, especially those of galloping inflation, grew worse. Even those opposed to Goulart came round to the view that the parliamentary system had to go. The legislature agreed to Goulart's request for an early plebiscite on a return to the presidential system, which was overwhelmingly approved by the voters in January 1963.

Although Goulart secured financial backing from the International Monetary Fund (IMF) with promises of an orthodox financial policy that would end the inflation, he waffled and wavered. In fact, he never met his commitments to the IMF and soon had to suffer the indignity of having to accept foreign aid agreements' being concluded directly with the state governments, since the federal government could not be trusted to live up to its commitments.

Goulart's policies.   Goulart's policies amounted to a disastrous combination of vacillation and demogoguery. Inflation was completely out of control, and Jango's purely verbal leftism aroused mass expectations and elite fears while accomplishing nothing concrete. Yet he made plans to succeed himself in the elections scheduled for October 1965 on the premise that the prohibition of reelection did not apply to a president who had not wielded the full powers of the presidency during part of this term. But more authentically leftist candidates were available, such as Miguel Arraes, the governor of Pernambuco, and Brizola. That was enough for the middle class.

For the military, the last straw came, typically, in the shape of a threat to military hierarchy and discipline. Trying to undercut a possible military move against him by seeking support among non-commissioned ranks, Goulart gave his support to a movement protesting the prohibition on non-commissioned officers' running for political office, which finally led to an unsuccessful revolt by sergeants in Brasilia. He further enraged the service commanders by pardoning naval non-commissioned officers who mutinied against their superior officers in Río de Janeiro.

MILITARY RULE

An Overview

The movement that overthrew Goulart in April 1964 was backed by a coalition of the military and the governors of the major states, São Paulo, Minas Gerais, and Guanabara (the city of Río de Janeiro, which had status as a separate state from 1960, when it lost its status as the federal district, until 1975, when it was absorbed into the state of Río de Janeiro). However, the military leaders of the new regime soon disappointed their civilian allies. Instead of limiting themselves to removing Goulart and other Getulistas from public life and then turning the government over to UDN politicians, the military abolished all parties and suspended the political rights not only of leading Getulista and leftist figures but also of centrists and anti-Getulistas accused of corrupt activities.

During the first ten years of military rule, as the regime confronted a variety of economic and political problems, the lines of cleavage shifted from Getulistas versus anti-Getulistas, to "liberals" versus nationalists, to democrats versus authoritarians.

Reorganization of the political system.   By a series of stages, through a process of trial and error, the political system became that of a dictatorship with a democratic façade, an institutional authoritarian regime dominated by the armed forces. Lists of those deprived of their political rights were published that eventually included not only Goulart and Brizola, but also Kubitschek, Quadros, and Carlos Lacerda.

Elections.   Presidential election was taken out of the hands of the voters and given first to the remnants of the national Congress that remained after its membership was purged, then to a Congress elected under the new rules, and finally to an electoral college modeled on that of West Germany, which consisted of members of the national legislature plus representatives of the state legislatures. In fact, the make-up of the electoral body did not matter, since the official candidate was designated by a caucus of generals, with only senior generals being considered eligible. Sometimes, the democratic façade slipped. In 1967, President Costa e Silva was incapacitated by a stroke. Legally, the presidency should have been assumed by the vice-president, a civilian, Pedro Aleixo. Nevertheless, after consultations within the armed forces, the military chiefs passed the word to the Congress to designate General Emilio G. Medici as the new president.[7]

Political Parties.   The party system was also reconstructed by decree, with no more than two parties to be officially recognized, although, of course, unofficial factional groups developed within the recognized parties. The pro-government party, the Aliança Renovadora Nacional, or ARENA, was based on the former UDN and the more conservative elements from the PSD and minor parties. The second party, the Movimento Democrático Brasileiro, or MDB, was based on elements of the PTB and the left of the PSD who still retained their civil and political rights. The ground rules of the dictatorship gave the MDB only a restricted area of maneuver, and for the first two presidential elections under the new system, the party even refrained from nominating a candidate. Brazilians sardonically remarked that under the new system, the country had two parties: the "yes" party, and the "yes, sir" party.

Repression and torture.   Outside the formalistic democracy of a legislature with an opposition party and elections for governships and for state legislatures, however, the dictatorial face of the regime was clear. The military courts tried political cases; a great many political offenders never reached the court system in any case, simply disappearing into the prisons, torture chambers, and graveyards of one or another

[7]The "inside story" is told in detail by Carlos Chagas in a series of articles entitled "Impedimento e morte de Costa e Silva," which ran in *O Estado de São Paulo* from January 7 to February 7, 1970.

of the secret police forces. The widespread and deliberate use of torture was countenanced by the regime for a long time, providing wide protests abroad, including one from the Pope. When the reaction against these excesses of the regime helped contribute, in 1974, to the election of a general of moderately democratic inclinations, Ernest Geisel, the structure of repression had become so implanted that it resisted the president's efforts to bring it under control.

Lawlessness at the top legitimized lawlessness at the bottom. Especially in São Paulo, local police forces organized "squadrons of death" that assassinated petty criminals without benefit of arrest, evidence, or trial. Needless to say, these activities became elaborated into a protection racket under which criminals who could pay off the police were left alone. Honest prosecutors who attempted to take action against the squadrons of death were removed from office, and the police assassins they had arrested were allowed by their colleagues to escape from jail.

The Economy

Nevertheless, many members of the middle class were prepared to accept the dictatorship and even ignore the torture and assassinations because of the striking success of the regime's economic policies. It is true that perhaps the greatest factor in Brazil's economic success is not government policy but the nature of the country itself. The country presents to the potential investor and entrepreneur a combination of a huge domestic market, the availability of technical and managerial skills, an unlimited supply of cheap labor, and a wealth of natural resources. Of course, excessive reliance on a single export creates an unhealthy situation, and historically the Brazilian economy's booms have been punctuated by collapses as the foreign market for the major product disappeared or was captured by a competitor. Nevertheless, one might almost say that the normal condition of the Brazilian economy is one of boom, and only the inflation left by Kubitschek and the confusion and vacillation of the Goulart period caused a temporary cessation of growth, which was then resumed in 1964.[8] Brazilians had the saying "the country grows at night, while the politicians are sleeping" before Goulart. Nevertheless, it remains true that the economic policies of the military regime have contributed to the Brazilian "economic miracle," under which annual rates of growth averaged about ten percent until the severe blow dealt the economy by the Organization of Petroleum Exporting Countries' raising of oil prices in 1974.

[8]Albert O. Hirschman documents this view in *A Bias for Hope: Essays on Development and Latin America,* New Haven, Conn.: Yale University Press, 1971.

Exchange rate policy.   Economic policy, largely the creation of the finance ministers Roberto Campos and Antonio Delfim Neto, supplemented classical economic theory with strategic government intervention. Instead of the pre-existing pattern, then followed by most countries, of attempting to maintain the exchange value of the national currency, even when movements in international trade relations made its value unrealistic, thus leading to speculation against it that forced eventual devaluation by a substantial amount, the Brazilians accepted the necessity of devaluation but made frequent devaluations by small amounts, thus rendering it not worthwhile to speculate against the cruzeiro. This highly successful policy prefigured the movement of other currencies away from fixed exchange rates.

Incentives to manufacturers.   Every incentive was given to the development of the manufacturing sector. In a shift away from dependence on coffee exports, not only was the export of iron ore and other minerals developed, but so were exports of manufactured goods, so that soon Brazilians could boast that they were exporting watches to Switzerland, computer components to the United States, and shoes to Italy.

Problems.   Nevertheless, criticism of the regime's economic performance, remarkable as it was, could still find some basis. It was clear, for example, that the benefits of the boom went principally to the upper middle classes. The power of the labor unions had been broken by the military regime, and a substantial number of union leaders, many of whom had been PTB or Communist party members, were on the lists of people deprived of their political rights. Wage increases were limited on the whole to an amount necessary to catch up with the *previous year's* inflation, which the regime managed to reduce from the levels of the Kubitschek and Goulart periods, but which still ran at least twenty or twenty-five per cent per year, even in the government's manipulated figures.

There were also nationalist criticisms of the extent to which foreign investment was welcomed, and one common theme of left-wing commentary was that Brazil had become a sort of branch operation of the United States, a "sub-imperialist" power, in charge of exploiting the economies of the other Latin American countries.

Mistrust of Brazil by Neighbors

The other countries of South America do, indeed, regard the Brazilians askance. Brazil's new economic power has enabled it to exert influence in the smaller countries neighboring both Brazil and Argentina (Uruguay, Paraguay, and Bolivia) where Brazilian influence is in the ascendant over that of Argentina. The Venezuelans have also shown some nervousness about their unclearly demarcated frontier with the giant power to the south. It is true that leaders of the regime have grandiose ideas about making Brazil a world power, pursuing an active foreign policy not only in South America but also in Africa and Western Europe. One of the pet projects of the military government is the opening up of the Amazon region, and it has not escaped the notice of Brazil's neighbors that the roads that are built to open up new regions and attract settlers can also be used to transport troops.

Geisel and Figuieredo

Frustrated attempts at reform.   With the designation of Ernesto Geisel for the presidential term beginning in 1974, the opportunity was provided to ameliorate the most unpopular features of the military regime and to begin the process of restoring Brazil to some kind of normality. On economic policy, Geisel tended to be more "nationalist" than "liberal," and he removed Delfim Neto, who had become the symbol of the liberal policies, from his post as finance minister. But Delfim's successor, Mario Henrique Simonsen, was of the same school of thought; indeed, it was hardly to be expected that policies that have proved so successful would be changed other than in matters of detail. Geisel was also of the democratic rather than the authoritarian camp. He tried to allow somewhat greater freedom of the press and assembly and attempted to eliminate arbitrary arrests and torture. But these practices had become so entrenched that they continued anyhow. For example, people were arrested without the secret police agency responsible identifying itself to the victim's family or bystanders, using plainclothes and unmarked cars. The arrest was not noted in any agency documents, so that it could not be traced. Terror was driven underground, and reduced, but not eliminated. Geisel thus found himself, like President Echeverría of Mexico, in a position of trying to democratize a system that proved to be resistant to presidential control.

Other problems.   At the same time, President Geisel's position was weakened by the world economic situation. Worldwide inflation and trade and balance of payments difficulties, together with a huge increase in the price of petroleum imports, got Geisel's economic policies off to a bad start. Heroic efforts were made to prospect for oil, to produce vegetable alcohol for motor fuel, and to expand exports. Some petroleum was found, especially offshore near Rio de Janeiro, but the hoped-for colossal finds in the Amazon refused to materialize. The alcohol program was able to substitute for part of the imported oil, although at very great expense. Exports grew, especially of soybeans, which rivalled coffee as a producer of foreign exchange. But while all of these measures ameliorated the balance of payments problem somewhat, they were not able to close the gap created by the explosion in petroleum prices, and Brazil had to resort to heavy foreign borrowing. Payments on the foreign debt became an increasing burden, although some relief to the balance of payments came in 1981, when oil prices weakened due to world oversupply.

Nevertheless, it was possible to continue the process of *distensão*. A "hard-line" attempt to call off the process, led by General Silvio Frota, was blocked by Geisel in the run-up to the 1979 presidential elections. The fact that the presidency did change hands every five years—even if only between five-star generals—made for situations in which rival candidates tried to line up support and, in so doing, made alliances with civilian groups and listened to civilian pleas for greater openness and less repression in the system.

The former cavalry officer and chief of military intelligence, João Baptista Figueiredo, was designated to succeed Geisel in 1979. Figueiredo was committed to continue the gradual democratization of the system, now referred to as the *abertura democratica*. In fact, Figueiredo's election had even been contested (by another four-star general, Euler Bentes Monteiro, whose position was politically and economically further to the left). As Figueiredo saw it, the democratization process would continue, but it would remain controlled and it would never actually threaten the continuance of the regime. Thus, for example, a new law governing political parties was adopted which eliminated the former limitation of legally recognized parties to only two. While this seems a liberalizing move, it grew out of the fact that the opposition party, the MDB, had seemed about to defeat the government party in legislative and gubernatorial elections. By opening up the party system, President Figueiredo's advisors, especially the former aide to Marshal Castello Branco, General Golbery, believed that the new law would splinter the opposition party but not split the government party. This perception was correct in the short run, and the fractionalization of the opposition was further promoted by the government's permitting the return from exile and amnestying of various pre-1964 political leaders, including Brizola and Arraes. Goulart and Kubitschek had died in the interim, although Quadros was still active. However, it seemed clear that further fiddling with the rules would be necessary to prevent an eventual opposition victory, especially after Golbery, the regime's cleverest political operator, was forced out of power by rivals.

Economically, Figueiredo inherited a difficult situation and was forced to recall the old magician Delfim Neto. This was a new Delfim, now prepared to acknowledge that workers should increase their wages faster than purchasing power was taken from them by inflation, and emphasizing the development of agriculture and raw material exports rather than industrial production. Nevertheless, the foreign debt was colossal and continued to grow.

The search for alternative energy sources had led to an emphasis on hydro-electric power and fuel alcohol, and also on nuclear energy. Because of Brazil's refusal to sign the nuclear non-proliferation treaty, nuclear cooperation with the United States was not possible, and technical assistance in these matters came principally from West Germany. Some observers believe that one of the reasons for the continuation of *abertura* was West German reluctance to be seen giving such critical aid to a country without at least some pretensions to democracy.

The constitutional façade was put to some strain in September 1981, however, when President Figueiredo suffered a heart attack. The last time a president—Costa e Silva—had been incapacitated, the generals had not let the civilian vice-president succeed, but had instead picked another military president. This time, despite the opposition of the powerful chief of military intelligence, General Octavio Aguiar de Medeiros, the civilian vice-president, Aureliano Chaves, was allowed to become acting president, if only for the few weeks it would take Figueiredo to recover sufficiently to resume his functions.

There were clearly elements of instability in the pseudo-democratic authoritarian system the generals had created. There existed tension between the relative freedom of the press and the considerable impunity of military intelligence and security forces in con-

PRESIDENTS OF BRAZIL, 1930–82

1930–45	Getúlio Vargas
1945–50	Enrique G. Dutra
1950–54	Getúlio Vargas
1954–55	José Café Filho
1955	Carlos Luz
1955–56	Nereu Ramos
1956–61	Juscelino Kubitschek
1961	Jânio Quadros
1961–64	João Goulart
1964–67	Carlos Castelo Branco
1967–69	Arthur Costa e Silva
1969–74	Emilio Garrastazú Médici
1974–79	Ernesto Geisel
1979–	João Baptista Figueiredo

ducting "anti-subversive" operations which now, however, only rarely resulted in deaths and disappearances. It remained unclear how long the regime could manage the political juggling acts which allowed opposition parties to compete in legislative and gubernatorial elections without excessive success. The limited freedom that had been given labor organizations was monitored carefully to see that significant strike activity did not occur.

Although the system seems an unstable mix, most Brazilians have by now known nothing else. By the time General Figueiredo assumed the presidency, half of all Brazilians then living had had no personal experience of living under a popularly elected civilian president.

SUMMARY

Brazil's distinctiveness from the rest of Latin America extends not only to its vast size and the fact that the national language is Portuguese but also involves the national character of its people, who are typically relaxed, easy-going, informal, and generous. There are substantial regional differences, with the northeast a region of plantations, export agriculture, and black sharecroppers, while the center-south, focusing on the city of São Paulo, is fairly modern and industrialized, with relatively high living standards.

The government of the empire (1822–89) was a moderating influence, regulating the competition of regions and factions. Under the first republic (1889–1930), the federal government played a limited role, with the centers of power in the principal states. The Vargas regime (1933–45) centralized power in the federal government, whose role was vastly extended as a manager of the economy and provider of welfare. In the second republic (1945–64), politics were chaotic as the economy deteriorated and inflation grew. The gradual mobilization of the masses produced more left-wing and nationalist policies until a right-wing reaction brought a military government to power in 1964. The military regime embarked on sophisticated and generally successful economic policies of modernization and industrial growth, based on foreign capital. However, the success of these policies was premised on the holding down of wages below the rate of inflation, which led to the increasing misery of the working classes, and the repression of labor organizations, and was accompanied by the intimidation of opposition elements through torture. In the late 1970s, the government embarked on the difficult task of evolving to a more moderate position, which would allow freer political and labor-union activity while still maintaining the political and economic control of the military.

9

In Conclusion

POLITICAL DEVELOPMENT
AND
MILITARY INTERVENTION

In the introduction to this book the concept of political development was discussed. In the politically more developed countries, it was said, a greater proportion of political conflicts are settled in the constitutional arena; that is, legislatures and courts more frequently have genuine, autonomous roles, free elections take place at regular intervals with unrestricted participation, those elected take office as scheduled and serve out their appointed terms, and military and bureaucratic officials are subordinate to the elected officeholders.

Quite clearly, there is nothing inevitable about political development in this sense; it represents a possible line of development that may occur under certain circumstances. Experience in Latin America and elsewhere indicates that one of the most important of these circumstances favorable for political development is steady economic growth;[1] that is, it is easier for peaceful democratic procedures to be maintained, and for democratic governments to acquire the legitimacy that comes with sustained popular satisfaction, if the economy is growing so that the demands placed on government by democratic electorates can be met more or less satisfactorily. If the economy does not grow, or if levels of national income decline, dissatisfaction grows, competition over shrinking resources becomes more acute, and it is more likely that consensus will break down into violence and that the classes possessing wealth will use force as the only means of maintaining their privileged position. The example of Venezuela indicates how much easier it is for a country to become democratic when its national income is rising; the cases of Argentina and Uruguay show how economic stagnation and decline contribute to the breakdown in democratic procedures, violence,

---

[1]For a demonstration of this point, and a more detailed discussion of the problems involved here, see the author's *Political Development in Latin America: Instability, Violence, and Revolutionary Change*, New York: Random House, 1968.

and imposition of dictatorship. Let us examine the processes involved in greater detail.

One of the great constants of political life in Latin America is the seizure of power by the military. While there has not been much variation over the years in the frequency with which military forces have overthrown governments, there has been a difference in the political significance of such seizures of power. In the late nineteenth and early twentieth centuries, the military often aligned themselves with liberal middle class forces unable to come to power through electoral means in the face of elections rigged by conservative and landholding elements. In the middle of the twentieth century, however, in most countries it was no longer a case of admitting the liberal middle class to participation in the political system, but the populist lower classes.

Now military men can be found, at different times, in alliance with different social classes and interests. In fact, any military intervention represents a coalition between civilians and different groups of military officers, the soldiers varying among themselves in the motivations for which they entered the coalition, while other officers opposed to the intervention may have been outmaneuvered or may have remained silent out of reluctance to split the armed forces. Nevertheless, one can say that during the middle of the twentieth century most military interventions that had social significance, that represented more than a simple jockeying for power among ambitious officers, had the objective of frustrating popular participation. There are radical military officers, and very occasionally they may happen to have the key positions in a seizure of power—as occurred with the 1968 seizure of power in Peru, led by General Velasco Alvarado—but for the most part they are in a very small minority. Extreme right-wing or fascist military officers are more common, and military governments will frequently reflect those tendencies. However, the bulk of military opinion is amorphously conservative or politically apathetic. As a result, most of the times when a military conspiracy to seize power is in process of formation, it is necessary for the politically committed officers, and the civilian politicians and representatives of economic interest groups soliciting the intervention, to appeal to officers not solely, or not at all, on the basis of political principles or social class interests, but instead to indicate how the institutional interests of military officers themselves make military intervention necessary. That is, the immediate precipitating motives for a coup are almost always self-interested.

There are various ways in which such military interests can be portrayed as being threatened by progressive popular governments. Sometimes there appears to be a threat, real or imagined, to the military budget, either to its current size or to its hoped-for rate of increase. In

Peru, no civilian governments that proposed to cut military expenditure as a percentage of total government expenditure have remained in power. Political "interference" with the military seniority system is especially resented. Arnulfo Arias remained in office as president of Panama for only eleven days in 1958 when he passed over the two ranking officers of the National Guard in appointing the Guard commander. Military institutions are especially jealous of presidential attempts to create popular militias which could eliminate their monopoly of the legitimate use of armed force. President Arbenz's attempt to organize such a militia was the principal reason that the Guatemalan armed forces refused to fight the tiny CIA-sponsored invasion force in 1954.

In addition to these and similar specific complaints that armed forces may have against popularly elected progressive governments, there exists a general military concern that such a government's toleration or encouragement of popular mobilization and especially its complaisance towards the growth in the strength of labor organization imply a breakdown of law and order. This not only is unattractive in itself but may also raise the possibility that military forces will be used to maintain domestic order in situations that will only make them unpopular.

THE "NATIONAL SECURITY" DOCTRINE

One of the major reasons for the frequency with which military forces have acted against popular mass movements or progressive governments in the second half of the twentieth century has been the acceptance and elaboration by Latin American militaries of strategic doctrines propagated by the U.S. military according to which national security is threatened not only, or not primarily, by armed attacks from neighboring states, but by internal subversive movements "acting under the direction of foreign powers," that is, the Soviet Union and revolutionary Cuba. In extreme versions of this point of view, any agitation to change existing social conditions in the direction of greater equality in income distribution, land reform, or improvement of the lot of peasants and workers uses the same kind of language that Russians and Cubans do, thus serves their purposes and is probably under their direction, and is therefore a threat to national security. Absurd in itself, this view leads to absurd consequences: A military officer engaged in the repression in El Salvador in 1982 told a foreign reporter that most Salvadoreans were subversive.

Under this "national security doctrine," as it was understood by the Brazilian military, in order to defend the "ideological frontier" it was necessary not only to stamp out political parties and movements of the left and center-left, and bring an end to trade union autonomy, it was also necessary to end the social and economic conditions which, it was thought, gave rise to revolutionary sentiment. This entailed not only the military's seizure of control of government and repression of civilian opposition, but also military management of the economy, which, in turn, implied the indefinite retention of political control by the armed forces. The Argentine military adopted the same idea in rather more incoherent form, and they were then followed by the Chileans and Uruguayans.

In adopting the "national security doctrine," these South American armies have, as was indicated, followed a lead given them by the United States military. On the whole, they were also acting in keeping with the preferences of the United States government. Now of course it is somewhat difficult to generalize about United States influence as a whole. The United States is a large and complex country with a large and complex government. There are smaller or greater divergences among the lines being followed by the State Department, the Department of Defense, other government departments, various "intelligence" agencies, and groups and cliques within each of these; and between them and business interests, which play a major role in the region.

Moreover, there are changes over time and with different administrations. For the two and a half years of the Kennedy administration the President and the State Department expressed support for the holding of free elections and the introduction of progressive social policies in Latin America; during the administration of Gerald Ford and part of the administration of Jimmy Carter the Department of State, or at least some of its elements, took often effective action in defense of human rights in the region. For most of the last 30 years, however, the general thrust of United States policy has been to view Latin America as a battleground of the cold war and to oppose political forces favoring redistribution of wealth and income as crypto-Communist, therefore on the wrong side in the cold war, and therefore subversive and liable to the most repressive measures.

Ironically, these attitudes persisted even when Latin American Communist parties took fairly moderate positions on social issues, espousing gradualism and peaceful methods.[2] Further ironies abounded. Since the influence of the United States is all-pervasive in the area, in

[2]See Martin C. Needler, "Détente: Impetus for Change in Latin America?" *Journal of International Affairs,* vol. 28, no. 2, 1974.

political, economic, and cultural spheres, a patriot, one desiring true national autonomy, must advocate the limitation of United States influence. To those who interpreted events in terms of the international civil war, however, anyone who wanted to limit United States influence must necessarily have been working for the international Communist movement and was thus subversive. In this perspective, therefore, true patriots were defined as subversive; those regarded as the real patriots were, on the whole, those most servile in accepting the tutelage of the United States.

THE CHARACTER OF U.S. HEGEMONY

Despite the predominant role of the United States in the region, however, it should not be thought that the United States simply "gives orders" or that everything that happens in Latin America happens the way it does because the United States wants it so. The hegemonic relationship is more complex than that.

The influence of the United States in Latin America is exerted, in the first instance, by the penetration of United States ideas and attitudes that occurs automatically without anyone's planning or working to that end. There is a continuous North American presence, because events in the United States make news, because the wire services that feed news to the papers of the region are themselves principally United States entities, because North American books, companies, technologies, salesmen, government personnel, missionaries, and tourists are everywhere. Large numbers of Latin American professionals have attended school in the United States. The cultural predominance of the United States, using "culture" in the widest possible sense, exerts great influence on the way people think, they way they perceive the world, and the way they act.

However, it is also true that these natural types of influence are intensified by deliberate polices of the United States government. The Department of State brings promising younger leaders from the area to the United States on exchange programs, and the Pentagon does the same with young military officers; the American Institute for Free Labor Development, ostensibly an independent operation of the AFL–CIO for training Latin American union leaders, actually works closely with United States government agencies and in parallel with their purposes. The Central Intelligence Agency spends money freely in subsidies to group and individual actors in the political process.

Within this framework of generalized influence, both contrived and natural, there are of course specific attempts by specific United States governments, or by corporations based in the United States, or sometimes by both together, to influence the actions of Latin American governments. A great deal of this is accompanied by economic pressures, in the granting or withholding of "aid," credit, and trade, either on a direct bilateral basis, or in the instructions given to United States representatives on the boards of international financial institutions such as the World Bank or the International Monetary Fund. There is a pious convention that the decisions of such bodies are made solely on economic and never on political grounds, but one should not allow oneself to be fooled by statements of this tenor. For most of the time, however, it is not necessary for any specific pressures to be brought. Political leaders in Latin America understand the "realities" of their economic situation, with its heavy dependence on the United States as a market for their goods and a source of credit, and they know how much their economic well-being can be affected by actions of a displeased United States government with respect to tariffs, quotas, the encouragement or discouragement of investors, and so on. Officials of international financial institutions sincerely feel that they can only grant the loan applications of those whose economic policy-making is "responsible," which includes policies promoting international trade and attracting foreign investment. Thus it may not be necessary for the United States to take specific actions in order for its influence to be felt and to be effective.

To be sure, there are occasions when neither generalized influence nor specific economic pressures are effective, and in these rather infrequent situations direct political action has occurred. This, too, can be of different degrees of intensity, from the expenditure by the CIA of large sums of money in the attempt to influence elections, to the procurement of military *coups d'état,* to the organization of exile invasions, to the actual dispatching of United States troops. The last of these actions is of course undertaken with great reluctance because of its negative political repercussions, and it is rare that affairs get to that point, but it does occasionally occur nevertheless, as when United States Marines were sent into the Dominican Republic in 1965.

It would be a mistake, however, to focus only on these rare and extreme cases of intervention as evidence that the United States runs Latin America by remote control. For most of the time such extreme forms of action do not occur. For most of the time, they are not necessary. That is, they occur only when political and economic events in the region pass the boundaries of what is acceptable to the United States, not having been contained by the normal lower-level forms of influence. For most of the time, the political life of Latin America occurs within those boundaries and therefore Americans take little interest in what goes on. For most of the time, therefore, the political life of the countries of the region moves by its own logic. Governments and policies come and go; the influences, natural and contrived, emanating from the United States are part of the picture, but extreme cases calling for overt acts of intervention occur infrequently.

While of course the United States government continues to act in the defense of the economic interests of its citizens when these are threatened by policy decisions in Latin America, as any government feels it its duty to do, the more extreme forms of pressure or intervention are provoked only when a Latin American government appears to be going off the reservation entirely, that is, when it appears to be seceding from the norms of the international capitalist economic system or abandoning loyalty to the United States in questions of international politics.

Now of course there are disagreements among observers as to whether the behavior of a specific government does indeed pass the limits of acceptability, and United States governments differ in how wide the bounds of acceptability are set. The government of Franklin D. Roosevelt, for example, tolerated socialist economic policies by the government of Mexico under Lázaro Cárdenas that the later governments of Lyndon Johnson or Richard Nixon would have found intolerable.

CHANGES IN THE HEGEMONIC RELATIONSHIP

At the same time, circumstances are developing which appear to be changing the character of the United States hegemony in the region. After all, the United States has been the dominant power in the area for less than a hundred years. Spain was still a factor in the Caribbean until 1898. United States investment only surpassed that of Britain after 1916 in Mexico, between 1919 and 1940 in most of the region, and only after 1950 in Argentina. It is not an eternal truth, that is, that the United States must be absolute sovereign in the Western Hemisphere. Today there is a rapid increase in Japanese economic influence, but that will not have political repercussions for some time. More important is the resurgence of the European role, spearheaded by West Germany and France. This is not only an economic role but a directly political one. The Socialist International, led by French and West Germans, but with important participation from Spain, Portugal, Austria, and Sweden, has become a factor of significance, for example in attempting to prevent a victory of right-wing forces in the Salvadorean civil war. Brazil's growing economic power is enabling her to play a more independent role, defying United States preferences with respect to nuclear energy policy, for example. Mexico's oil has purchased for her an increasing autonomy of action, especially with respect to Central America. Another force making for increased autonomy has been the progressive movement within the Roman Catholic Church, a movement of consciousness-raising and grass roots mobilization that has recovered some of the original meanings of Christianity, which had become for many no more than passive obedience to the requirements of ritual.

While forces such as these are acting to restrict or qualify United States hegemony in the region, that hegemony is continuing to extend itself into marginal areas hitherto not completely incorporated into the hegemonic system. United States overlordship is replacing that of Britain as the former British colonies of the Caribbean region become independent. The prime minister who came to power in Jamaica in late 1980, Edward Seaga, was born in the United States and looks to the United States rather than Britain as his patron. Britain's last colony on the American mainland, Belize (British Honduras), became independent in September 1981. United States influence continued to grow, along with Brazilian, in Paraguay, which had been until the second half of the twentieth century a dependency of Argentina.

Similarly, in El Salvador one of the results of the extended civil war of the 1980s was that the Salvadorean military were forced to look to the United States as a source of funding, munitions, training, and moral support. This, plus the fact that the psychological warfare adepts of United States intelligence believed that a land reform was a necessary ingredient in a campaign to capture the hearts and minds of the Salvadorean peasantry, led the Salvadorean military to transfer its allegiance from the traditional oligarchy within the country, the "fourteen families," to the government of the United States. This development paralleled what had occurred in the countries of Central America and the Caribbean that had known United States occupation earlier in the century. The long United States occupation of Nicaragua had resulted in the creation of a National Guard which looked to the United States as its fundamental constituency; the same was true of pre-revolutionary Cuba and the Dominican Republic. In each of these countries the military maintenance of the status quo was not designed in the first instance to serve the interest of the local oligarchies; in these countries the military institutions served their own interests and the interests of their commanding officers, within the framework of a general allegiance to the United States.

Although United States concern was strongest with respect to the countries that had known direct U.S. rule, in the Caribbean region that was the area of primary concern to the United States, the United States' own "backyard," following World War II the United States extended its hegemony to South America as well. In Chile, Ecuador, and Brazil, for example, when governments appeared to be moving "off the reservation" by flirting with communism domestically or internationally (in 1973, 1963, and 1964 respectively), United States officials conspired with local military officers to overthrow those governments.[3]

SOCIAL MOBILIZATION AND AUTHORITARIAN GOVERNMENT

However, the fundamental problems of Latin America are not the result of the deliberate manipulation of events by agencies of the United States government or anyone else but grow out of the underlying social and economic structure of the region and the fundamental changes occurring in demographic, social, economic, and psychological dimensions. In Latin America today these changes take the form of population growth, urbanization, and rising expectations. In the Soviet Union and in Western Europe, these tendencies took hold at the same time as the industrial revolution. Industrialization occurred at great human cost, in shortened and blighted lives, in child labor, in an exploitation that was not merely a figure of speech. In Latin America, the labor of Indians and blacks was exploited in similar fashion, but the proceeds of their labor did not go to create machinery, factories, and accumulations of capital that could make industrial growth a continuing self-generating process, but mostly went abroad, where they contributed to capital accumulation in Europe, supported an opulent style of life for a favored few, or went uselessly to finance an inflation that was the economic ruin of Spain. The portion of the profits of the colonial economy that remained in the Americas was absorbed by the patterns of consumption of the upper classes.

The great demographic and psychological changes of the twentieth century made it more difficult to operate regimes of pure exploitation. Mass mobilization and heightened political consciousness made the lower classes increasingly assertive and began to give relevance to the

[3]"Alleged Assassination Plots Involving Foreign Leaders," Report of the Senate Committee on Intelligence Activities, Washington, D.C.: U.S. Government Printing Office, November 20, 1975; Jan Knippers Black, *United States Penetration of Brazil*, Philadelphia: University of Pennsylvania Press, 1977; conversations between the present author and United States diplomats serving in Ecuador in 1963.

promises made in the constitutions written during the independence years and rewritten countless times since then, of equality, liberty, and democracy. Politics is passing out of the "private" arena and is finding its home more often in the streets and in the polling booth. Governments increasingly concerned about popular demands, whether they yield to them or repress them, no longer assume an automatic posture of subordination to the United States as the dominant hemispheric power, but are increasingly nationalist.

In most countries of the region, rising mass demands have passed the point where they can be met, or even palliated, out of any increases in national income that have been occurring. Increasingly, therefore, the possibility is raised of policies that will redistribute income and wealth; policies, that is, which threaten the economic well-being of upper status groups. Governments are therefore called into being with the mandate of repressing mass participation and demands and of crushing labor organization and peasant mobilization. The United States is enlisted as supporter of such governments on the premise that the threat is not simply of a more just distribution of wealth and income, but of "communism," and thus of an extension of Russian power.

The military regimes placed in power may, like the demons summoned by the sorcerer, not always obey him, and military governments may prove to have their own way of ruling, not necessarily to the liking of the propertied classes that had solicited military intervention against popular movements. Such regimes may make their own arrangements with the United States, or they may have nationalist and socialist ideas of their own, though most often their rule remains in the conformity with the political and economic preferences of the propertied classes.

Traditionally, Latin America was the region of the formally democratic regime that masked economic oligarchy; of military coups that went no deeper into society than a game of musical chairs; of a passive and obedient peasantry. This older Latin America still exists in the more out-of-the-way corners of the region. In the mainstream, however, one is more likely to witness ferociously repressive authoritarian regimes; an occasional wealthy democracy or nationalist and mildly progressive authoritarian government; or a very occasional revolutionary regime, precariously surviving harassment by its neighbors and by the United States.

For Further Reading

CHARLES W. ANDERSON, *Politics and Economic Change in Latin America*, Princeton: Van Nostrand, 1967.

SOLON BARRACLOUGH and JUAN CARLOS COLLARTE, *Agrarian Structure in Latin America*, Lexington, Mass.: Heath-Lexington Books, 1973.

R. ALBERT BERRY, RONALD G. HELLMAN, and MAURICIO SOLAUN, *Politics of Compromise: Coalition Government in Colombia*, New Brunswick, N.J.: Transaction Books, 1980.

CYRIL E. BLACK, *The Dynamics of Modernization: A Study in Comparative History*, New York: Harper & Row, 1966.

DAVID E. BLANK, *Politics in Venezuela*, Boston: Little Brown, 1973.

COLE BLASIER, *The Hovering Giant: The United States and Revolutionary Governments in Latin America*, Pittsburgh: University of Pittsburgh Press, 1976.

RODERIC A. CAMP, *Mexico's Leaders: Their Education and Recruitment*, Tucson: University of Arizona Press, 1980.

WILLIAM REX CRAWFORD, *A Century of Latin American Thought*, 2nd ed., New York: Praeger, 1966.

JORGE DOMINGUEZ, *Cuba*, New Haven: Yale University Press, 1979.

LUIGI EINAUDI, et al., *Beyond Cuba: Latin America Takes Charge of Its Future*, New York: Crane, Russak, 1974.

KENNETH P. ERICKSON, *The Brazilian Corporative State and Working Class Politics*, Berkeley: University of California Press, 1977.

SAMUEL E. FINER, *The Man on Horseback*, 2nd ed., New York: Praeger, 1974.

ROGER HANSEN, *The Politics of Mexican Development*, Baltimore: Johns Hopkins University Press, 1971.

SIMON P. HANSON, *Dollar Diplomacy, Modern Style*, Washington, D.C.: Inter-American Affairs Press, 1966.

TERESA HAYTER, *Aid as Imperialism*, London: Penguin Books, 1971.

PEDRO HENRIQUEZ URENA, *A Concise History of Latin America Culture*, New York: Praeger, 1966.

OSVALDO HURTADO, *Political Power in Ecuador*, trans. Nick Mills, Albuquerque: University of New Mexico Press, 1980.

JACQUES LAMBERT, *Latin America: Social Structures and Political Institutions*, Berkeley and Los Angeles: University of California Press, 1967.

PENNY LERNOUX, *The Cry of the People*, Maryknoll, N.Y.: Orbis Books, 1981.

ABRAHAM LOWENTHAL, ed., *The Peruvian Experiment: Continuity and Change Under Military Rule*, Princeton: Princeton University Press, 1975.

MARTIN C. NEEDLER, *Political Development in Latin America: Instability, Violence, and Evolutionary Change*, New York: Random House, 1968.

————, ed.,   *Political Systems of Latin America,* 2nd ed., Princeton, Van Nostrand Reinhold, 1970.

DAVID SCOTT PALMER,   *Peru: The Authoritarian Tradition,* New York: Praeger, 1981.

OCTAVIO PAZ,   *The Other Mexico: A Critique of the Pyramid,* trans. Lysander Kemp, New York: Grove Press, 1974.

THOMAS E. SKIDMORE,   *Politics in Brazil, 1930–1964: An Experiment in Democracy,* New York: Oxford University Press, 1967.

PETER SNOW, ed.,   *Government and Politics in Latin America,* New York: Holt, Rinehart, and Winston, 1967.

————,   *Political Forces in Argentina,* New York: Praeger, 1979.

ALFRED STEPAN,   *The Military in Politics: Changing Patterns in Brazil,* Princeton, Princeton University Press, 1971.

ARTURO VALENZUELA,   *The Breakdown of Democracy in Chile,* Baltimore: Johns Hopkins University Press, 1978.

HOWARD J. WIARDA and HARVEY F. KLINE, eds.,   *Latin American Politics and Development,* Boston: Houghton Mifflin, 1979.

EDWARD J. WILLIAMS,   *Latin American Political Thought: A Developmental Perspective,* Tucson: University of Arizona Press, 1974.

————, and FREEMAN WRIGHT,   *Latin American Politics: A Developmental Approach,* Palo Alto, California: Mayfield, 1975.

Index

2012

980.03
N   16279

Intro. to Latin American Politics

DATE DUE		
NOV 21 1992		
OCT 08 1996		
DEC 11 1997